PENGUIN BOOKS

POVERTY AND THE UNEQUAL
SOCIETY IN HONG KONG

Gary Lai is an economist whose writing has appeared in the *South China Morning Post* (Hong Kong), the *Daily Caller* (USA), the *Toronto Star*, and the *Daily Monitor* (Uganda), among other publications, on topics ranging from Aboriginal employment in British Columbia to girls' education in Hong Kong.

Gary's interest in poverty issues led him to found the anti-poverty campaign TKO Poverty at Columbia University in 2005.

Gary received a Bachelor of Arts in Economics from the University of Southern California and a Master of Economics from the University of Hong Kong. He also attended the University of British Columbia Allard School of Law and Columbia University. Lai was shortlisted for a Chevening Scholarship and was nominated for a JCI Hong Kong Ten Outstanding Young Persons Award in 2016.

Poverty and the Unequal Society in Hong Kong

Gary Lai

PENGUIN BOOKS

An imprint of Penguin Random House

PENGUIN BOOKS

USA | Canada | UK | Ireland | Australia
New Zealand | India | South Africa | China | Southeast Asia

Penguin Books is part of the Penguin Random House group of companies
whose addresses can be found at global.penguinrandomhouse.com

Published by Penguin Random House SEA Pte Ltd
9, Changi South Street 3, Level 08-01,
Singapore 486361

Penguin
Random House
SEA

First published in Penguin Books by Penguin Random House SEA 2021

Copyright © Gary Lai 2021

All rights reserved

10 9 8 7 6 5 4 3 2

The views and opinions expressed in this book are the author's own and
the facts are as reported by him which have been verified to the extent possible,
and the publishers are not in any way liable for the same.

ISBN 9789814914048

Typeset in Adobe Garamond Pro by Manipal Technologies Limited, Manipal
Printed at Markono Print Media Pte Ltd, Singapore

www.penguin.sg

Contents

Introduction

The Central district, the commercial heart of Hong Kong,
epitomizes the income inequality in the city.
Source: Wikimedia Commons

Hong Kong is a dynamic city. But the contrast between the
well-off and the poor is stark. In the 1980s and 1990s, and to
a lesser extent in this century, luxury brand bag-toting women
can often be seen walking past beggars on the sidewalks of busy

streets. Poverty has always existed in the city. Where else can we find it and is it getting worse? Does it matter?

To the first question, the government in Hong Kong has occasionally released useful statistics on the nature of poverty in the city. They are self-initiated and their effort must be applauded. They centre on the staples of economic analysis, for example trade, wages, and education. But there are special thematic reports, like one on the Internet that tells a good story about the digital divide and the challenges that the poor face.

As to the second and third questions, statistics seem to show a slow increase in Hong Kong's poor population. But in terms of inequality—the gap between the rich and the poor—the trend has been steadily increasing from 1976. Poverty makes people more vulnerable and corruptible, whether to choosing bad leaders or committing violence. Kenneth McVay, editor of the Holocaust-themed Nizkor Project, once explained that Adolf Hitler's success in mobilizing millions of people to war lied in 'poverty and unemployment'. Ben Taub, in a *New Yorker* article, wrote this about Chadian nomads who are kept from crossing international borders to make a living: 'If they are denied the freedom to move with the seasons, their cattle will die. In recent years, as the Sahelian climate has worsened, many herders who had bought weapons to protect their animals have turned to jihad.' Thomas Friedman, in *From Beirut to Jerusalem*, opined about 'the young men who actually carry out the suicide car bombings or guard the hostages or walk through the minefield. These young, urban poor are economically, socially, and psychologically vulnerable to promises of the millennium, to the intoxication of sacred religious texts or to the illusion of a quick fix.'

The motivation of this book is to ascertain the extent of poverty in Hong Kong in the context of the experiences in other parts of the world. Doing so can serve as a comparative gauge or measure to identify the unique challenges faced by Hong Kong's poor. And only by grasping the facts of Hong Kong's destitute can one help them.

The thesis to my book is: inequalities exist in Hong Kong, and they are the cause of a wide range of socio-economic problems. The meditations in this book are not meant to be encyclopedic. They are a sample of the unique challenges that exist in different parts of the world. In Europe, violence and conflicts caught my attention. Africa is a large continent with over one billion people. It is a large battleground for the fight against extreme poverty and suffers from corruption, the resource curse, a lack of good leadership, and unfair farmer compensation. Microfinance, business-friendly policies, and climate change are urgent and timely topics to discuss.

My focus in the Americas includes western alienation, a persistent regional problem. The marginalized Aboriginals in British Columbia, Canada, has been fighting for inclusion on the national agenda. In the United States, the focus is on the urban poor, illegal immigrants, and military veterans.

In Asia and the Pacific, I survey Australia and the Dutch disease, India in the US-China trade war, Japan and its business culture, and China and its energy supply. Vignettes about these places serve to contrast with the contemporary problems faced by Hong Kong.

By considering how different countries deal with their indigenous problems, I have found a stock of tried-and-true templates for dealing with the problems in Hong Kong, like education and inequalities, as well as what may be inapplicable in Hong Kong, like chronic corruption.

I do not condone violence, and this book does not take a stand on the recent political protests against the diminishing freedom and autonomy imposed by Beijing in Hong Kong, although it may proffer underlying causes for the demonstrations. Inequality is a recurring theme, so are the social chasms that the wealth, education, and digital gaps created. Education can remedy them, so can government accountability (I do not say democracy). Government accountability does not require democracy, and while the latter is prescribed by organizations like the World Bank to alleviate poverty, the experiences of China, India, and Brazil on the lead up to the Millennium Development Goals' deadline in 2015 proved that there is no singular political or economic system that can lift millions of people out of extreme poverty. Countries often know best how to help their own citizens.

I have selected a few topics, again not meant to be exhaustive, for discussion about Hong Kong. I will estimate as well as describe the economic effects of gender equality in the city. Inheritable and elderly poverty exist, so do the possible solutions to alleviate their effects. Poor people are disadvantaged in the job market and in a technologically integrated future, made even more apparent during the COVID-19 pandemic, but there are fixes. People can create a 'poverty friendly' labelling to compel businesses to help the poor. The Greater Bay Area is becoming a solution to poverty in Hong Kong. The poor should not underestimate the importance of education, in the form of retraining programs, vocational schools, and universities.

Hong Kong is filled with entrepreneurs and different ways to finance the poorest of them. Next, I offer my opinion on housing and healthcare in the city, which are perennially hot topics. Finally, I cover the extent of philanthropy in Hong Kong. They all involve a wide variety of problems and solutions which I will attempt to divulge and delve into throughout this book.

Part I

Europe

1

The Culpability of Hjalmar Schacht

The Enigma code machine is displayed in the Army Museum in Paris,
France. Like cryptography, poverty elimination enabled Adolf Hitler
to take up arms in the Second World War.
Source: Gary Lai

The holy grail of economics, some scholars argue, is
understanding the Great Depression. It is not without good
cause. In Germany, the depression, coupled with the humiliation
of the defeat in the First World War, gave rise to one of the
worst dictators of the twentieth century. Understanding how
Hitler's banker, Hjalmar Schacht, transformed the country
into a war economy through public works projects, a grasp

of production, the New Plan, the war economy, investments, taxations, and bond issuance, is certainly an indispensable history lesson in poverty fighting—and, not least because of its insistence on self-sufficiency, what not to do to steer Hong Kong's economy.

Hjalmar Schacht's Challenge

'But Schacht, don't you realize how fond I am of you?' ('*Aber Schacht, ich liebe Sie doch*'.)

This affectionate statement came from the most unlikely source and that is Hitler, the chancellor of Germany in 1937. Who could have made one of the most brutal dictators ever express so much admiration? The receiver was Schacht. As Hitler's banker, Schacht implemented some of the most original economic programs in Germany from 1933 to 1937. Concerning Schacht's significance in the Nazi Party's success, there are two dominant schools of thought. One, which hails Hitler as the 'Great Man,' would argue that the supremacy and endurance of the Nazis were the direct result of the dictator alone. But that view has mostly given way to another school, which believes that Hitler alone could not have accomplished everything, at least without the help of people like Schacht. His role then, was to reinforce, through his economic policies, Hitler's totalitarian rule financially and morally.

To understand Schacht's role in upholding Nazi Germany, one must first analyse his economic policies. In March 1933, Schacht was hired by Hitler, then the new chancellor, to the presidency of the Reichsbank; 17 years later, Schacht also held the position of the German Minister of Economics.

At that time, the country had been, according to the German journalist Otto Tolischus, 'bled white of all capital' and lacked the crucial 'effectiveness of the army and the morale of the nation'. As the head of the two largest financial institutions in the country, Schacht was responsible for the complicated duties of any economic minister, such as the allocation of the government's expenditure, tax regulation, and production rate of businesses. Moreover, he attempted, with success, many unique policies, including those of the public works projects, Mefo bonds, and the New Plan. One can see, in the scheme of the regime's major goals of supporting and strengthening Hitler and his party with financial backing and programs that instilled trust in the German people, how they fit into the picture of Nazism and strengthen it like the pillars of a Greek temple.

Public Works, Employment, and the Military

When Adolf Hitler recruited Schacht, Hitler's foremost concern, unemployment, became Schacht's first challenge. When Schacht took his position at the Reichsbank in 1933, 6.5 million Germans, out of 65 million in the total population—of which 30 million belonged to the work force, were without jobs. Having barely warmed his seat at the Reichsbank, Schacht, as his decision, endorsed the government's Operation Reinhardt. Agreeing to invest a billion marks, the bank hoped to stimulate the housing industry through this factories and urban renewal plan. Along with Schacht's own autobahn project (Schacht pledged 600 million marks for loans)—building a network of modern highways and freeways across Germany—the public works provided millions of workers with the desperately needed jobs. If not already enrolled in the armed forces, all young able Germans had to serve six months in the newly established 'ditch digging' Labor Corps or the flourishing armaments industry.

These projects were definitely not entrepreneurial ventures; Schacht invested *for* Hitler. As soon as the Reichsbank's loans had been repaid, Schacht pulled his institution out of the projects. His purpose was to help *Herr Chancellor* (the name by which Schacht preferred when addressing Hitler, instead of *Mein Führer*), gain popularity with the Germans by providing millions of people with work. Being trusted by the people was the hope of any leader, let alone one who was preparing to take his nation into battle less than a decade later.

By the end of his first year, Schacht had reduced unemployment by 2 million; by 1936, there were 1.6 million unemployed. By 1937 there were only 912,300 left. There were rises, though, in a person's working hours per week—from 41.46 to 47.04 hours. Having job security, Germans neither minded the decreased pay of 25 shillings a week nor the taxes that took as much as a quarter of their income, that went the same for higher taxes and 'contributions' to the Nazi party.

Meanwhile, projects such as the autobahn strengthened the German military—an aspect of the totalitarian state that its citizens were once truly proud of. Before the construction began, the country already possessed one of the best railway systems in Europe; the autobahn was icing on the cake. Laying the modern superhighways, the military could, nonetheless, maneuver with greater efficiency, reaching battle zones and rebellion sites faster than ever. With purely good intentions, Schacht showed his loyalty through his plans that complemented Hitler's ideology.

Control of Production, Command Economy, and the Military

In terms of economic theory, not only did Schacht control the market demand through job creation, the Minister of Economics commanded the supply as well. Even saying that Schacht controlled the production of goods was an understatement; his power stretched from the extraction of raw materials to the amount and type of goods to be produced. Even at the marketplace, the Ministry determined where the products should be sold and for how much money. Guidelines were prescribed that stated the types of raw material that could or could not be used in making a commodity; red tapes of bureaucracy prevailed in this economy. Scarce materials were ordered to be mixed with a set amount of abundant ones, while synthetic materials were produced to substitute those which must otherwise be imported. In the words of Schacht, the 'exact instructions for every individual commercial undertaking [was] laid down by a central authority'.

Obviously, this centrally planned method of production was beneficial to the Hitler's totalitarian rule. All aspects of the market supply were pre-determined and planned by Schacht and the Ministry of Economics, which generally had the same interests and values. Moreover, the new implemented government plans would very unlikely result in a negative feedback from the market. If it were a free economy, and the government chose to raise production costs, manufacturers might choose not to continue production due to a conflict of interests; this potential source of conflict was eliminated in the 1930s. Compared to a capitalistic society, Schacht's command economy was much more stable.

[For instance], if [one] expand[s] credit on a large scale
in . . . a free, capitalistic national economy, . . . the
standardized kind of results [would be that] production
increases; unemployment declines; prices, wages, dividends,
and interest rates go up; the national income rises; imports
tend to increase and exports to fall. [And] if one expands
credit too far under these circumstances, [one] is liable to
cause an uncontrollable inflation, with panic flights from the
national currency into goods and other currencies, runs on
banks, bank failures and soaring prices. Schacht's economy
would never succumb to the phenomenon of the free market
under the same conditions. They [had] increased production,
employment, and the national income. But they [had] kept
prices, wages, dividends, and interest rates within limits
which, considering the circumstances, [were] remarkably
narrow. (Deuel 1942, p.349)

The beauty of the centrally planned economy is that the results
are within Hitler's control. Once again, stability equals to power.

Victims to this controlled, guns-before-butter program
included giant Ruhr and industries such as Krupps and I.G.
Garben. The larger corporations, nevertheless, were supportive
of the system, due to the much increased profits; from 1933 to
1938, their profits, on average, jumped 146 per cent.

What must be stressed about Schacht's controlled
production technique was that it was relatively efficient. With
a structured organization, there was minimal resistance to even
revolutionary changes; if Hitler, or any high official, wanted to
change the economic strategy, for example, to prepare for a war,
the transition would be smooth and quick. When Germany
began experiments on autarky—economic self-sufficiency,

factories quickly produced synthetic material. This saved the government from unnecessary import capital and resources (e.g., transportation). In 1934, described McVay, the investigations initiated by the Raw Materials Commission and the measures introduced for enlarging Germany's raw materials basis through home production as well as for furthering the production of substitute materials would directly benefit war economy preparations. Only through this type of economy could a strong, economically independent totalitarian state exist.

The New Plan, Autarky, and the Military

Based on this line of thought, Schacht developed the New Plan and proposed it in September 1934. Taking control of the monetary current, Schacht and his ministry aimed to reduce the citizens' demand for foreign currencies in purchasing consumption goods from other countries and then to use these currencies for the sole purpose of purchasing essential imports, which could not be acquired within Germany. Now, the exchange of international currencies was not available, and the government decreased the demand for foreign moneys, in McVay's words, 'by various measures suspending the service on Germany's foreign indebtedness, by freezing other claims of foreigners on Germany, by a stringent system of export controls and by eliminating foreign travel and other unessential foreign expenditures'. By reacquiring all foreign currencies, Schacht sought to drastically increase the size of the Reichsbank's foreign reserve.

In this simple way, the German government could purchase the material it needed using only the foreign currencies it already had, and the country did not need to bring in unnecessary capital—those not in German marks.

Eventually, through a new clearing system, Schacht made it possible for German businesses to accomplish international trades without using foreign currencies. A variation of the system was the introduction of aski accounts (or *Auslander Sonderkonten fuer Inlandszahlungen)*—foreigners' special accounts for inland payments. Instead of paying foreigners with their currency or the German mark, they were given 'special' aski marks. This currency could only be used to purchase German exports to the country of the aski marks' holder, and they could not be converted into a major international currency.

The plan reflected the fact that as much as obtaining German autarky was important, there were still needs to bring in imported raw materials for manufacturing arms. There was minimal reliance on other countries, as there were no extra foreign currencies entering the country. Acquiring 90 per cent autarky during Schacht's tenure already reflected a much more stable Germany, which was increasingly less affected by external economic turbulence; Germany was Europe's largest consumer at a time when an overwhelming majority of the continent's nations succumbed to the effects of the 1930s global economic depression. This was good news for Hitler, since the facts showed that a totalitarian government provides the most stability and economic control compared to its political counterparts in countries such as France and Italy. History had shown that the population would be willing to trade its freedom for a little more stability in life like now.

Under the new clearing system, by 1937, Germany's imports were worth 500 million Reichsmarks more than they should have received, bringing in more capital for armament use. In the midst of the confusion, Schacht borrowed enormous amount of capital from neighbouring countries, exploiting especially the Western European countries. Using the status of Europe's largest consumer at the time, Germany used the aski accounts to force nations into importing only German products. About a fifth of all German imports in 1935 were paid in this arm-twisting manner. Of course, none of these schemes were without benefits. From 1934 to 1937, the import of petroleum increased by 116 per cent, rubber by 71 per cent, finished products by 63 per cent, grain by 12 per cent, and of ores by 132 per cent. The New Plan was a great step towards German autarky, which was a big goal of Hitler's totalitarian rule.

Preparation and Plans for the War Economy and the Military

Hitler's goal of establishing an even stronger German state inspired Schacht's policies on the war economy (*Wehrwirtschaft*). Appointed the General Plenipotentiary War Economy by Hitler through the Reich Defense Law of 1935, Schacht became the virtual economic dictator of Germany; he now controlled all economic planning and preparation for war, putting 'all economic forces in the service of carrying on the war and to secure the life of the German people economically'. Under the law, the Ministry of Economics was placed higher in the government's hierarchy than the Ministries of Food and Agriculture, Labour, and Forestry, though Schacht must accept sole responsibility for his counterparts in those departments. In Schacht's preparation, he ordered intensive studies of statistics, such as 'the composition of the labour force as to sex, age, and training, the consumption of raw and auxiliary material, fuels, power, the productive capacity, the domestic and foreign trade as well as the supply of material and products in the beginning and at the end of the year'.

His dedication to his policies was shown when he carefully planned different scenarios. For example, Schacht held real-life military maneuvers to determine where equipment and power sources should be placed, functioning even when accidents (i.e., power shortage) occurred. When necessary, evacuation of military troops and equipment, technicians, and livestock were all worked out to the smallest detail; each entity was marked and registered with the *Wehrkreiskommandos* by the field offices of evacuation and salvaging plans. As for the German people, they were well considered by Schacht too. Authorities, within twenty-four hours after troop mobilization, would distribute the 80 million food cards throughout the country, for the purpose of food rationing.

Again, placing one individual in charge of such an important aspect of the German economy, that of wartime, was rather risky. However, Hitler must have known that only a bold, competent man would bear the responsibility of so many colleagues. The return, however, would be a great increase in efficiency for Germany; having one ministry as the superior meant fewer conflicts during national emergency, namely a war. Schacht's detailed work on the preparation of Germany in war was extremely useful for the country; the plans described 'the needs of the Armed Forces and the civilian minimum needs in wartime . . . compared with the covering thereof by supplies and production'. Furthermore, sufficient resources, such as fuel, were available for war at the spur of the moment. These precautions would prevent chaos and confusion at times of war, for everyone would know where to go and what to do.

Investment of Oppositions' Money and the Military

Strangely, one of Schacht's economic plans called for oppositions to invest on the Nazi party. How was that possible? As the president of the Reichsbank, he had the power to control the flow of the money that had been deposited in the bank. Interfering with the capital of any account, even those belonging to Hitler's critics, Schacht redirected the funds to arms manufacturers. He confirmed the plan with Hitler in 1935: 'The Reichsbank invested the major part of Reichsbank accounts owned by foreigners, and which were accessible to the Reichsbank, armament drafts. Our armaments are, therefore, being financed partially with the assets of our opponents.'

Taxation and the Military

A master of monetary diversion, Schacht accomplished similar feats as the Minister of Economics. Like any country, inter-war Germany received most of its income through taxes and public debt. Schacht, during his tenure, increased the public debt from 10.4 billion marks in 1932 to a stunning 19 billion marks 6 years later. The extra cash, in return, was discreetly transferred to the Nazi's rearmament Program and Hermann Göring's Four Year Plan, which was later revised as the Three Year Plan. Putting the entire process under his control, Schacht did not let unnecessary capital drain into the hands of private institutions that competed for the same monetary pool.

Mefo Bonds, Unemployment, and the Military

Early on in his term, Schacht introduced the Mefo bonds. This scheme was based on the establishment of the

Mefo Corporation (*Metallurgische Forschung GmbH*—Metallurgical Research Company). Initially funded by a nominal capital of 1 million Reichsmarks, the shell companies distributed bonds that paid 4 per cent interest and matured in 5 years, to 4 leading industrial companies: Gutehoffnungshütte, Krupp, Rheinstahl, and Siemens. The bonds were redeemable at any time and their payment was guaranteed by the Reichsbank, which in turn was backed by the Foreign Conversion Fund.

The Mefo bills clearly served an underlying cause; that the Mefo Corporation was capitalized with 1 million marks should have raised an eyebrow. As events revealed, they were a part of a larger scheme for rearmament; much of the money ended up in large government contracts for that purpose. The Mefo Corporation was really a middleman. After military contractors received payments by the government in Mefo bonds, they turned to Mefo, which in turn helped these manufacturers to obtain cash from the Reichsbank, including the 4 per cent interest that the bonds offered. As previously mentioned, these payments were guaranteed, so the bank could draw capital out of the corporate capital reserves, which were supposedly used for emergencies only. The popularity of the Mefo bond drew much needed money for rearmament; the original 1 million mark bonds reached 12 billion marks 4 years later, in 1936.

Another desirable side-effect was, of course, the creation of employment; Schacht called the Mefo plan 'an inventive way of priming industrial production and wiping out unemployment'— as reported by Weitz. Many observers, most of whom are apparently cynics, believe it 'a well-camouflaged ruse for cranking up armament production without much visible accountancy or unduly alarming the outside world. Like the various taxation methods and usage of bank investments, the Mefo bills helped finance the German rearmament program, which supported the Nazis' primary foreign objective—turning the country back into a major military power.

Given its wealth of talents, there is no lack of financial 'wizards' in Hong Kong (*Confessions of an Old Wizard* was the title of Schacht's autobiography), even in times of great economic turbulence. Nazi Germany was a case of what Hong Kong is not, and hopefully never will be. It is a free, economically vibrant economy. It never raises employment rate by shutting itself off from trade with China and its neighbours in Asia. It does not craft trading accounts to extract export money from others. Knowing that Hong Kong has little in common with inter-war Germany is probably a good thing.

What became of Schacht? Considering Schacht's policies drawn in such a short period of time, it is hard to deny his relevance and contribution to the Nazi party. George S. Messersmith, the US Consul General in Berlin from 1930 to 1934, shared this view:

> It was [Schacht's] financial ability that enabled the Nazi regime in the early days to find the financial basis for the tremendous armament program and which made it possible to carry it through. If it had not been for his efforts, and this is not a personal observation of mine only but I believe was shared and is shared by every observer at the time, the Nazi regime would have been unable to maintain itself in power and to establish its control over Germany, much less to create the enormous war machine which was necessary for its objectives in Europe and later throughout the world. The increased industrial activity in Germany incident to rearmament made great imports of raw materials necessary

while at the same time exports were decreasing. Yet by Schacht's resourcefulness, his complete financial ruthlessness, and his absolute cynicism, Schacht was able to maintain and to establish the situation for the Nazis. Unquestionably without this complete lending of his capacities to the Nazi Government and all of its ambitions, it would have been impossible for Hitler and the Nazis to develop an Armed Force sufficient to permit Germany to launch an aggressive war. (McVay 2019)

Weitz observed that, from the beginning, 'the Reichsbank [had] been aware of the fact that a successful foreign policy can be attained only by the reconstruction of the German armed forces'. Schacht represented this belief, which permeated throughout his economic policies. They strengthened Hitler's totalitarian rule indirectly by financial and social means. To put it simply as a *Business Week* article at the time, Schacht '[played] a dominant role in formulating government economic and financial policy' in Germany.

The power now rested in the dictator's hands; it had been demonstrated that security, to the people, meant more than liberty. Eventually, it would be proven that Hitler's success indeed lied in poverty and unemployment, as McVay puts it.

2

To Fight Terrorism, France Needs to Focus on International Cooperation and Marginalized Groups

People gather to see the Arc de Triomphe, a major tourist attraction in Paris, France. Like other sectors of the economy, terrorism strikes tourism harder in some countries than others. *Source*: Gary Lai

Recently, there has been a surge of high-profiled acts of domestic terrorism in France. A paper by two American academics offers a view on the controversial relationship between terrorism and the economy. Terrorism and militarism in inter-war Germany seem

17

to be quite different; according to the authors, there does not seem to be a link between poverty and terrorism, which should reassure Hong Kongers as well as everyone else. However, there is a case to be made for caring about marginalized religious and other social groups and cooperating with international policing groups like INTERPOL.

The nature of terrorism has changed drastically in the past 30 years in France and worldwide, driven by the rise of religious fundamentalist groups like Al-Qaeda, Boko Haram, and Al-Shabaab. So has the trajectory of academic discourse on the topic. Two economists, Khusrav Gaibulloev and Todd Sandler, summarized the latest findings in a recently published paper in the 'Journal of Economic Literature'.

Alleged Causes of Terrorism

According to Gaibulloev and Sandler, there are several widely speculated causes of terrorism. One is globalization, which is the increased economic integration of countries that may lower the cost of international terrorism, help raise money for illegal activities, and exacerbate the problems caused by income inequality—among other effects. But, according to data, there seems to be no direct relationship between globalization and terrorism.

The second possible cause is poverty. It is a somewhat a well-known fact among scholars that Palestinian terrorists, as a group, were well-educated and wealthier than their target populations. In fact, there is no agreement on whether increasing per capita GDP lowers the amount of terrorism. However, researchers found that the lack of civil liberties, the third alleged cause, seems to drive terrorism.

The Economic Effects of Terrorism

What is the effect of terrorism on an economy? While a terrorist attack tends to reallocate resources from investments to government spending, its effect on economic growth is small and transitory. The effect is even smaller if the terrorist activity is domestic rather than from abroad. Small economies frequently hit with terrorism, for example the Basque Country in the 1980s and 1990s, do feel the effects on their GDP.

In general, bilateral trade is negatively affected, though not by a great magnitude, by terrorism. It increases the costs of doing business, due to greater uncertainty, higher insurance and wage premiums, and other transaction costs. Studies also found that stock markets in industrialized countries recover quickly from a terrorist incident, so long as there is liquidity and fiscal stimulus from the government.

Since people typically look at a country's terrorist risk when they invest, terrorist incidents tend to lower FDI. But if the amount of terrorist activities is small, like in France, so the effect is small relative to the GDP.

While the tourism industry is particularly vulnerable to terrorist attacks, France, looking at data between 1970 and 1988, did not suffer monetary losses. Countries like Austria, Greece, and Italy, however, did. But a number of studies using data from 1970s onward show that there is a general negative effect. Moreover, it seems that the neighbouring countries of a terrorist target suffer a decline in tourism income.

International Cooperation and Counter-Terrorism

To policymakers, this means there is a great economic incentive to cooperate with countries that neighbour France. While poverty would not lead to terrorism in Hong Kong, Gaibulloev and Sandler suggest that terrorism, whatever its causes, would have an economic impact on the city. This calls for action on its part, through greater involvement in the IMF and the Financial Action Task Force (FATF) on money laundering to cut off terrorists' funds—and the INTERPOL to monitor their movements between countries.

The French and Hong Kong governments can, in the meanwhile, work on domestic policies that would be more inclusive of different religious and marginalized social groups and prevent terrorist cells from forming.

3

As Catalonia Prospers, Its Crime Rate Increases

Barcelona, which draws millions of tourists each year,
has a problem with crime.
Source: Gary Lai

What often gets in the way of an economist from getting to the truth is the lack of data. As I will show later in the book, the Hong Kong government provides a wealth of information on the welfare of its people. Catalonia seems to offer some interesting figures on crime, which would allow me to finish this part on Europe by illuminating the relationship between minimum wage and crime in this part of Spain and comparing it with the experience in Hong Kong.

Minimum Hourly Wage and Crime

Catalonia is the land of Gaudí, Michelin-starred restaurants, and top-rate soccer, but an equally relevant, everyday issue is crime. Specifically, what contributes to it in the autonomous region? From official statistics, there is a plausible candidate: the minimum hourly wage. From the available years, from 2004 to 2017, the minimum wage in Catalonia is always above the national average. It ranges from, unadjusted for inflation, 12.1 euros in 2004 to 16.06 euros in 2017. There is no fixed, national hourly minimum wage in Spain. The lowest rate is, unadjusted for inflation, 11.2 euros in 2004, and the highest is 15.13 euros in 2017.

In these available years, there was a rise and fall in prison population—an indicator of crime—in Catalonia. The population in prison reached a peak of 10,525 in 2009, and the decline may be partly due to the nation-wide shortening of drug trafficking sentences and empowerment of courts in deporting foreigners in Spanish prisons in 2010. The change in policies in the latter has implications in Catalonia, where a whopping 44.5% of criminals in prison are foreigners in 2018, most of whom hail from outside the EU like the Maghreb and South America.

How Crime Responds to Spanish and Catalonian Wages

To explore minimum wage and crime's cause-and-effect relationship statistically, I look at the correlation between minimum hourly wage and the Catalan prison population. I do not consider the reverse, that is, the prison population affecting the minimum wage, since that is highly unlikely. The minimum wage in Spain represents the economic conditions of the whole country. Regressing it with the Catalan prison population will reveal the relationship between crimes in Catalonia with the income of Spaniards outside the region. As it turns out, the prison population increases when people earn more at the lowest rung—for a 1 euro increase in minimum wage, there is an increase of 248 prisoners in Catalonia.

If I regressed Catalan minimum wage with its prison population, we get similar results. Here, an increase of 1 euro in hourly minimum wage leads to an increase of 263 prisoners. In this province, crime is positively correlated to wage increase. When Catalans earn a higher income as measured by the minimum wage, more people land in prisons.

Explanation and Prescriptions

Why does setting the minimum wage higher lead to more criminals? There are two possible explanations. People earning low wages may be more vulnerable to criminal activities than other demographics. When they receive a higher wage as a result of the labour policy—and without being instructed on how to use that money wisely—they will be empowered to commit further criminal activities.

Another effect of the minimum wage is that some low-wage workers will lose their jobs. They will also turn to criminal activities. This means the government should establish financial literacy courses for low-income Catalans, as well as education programs for poor, unemployed workers who need to upgrade their skills or retrain.

Given the strong correlation we found in this pair of variables, and the continual growth of the Spanish economy (the Bank of Spain predicted 1.7 per cent growth for 2020), one should ask the logical and more practical question: will there be enough policemen in Catalonia?

Is there Enough Police on Catalonian Streets?

Official statistics for the police force is only available between 2010 and 2018. There was a decrease in the number of policemen from 11,027 in 2010 to 10,586 in 2013, and an increase to 10,968 in 2018. If I regress the number of policemen and the number of Catalan prisoners, I find that for each additional prisoner in Catalonia, there is an increase of 0.0135 police. This is only a small, positive correlation between the number of prisoners and police. In other words, the government is not responding well to increases in criminals by putting more cops on the streets.

This view is affirmed by looking at the increases and decreases of street-level officers. Despite making up the largest contingent in the police force, the relative proportion of officer-rank policemen has not budged, hovering perennially between 81.2 per cent and 84.3 per cent. Using these statistics as a guide, the Catalan police should put more police officers on the streets, at an overwhelming rate when necessary, to control the crime rate and reduce the number of convicts in prison.

The Hong Kong Experience

However, the minimum wage-crime rate connection is not universally true. In Hong Kong, for example, there is a negative correlation between the two variables. From 2011 to 2019, when the minimum wage rose from HK$28 step-wise to HK$37.5, the annual crime rate decreased steadily by 40.3 per cent from 75,936 to 45,334 incidences, according to figures released by the Hong Kong Police. Increasing minimum wage, therefore, reduces crime in the city. This seems to support a study published in 2016 by the US Council of Economic Advisers that found a 10 per cent to 20 per cent reduction in crime rates among non-college educated men for a 10 per cent increase in wages. So the trend continues; what works in one country in poverty alleviation may not apply to another, like Hong Kong. There will be more examples of that on the next continent, Africa.

Part II

Africa

4

More to Global Poverty than Jeffrey Sachs

Muhammad Yunus received the Nobel Peace Prize for his work providing credit to the poor. Many lesser-known economists have important things to say about poverty alleviation.
Source: Wikimedia Commons

This chapter is a word of caution not only of quick fixes in poverty alleviation, but also high-profiled economists. The chapter's title is in reference to the well-known economist Jeffrey

Sachs, who built a smattering of Millennium Villages in Africa and was recruited by Columbia University in the early 2000s. There are other, lesser-known economists who deserved to be heard for their scalable approaches, including Hernando de Soto and Muhammad Yunus. They should form a panel to solve the toughest poverty issues. Hong Kongers can learn from them, too.

Hernando de Soto and Property Rights for the Poor

Who in the economist community have the greatest ideas? Jeffrey Sachs should count as one. The Peruvian economist Hernando de Soto has done a great job. He has observed that many poor people in the developing world have property that can be turned into capital if a legal property system is in place to formalize their ownership. If realized, he estimates that 5 trillion dollars of assets can be created in those poor countries—capital that people can use to mortgage in order to create businesses and economic speculations.

His think tank in Lima, Peru, the Institute for Liberty and Democracy (ILD), promotes the work he has been doing in helping people obtain these property rights. *The Economist* has called the ILD one of the two most influential think tanks in the world. President George Bush has endorsed it, and President Bill Clinton has repeatedly endorsed the economist as doing important work—giving credibility to an initiative that could easily be dismissed as a radical program to transfer billions in capital from the government to the people around the world. Likewise a group of well-intentioned and apolitical economists who are intent on solving one of the world's most persisting (and probably never-ending, since poverty still exists relatively) problems will doubtlessly attract the philanthropy of smart, well-educated, and most importantly reasonable donors.

Muhammad Yunus and the Others

What admires me about economists is the methodical, rational way that they have approached their subjects. Though in the case of Lawrence Summers, who once publicly claimed that men may be more predisposed to science than women, this has gotten him into trouble, here, in fighting poverty, it is obvious that Third World poverty has gotten to a level where NGOs and foreign aid are still chronically required. There are at least several economists who are very high profiled who have big, systemic ideas to this problem. Apart from Sachs, there are microfinance specialists (the Grameen Bank in Bangladesh) who are working on commercial lending to the poor, and Amartya Sen, who also won a Nobel Prize and had important things to say about infrastructure-building in Africa.

The influence of economists like Yunus cannot be understated. Unique among his peers for eschewing flashy suits, he worked tirelessly to be the banker for the poor of the world. His ideas on microfinance, which originated with the revelation that women in groups who lend small amounts of money have high repayment rates, have expanded to urban microfinance (with operations in the US and Japan), prompted multinational banks to set up charitable and for-profit micro-lending arms, and inspired offshoots like the micro-insurance organizations. In serving the poor, Yunus united even more under his organization's banner.

A Concerted Fight against Poverty

With these myriad approaches to a persisting humanitarian problem, it is time that someone put together a concerted effort to attack it. There needs to be a focused institution other than the UN (to which Sachs is affiliated as a special advisor), which for all its accomplishments is not a poverty-fighting institution. It is also not run by economists and is prone to give grandiose twenty-year, poverty-fighting objectives that one may hardly take seriously (you can read any edition of the UN Human Development Report for further information). This is as good a time as any for institutions like the Earth Institute or the Institute for Liberty and Democracy (which de Soto directs) or the Grameen Bank to sit around a table and to find a solution— one that the most influential economists can agree upon.

Economists now have warned the public that there are no silver bullets to poverty alleviation. They should also warn them that there are no prophets either. President Clinton said in a speech in January 2003 at NYU that more institutions and 'frameworks within which people have an interest in working together' are needed in a world of integration. While the president's advice is not directed at the economics profession, but it is suitable. Now is the time for an institution to be created, one by the top economists for combating poverty, in Africa or, as a matter of fact, in Hong Kong. By working together to integrate big ideas within a rationalistic framework, great things like having an effective and serious approach to eradicating poverty can perhaps be achieved in our lifetime.

5

The Virulent 'New World Syndrome'

Developing economies import an enormous amount of unhealthy foods that
are high in sugar and sodium.
Source: Wikimedia Commons

There is a wave of westernization of global diets, and the chronic
diseases that come with it. Obesity is on the rise in Chile and
North Africa. In Asia, there is an increase in fat, sugar, and oil
intake. Couple that with a more sedentary lifestyle, a country

like China might have already lost US$4.5 trillion to the 'New World Syndrome'. Hong Kongers have a similar diet, which means that both should take the experts' recommendation of collecting better medical data, procuring more fresh fruits and produce, and dispensing affordable medication for the poor.

The WHO estimated that by 2015 approximately 2.3 billion adults would be overweight and more than 700 million would be obese. Obesity is a major risk factor in a host of diseases, like cardiovascular diseases, diabetes mellitus and metabolic syndrome, and hypertension.

The Chilean Diet

Claudia Bambs, Jaime Cerda and Alex Escalona of the Pontificia Universidad Catolica de Chile reported a drastic shift in high energy food consumption in Chile, a developing country (which, according to the World Bank, is defined as having an annual GNP of US$9,075 or less). Corresponding to a drop in malnutrition there—from 37 per cent to 2.9 per cent among children younger than 6 years old between 1960 and 2000 and from 26 per cent to 14.1 per cent among pregnant women between 1987 and 2000— was a rise in obesity—20 per cent among 4-year-olds and from 12.9 per cent to 32.7 per cent among pregnant women during the same period. It should have been no surprise, since daily calorie intake increased—from 2.667 kilocalories per 11.159 Joules in 1980 to 2.844 kilocalories per 11.899 Joules in 1998.

The North African Diet

Najat Mokhtar, Jalila Elati, Rachida Chabir, Abdelatif Bour and their colleagues at the Ibn Tofail University, Global Food and

Nutrition and Johns Hopkins University reported the obesity level among women in Morocco between 15 and 60-years-old to be 17.8 per cent. In Tunisia, the obesity rate increased from 28.3 per cent in 1980 to 51 per cent in 1997—a threefold increase. One out of two Tunisian women will become overweight or obese. This is not helped by the urbanization—which promotes an inactive and bad alimentary lifestyle—experienced in these countries (Morocco's population doubled from 15 million in 1970 to almost 30 million in 1999). The paradox is the endemic malnutrition that still exists (24 per cent of children under five were malnourished in Morocco in 1992, while 18 per cent were in Tunisia in 1988).

Causes of the 'New World Syndrome'

S.U. Raymond, from Changing Our World—a New York-based philanthropy consulting firm—blames falling food prices and globalization of the economies as additional reasons for an increase in risk factors for chronic diseases.

Barry M. Popkin, of the University of North Carolina at Chapel Hill, blames the increase in obesity on changes in people's diet. He claims that the peoples of most countries in Asia, Latin America, North Africa, the Middle East, and the cities of sub-Saharan Africa have seen a huge shift in diet—in the amount of fat, sugar, and animal food product intake and a decrease in cereal intake and fibre—analogous to a Western diet. In Asia, there is an increase in oil in the diet.

Industrialization is going on all over the world, Popkin adds. An unpreventable consequence is the more sedentary lifestyle it leads to. Not only does work require less energy input, less physical effort is required in leisure activities. Household appliances have reduced energy expenditure at home—a marked difference to the agrarian era of human development.

The WHO claims that heart disease, stroke, and diabetes— the representatives of the 'New World Syndrome' afflicting developing countries—might have cost China US$4.5 trillion between 2005 and 2015.

Andrew Prentice, of University College London, argued that the factors contributing to the obesity pandemic were the low cost of highly refined oils and carbohydrates, the popularization of motorized transportation and the rise of sedentary types of employment.

Policy Recommendations

To fight chronic diseases on a policy level, Salim Yusuf, of McMaster University in Canada, Mario Vaz, of Rajiv Gandhi University of Health Sciences, Karnataka, and Prem Pais, of St. John's National Academy of Health Sciences in India, recommend better collection of data pertaining to people who died of cardiovascular diseases in developing countries and people who live in Asia, the Middle East and Africa, which had virtually no data on secondary interventions of cardiovascular diseases at the time of their report. They also believe that prevention of chronic diseases is key, and Western strategies are a good model to follow. Prevention may include adjusting agricultural policies, so that people can live more healthily (for example, by increasing the availability of fresh fruits and vegetables). Governments also need to tackle the problem of expensive medication in the developing world, whose prices appear to be pegged to developed countries (some countries' prices are relatively high, like Pakistan's to India's).

Stacey Rosen and Shahla Shapouri of the US Department of Agriculture would probably agree with Yusuf and his colleagues in advocating for prevention against chronic diseases caused by demographic and socio-economic changes in developing countries. For one thing, developing countries are poor; they cannot afford hospitals for treatment, offices for statistical gathering and analyses, and research centres for combating their unique variants of diabetes, cardiovascular diseases and hypertension.

The trade pattern between developed and developing countries has increased. The average ocean freight and port charges for US import and export cargo decreased 60 per cent in the two decades between 1970 and 1990. Refrigeration increased international trade; so did the eradication of trade barriers and the rise of global financing. Trade created dependence on foreign grown staples. The volume of processed foods traded increased five-fold between 1970 and 2005.

The stakes are high. Obesity, for one thing, reduces productivity. The healthcare systems of developing countries could be overwhelmed by sufferers of chronic diseases, burdened already by the host of infectious diseases afflicting different parts of the world and malnutrition with poor sectors of the population.

As I will return to the topic later in the book, the poor are generally in worse health than the rest of the population. This is expected to be no different in Hong Kong, without the added burden of the 'New World Syndrome'. To tackle the problem of rising chronic illnesses by limiting or shutting down international trade of foodstuff is impossible. As a city perennially open to trade, Hong Kong cannot refuse importing unhealthy food either. Any student of economics knows that all participants are better off when they engage in free trade. The best option to deal with chronic diseases stemming from urbanization and globalization—and more specifically Westernization—therefore is to invest in preventative policies and education campaigns. The good news is that most experts agree with that plan of treatment.

6

An Inclusive HIV/AIDS Prevention and Treatment Policy Should Benefit the Poor in Africa

An American official is helping raise awareness for HIV/AIDS at the Pongwe Clinic in Tanzania.
Source: Wikimedia Commons

Apart from the 'New World Syndrome,' there are other epidemics in Africa. The fight against HIV/AIDS gets a lot of attention. Decades after it was first identified, the disease can now be suppressed by antiretroviral therapy. With treatment, Africans are more productive at work. Its control is also a great example of public and private money coming together to combat a health crisis, notwithstanding issues with control over its supply and distribution. Hong Kongers can learn from their African friends in funding health programs for the poor.

The Medical Benefits of Antiretroviral Therapy

HIV/AIDS is not a death sentence any more. With the advent of antiretroviral therapy, HIV has become more of a chronic illness for millions of sufferers worldwide—and in Africa, where 23.8 million are infected with the virus. But recent medical research still insists that patients need to be confined to a lifelong, strict regimen of medications that is too costly and fraught with side effects for many, including Africa's poor. Even when they can afford it, there are still toxic side effects—chronic immune activation, inflammation, and immune dysfunction that interfere with the productivity of a patient. Facing decades instead of years to live, patients have to deal with increased instances of a host of complications—like cardiovascular, bone, liver, kidney, and neurocognitive diseases, cancers, metabolic imbalance, and organ damage—that are still being understood.

This is not to discredit the benefits of antiretroviral therapy. Mother-to-offspring transmission at childbirth, for example, is an important link in the epidemic. In South Africa, when the mother takes the required drugs, only 2 per cent of the births result in HIV transmission. Without taking the drugs, transmission is 45 per cent likely.

The Economics of HIV/AIDS

Most experts see the HIV/AIDS epidemic as a burden on the economy, as Simon Dixon and his colleagues at the University of Sheffield showed in African countries where the HIV infection rate is relatively low. HIV/AIDS tends to affect the young, the most productive age group, so it has a large impact on economic growth. In cities, the high infection rate among educated workers means that those infected with HIV have to finance treatment out of their own pocket, reducing per capita income growth. Some people disagree with this. For example, Alwyn Young, of the London School of Economics, believes that—using data from South Africa—the AIDS epidemic deters people from having unprotected sex and makes women's work hours more valuable in economic terms. Both lead to a lower fertility rate and increases per capita consumption in the future.

Aid for the Epidemic

One thing is for sure. There has been a large inflow of aid money into the continent. Under the Emergency Plan for AIDS Relief, more than $80 billion has been dispensed by the United States to fight HIV/AIDS in Africa since 2003. The Global Fund to Fight AIDS, Tuberculosis, and Malaria received pledges of $1.7 billion and $1.56 billion from the UK and the United States, respectively, in 2019. Sophie Harman, of Queen Mary University of London, believes that this injection of foreign precedes huge geopolitical changes in whole African regions. She takes Kenya, Tanzania, and Uganda as an example—the epidemic ravages East and southern Africa more than the other West and North Africa—and observes that the World

Bank's intervention has led to the introduction of new ministries, and quasi-governmental bodies, and civil society organizations. National leaders and supranational organizations correspondingly changed, too. This makes poor African countries vulnerable to Western intrusion, economically by turning them into dumping targets or an extractive state or through humanitarian means by transforming them into passive aid recipients in programs of foreigners' design.

This is a massive effort that stakeholders in Hong Kong's health sector can learn from. To support the millions living with HIV/AIDS in Africa, governments need to study which economic sectors are the most sensitive to the epidemic, whether the epidemic has an effect on income inequality, and how to best implement cost-effective, targeted prevention programs— including free HIV testing. For the infected, governments should follow the World Health Organization's advice to offer antiretroviral therapy for free, leaving out no social or economic group in the process. If something at this level of sophistication and inclusivity can be carried out by charities in Hong Kong, poor people HIV/AIDS there can benefit as well. Look to Senegal as a role model. Its current HIV infection rate is 0.4 per cent, much lower than the 4.3 per cent for all of Sub-Saharan Africa. Drug users there are handed free and clean syringes, and a vast social network educate fellow citizens and identify untested sex workers.

7

Malaria Eradication Must Consider Pregnant Women, Children, and the Effects of Climate Change

Malaria, which infects millions of Africans, is spread by the female
Anopheles mosquito.
Source: Wikimedia Commons

Alongside diarrhea, malaria is one of the most notorious but preventable ailments in Africa. Obviously, not treating it leads to premature death for millions of people, but studies have linked in utero and postnatal exposure to lower education attainment as adults. There are tremendous economic benefits if the disease is eradicated, or so most people believe. Continuing bed net distribution and attention to climate change is needed—lessons that Hong Kong can learn from Africa to control the noisome dengue fever and Japanese encephalitis, which are also spread by mosquitoes and take productivity away from poor people.

Malaria is a persistent disease. Of the estimated 216 million cases reported in 2016, 90 per cent are in Africa. Samantha Rawlings, of the University of Reading in the UK, argued that young men, who are among the most educated group, are most likely to die from malaria—even though vulnerable, unskilled women die at a significant rate as well.

The Mechanisms of Malaria Affecting Economic Growth

Malaria is not good for economic growth. The specific mechanism by which these two are linked is not well-established, although Jeffrey Sachs and Pia Malaney, both formerly of Harvard University, proposed various theories. They include malaria lowering worker productivity, causing premature death, and changing savings and investment patterns (due to the money spent on drugs and medical treatment), leading to lower income growth in aggregate.

Some experts argue that malaria influences growth via other factors, such as political institutions and fertility. The latter causes, according to Adrienne Lucas, of the University of Delaware, lower birth rate, which translates to a lower GDP in the future. Alan Barreca, of the University of California, Los Angeles, tells a slightly different story, but with the same conclusion, in utero and postnatal exposure to malaria leads to considerably lower levels of educational attainment as adults and higher poverty rates.

Hoyt Bleakley, of the University of Chicago, proposes that the connection between malaria and income growth is targeted public health intervention, in people's early-childhood. His study found that if malaria was eradicated in the wet, tropical parts of Africa in the 1950s, the region's GDP would have been 40 per cent greater than if it had not been eradicated.

In a classic study, malaria eradication was found to increase agricultural productivity, so the reverse—that malaria leads to lower agricultural productivity—should be true. Kwadwo Asenso-Okyere, of Ethiopia's International Food Policy Research Institute, and his colleagues explored the conjoining mechanism. First, malaria causes the loss of labour and slows the adoption of better farming practices, because many attract malaria-carrying mosquitoes. Second, certain existing farming practices and interventions are known to facilitate the spread of malaria and may have been avoided, even though they are agriculturally more productive. Given the importance of farming in Africa, this link between malaria and reduction in output gives the governments' great incentive to eradicate.

Arguments against Malaria Having an Impact on Growth

There are skeptics that malaria, which has an undoubtedly big impact at the individual and household level, has an additive effect—that it impacts economic growth at the regional and country level. One of these people is Randall Packard, of John Hopkins University, who argues that studies so far have been unreliable, because data is incomplete or unreliable—malaria deaths and economic productivity, for example—and the models on which previous conclusions were based could not separate the effects of malaria from other social and economic factors. These are valid academic arguments, which the collection of these figures in the future, along with better research methodology, will emerge to shed light.

Other skeptics are Sue Bowden, of the University of York in the UK, and her colleagues, who studied the decline in malaria in four Mediterranean countries and its effect on their labour force, the agricultural sector, and the tourism industry. They observed that while those countries' escape from poverty were likely caused by the advent of international trade, malaria did encourage their rise from low economic growth. But certainly African countries should eradicate malaria if that would, too, encourage their escape from poverty and low economic growth.

Located in sub-tropical climate, Hong Kong is host to many diseases carried by local species of mosquitoes. Their eradication should have the same desirable effect on worker productivity, which is a good thing for poor people who are more likely to work and play outdoors. The African experience seems to suggest so far that pregnant women and children are among the most vulnerable groups in the malaria epidemic and should be protected first. Distributing insecticide-treated, malarial mosquito-repelling bed nets work. The effects of climate change on malaria cannot be underestimated. Areas previously spared from the disease, like the East African Highlands, are now susceptible to it, along with the people living there. Researchers in Hong Kong, too, should use technology to track changes in mosquito population in rural and urban geographies due to long-term climate flux.

8

Can Africa Keep Its Doctors?

A doctor working in a Tanzanian hospital. Brain drain is a major issue in the
African medical sector.
Source: Wikimedia Commons

While Hong Kong has an advanced healthcare system, it has been
toying with the idea of importing foreign-educated doctors to fill
its needs. The poor suffer from the shortage, since many live in
rural areas that doctors avoid. Looking at the countries in Africa
can reveal several possible reasons—a heavy workload, career
prospects, for example.

There is a great shortage of doctors in Africa. This is a
shame, because increasing the number of them, according to

academic studies, greatly improves various health outcomes on the continent. John Robst, of the University of South Florida, argued that more doctors reduce the mortality rate in rural areas. John Anyanwu and Andrew Erhijakpor—of the African Development Bank and Delta State University in Nigeria, respectively—found that doctors reduce the under-five and infant mortality rates in forty-seven African countries. To experts, maternal health professionals are essential to meeting the United Nations' Sustainable Development Goals.

Shortage of Doctors in Africa

The WHO pegs the doctor density bar at two per 10,000 people, anything less means there is a physician shortage. According to the most recent data, only fourteen African countries meet the WHO's standard. Whereas there are 25.9 doctors for 10,000 Americans and fifty doctors for every 10,000 Swedes, there are only 0.4 doctors and 0.37 doctors for every 10,000 Tanzanians and Liberians, respectively.

Making the situation worse is the brain drain of doctors to wealthier countries, a trend that has increased in most African countries since 2002. According to Mawusse Okey, of the University of Lome in Togo (physician density: 0.49 per 10,000 people), the emigration of medical professionals contributes to lower human development in the country they left. Studies blame it for higher mortality rate, further medical personnel shortages, and higher incidences of diseases and epidemics, such as the 2014 Ebola outbreak in Liberia, Guinea (0.79 doctors per 10,000 people), and Sierra Leone (0.25 doctors per 10,000 people).

The Rise of Community Health Workers

The shortage of doctors has led to the training of many community health workers, who are laypersons trained to provide health services. They go by different names in various countries, indicating the health services most needed there: community drug distributor in Uganda, community reproductive health worker in Uganda, and village malaria worker and mother coordinators in Ethiopia. Their medical training is limited, and they are only qualified to treat minor ailments, having to refer more serious cases to the hospital.

Community health workers are only part of the solution. Retaining doctors should be a priority for African countries. For example, the UK's Department for International Development and the Global Fund to Fight AIDS, Malaria, and Tuberculosis funded the government of Malawi (0.16 doctors per 10,000 people) with over $100 million between 2004 and 2009 to retain physicians.

What Caused Physician Shortage?

Amy Hagopian, of the University of Washington, and her colleagues cited several areas for governments to work on low wages for doctors, poor working conditions, the badly funded healthcare system, limited post graduate training and job opportunities, the unfavourable economic and political environment, and family ties abroad. Using a survey in Zambia (0.91 doctors per 10,000 people), Jeff Gow, of the University of KwaZulu-Natal in South Africa, and his colleagues found that safe working conditions, a manageable workload, and career opportunity matter more than better pay. That explains their findings that underinvestment in schools, doctor migration, and health workers leaving the public sector and the healthcare industry contributed to medical personnel shortages. In 2005, Zambia had only 50 per cent of the workers needed to provide basic health services, with the situation worst in rural areas. In 2017, the Ministry of Health announced a shortage of 3,000 doctors, an increase from 1,439 in 2008.

Okey observed that, in fifty African countries, corruption encourages doctors to leave their countries. Dishonest bureaucrats in underdeveloped countries extract a significant amount of bribe for day-to-day and professional activities, enough so to reduce doctors' returns on education. While training doctors in Africa takes effort and resources, retaining them around may require restructuring entire societies to create a more hospitable environment for medical practitioners. Likewise in Hong Kong, while compensation and corruption are not big issues, doctors complain about heavy workloads. Coupled with the increasing number of doctors practicing in China, this may deter good doctors from staying in the city and serving those who cannot afford good healthcare—exacerbating health inequality among the poor.

9[1]

Africa Is Not Yet Ready to Stand on Its Own

Women sing at an event in Liberia.
Source: Wikimedia Commons

As the Millennium Development Goals (MDGs) approached in 2015, it was apparent that most African countries were not going to meet their targets, including their aim to reduce their share of extreme poverty. Debts still needed to be written off by

---

[1] This chapter appeared as an op-ed in the *Monitor* (Uganda) on October 29, 2015.

developed countries. The best way to achieve the MDGs was still debated by Canadian officials in 2013. Corruption was still a big issue. The poor in Hong Kong are like Africans. While aid is offered to them with the expectation that they will stand on their own, it is more likely they will be dependent on it for some time.

In November 1989, the World Bank issued a widely hailed study on Africa's long-term development, 'Sub-Saharan Africa: From Crises to Sustainable Growth,' urging policy changes across a wide range of economic and social sectors. The core of the strategy lay in raising agricultural production beyond the continent's record population growth rate. It also called for increased investments in industry, mining and human resources, a revival of the private sector, socially equitable growth with a focus on the poor and environmentally sound development as well as a strengthening of Africa's own capacity for policy analysis and a pan-African identity.

The Lead-up to the 1991 African Debt Write-offs

The World Bank also asked African governments to rein in reckless and corrupt spending, to do something about the lack of accountability, and to reverse the repression of basic freedoms. For the first time its indifference towards regional economic integration gave way to the rational endorsement of it. The bank had indeed gone far to appease its critics. The United Nations Economic Commission for Africa gave the report reluctant approval, and the bank encouraged a global coalition of donors to join in an economic rescue effort for sub-Saharan Africa.

Michael Chege, policy advisor at the Ministry of Economic Planning and National Development in Kenya, urged the external debt policy of Western creditor nations to be reviewed to help support sound economic management in new African democracies. By 1990 sub-Saharan Africa owed $161 billion, mostly to official bilateral and multilateral sources. Even with rescheduling and debt relief by European countries, debt servicing still amounted to 30 per cent of the region's export earnings. The Group of Seven leading industrialized nations agreed at the July 1991 London summit to additional debt write-offs for Africa's poorest reforming economies. Britain has since followed this agreement with debt reduction to better managed African economies as well.

The Private Sector Led Approach

While the West supported promoting democracy as a prerequisite to economic growth, some advocate a business approach to eradicating poverty. At a 2013 African Union conference of ministers responsible for mineral resources development Canada's Lois Brown and Christian Paradis argued that 'creating sustainable economic growth, led by the private sector, is the number one way to break the cycle of poverty. When managed properly, the extractive sector can generate substantial revenues for governments, which they can in turn invest in much-needed infrastructure and basic services, including health and education. Local businesses can also benefit, which leads to greater job creation.' Brown and Paradis, in other words, were calling for a benevolent, top-down business approach.

Was Africa on Track to Meet the Millennium Development Goals?

There is ample academic and political evidence that Africans want to stand on their two feet. Scholars Kanayo Ogujiuba and

Fadila Jumare argue that Africans need to wean themselves away from the economic prescription of the West. They observe that sub-Saharan African countries report high levels of growth and per capita GDP and yet they were unable to achieve the MDGs, such as quality education and health.

They argue that contrary to the sensibility of the economically focused West, a country's GDP might not be sufficient for measuring development because the funds obtained may not necessarily be used to improve the quality of life of worse off communities.

Using examples from countries such as Nigeria, it was evident that many countries in sub-Saharan Africa were unlikely to achieve their MDG targets because of the persistence of poverty and other challenges such as corruption. Moreover, the required growth to substantially reduce poverty is too high by international standards, showing Western organizations are not in touch with the unique economic challenges of Africa.

Ogujiuba and Jumare recommended that different countries' development strategies must take into consideration the national realities in each country, presumably understood best by local people, rather than adopting targets and policies from the Western world.

For instance, Africans have also been taking the initiative to form organizations to eliminate corruption. To build on the positive leadership examples like those in Botswana, a group of prominent former and current African leaders decided to establish the African Leadership Council. They established a Code of African Leadership with 23 commandments, issued a Mombasa Declaration promoting better leadership, and proposed a series of courses to train their political successors in the art of good government.

But is Africa really ready to stand on its own? The answer may still be no. Foreign aid continues to flow into the continent, and extreme poverty remains. For example, aid makes up 27.5 per cent of the Central African Republic's national income, according to the World Bank. Despite great steps taken by countries like The Gambia and Ethiopia, over 400 million Africans still live in extreme poverty. Paul Miller, Africa policy adviser for Catholic Relief Services said the World Bank Development Indicators 2007 report brought 'positive news about income growth and the number of people in poverty worldwide, but a number of nuances [made it] a less rosy picture'.

Systemic debt relief, along with the establishment of leadership organizations against corruption, financial mismanagement, and such seems to be the way to allow Africa to stand on its own again. While the poor in Hong Kong are not generally in massive debt, they are perennially held back by socio-economic obstacles like a lack of higher education, gender equality, and access to the latest consumer technology. They, too, need to be given opportunities to become economically independent.

10

Oil and the Resource Curse in Africa

Oil production facilities in Nembe Creek, Nigeria.
Source: Wikimedia Commons

It's hard to appreciate a good government. It takes an expert to understand the intricacies of a bureaucracy and how it keeps a country, or, in Hong Kong's case, an international city running. African countries, using Nigeria and Equatorial Guinea as the standard have shown what it's like when things really fall apart, squandering their oil and mineral wealth to kleptocrats—officials who use their power to steal—and corruption. Reforms take time. People who are insistent that the Hong Kong government is not doing enough now to help the poor should acknowledge the labour required to run a large economy.

Good governments and oil wealth do not go hand in hand in the world's second most populous continent. Promoting stable, benevolent regimes in Africa would ensure that, defying the resource curse, oil money will flow directly to the people instead of the ruler. In that way, economic growth will have a greater chance of being sustained in Africa.

Oil and Corruption in Nigeria

In 2011, Nigeria, the most populous African country with 140 million people, had its first legitimate change of power since independence in 1960. Then the world's eighth largest oil producer, one of its top exporters, and the only African member of OPEC, Nigeria became one of only a handful of established democracies in the continent.

The United States supported Nigeria; the latter supplies about 10 per cent of the former's crude oil import, amounting to 1.1 million barrels a day. This support is unrelated to the despotism that former military leader turned President Olusegun Obasanjo bred; the US was mainly concerned with securing its oil supply. The country—riding on almost a decade of record oil revenues in the 1990s—was peppered with crumbling infrastructure, plagued by a lack of access to the medical and educational system for its citizens, and suffered from lackluster economic growth.

During Obasanjo's 8 years in government, Nigeria earned $223 billion, 2.5 times the amount earned over the previous 8 years. Kleptocracy and rampant grafting kept the money away from its intended destinations, extending a streak of $400 billion in mismanaged funds since 1960. Nigerians who voted Obasanjo out of office finally asked why, despite their country's oil, their lives were so miserable.

This is symptomatic of the resource curse. Jean Herskovits, the late historian, observes that the 'real obstacle to progress is not a lack of resources; it is who controls them and how they are used'. For example, according to Human Rights Watch, oil-producing Rivers State's (population 5.1 million) budget in 2006 was $1.3 billion, but little development occurred there and the governor owned a private jet and invested heavily in South African real estate. The EFCC, an anti-corruption agency, in 2006 investigated 31 of Nigeria's 36 governors for corruption.

Equatorial Guinea: A Cautionary Tale for Oil Producers

Equatorial Guinea is the model of what not to do for governments in oil producing states. It is an oil producer (1 billion barrels of oil in reserves; 400,000 barrels produced per day since 1995) with rampant corruption, an unwieldy and unaccountable government, and chronic underdevelopment. This is sad for a country (population 700,000) with a per capita GDP greater than Japan, France, and the UK. Three-quarters of Equatorial Guineans live on less than US$2 per day, and it seems that those connected to the country's president benefitted from the oil.

Learning from Equatorial Guinea is vital for the rest of Africa. Oil is, of course, not concentrated in a few African countries. In the next 8 years, 25 billion barrels of exportable oil worth trillions of dollars will come from the East African Rift Valley and West Africa's Gulf of Guinea. They will bring in oil money to Ethiopia, Kenya, Malawi, Mauritius, Tanzania, and Uganda in East Africa—and The Gambia, Ghana, Liberia, Sao Tome and Principe, Senegal, and Sierra Leone in the West. Some of the reserve estimates are 0.5 billion barrels in Ethiopia, 3 billion barrels in Kenya and Tanzania, and 3.5 billion barrels in Uganda. Countries that are already oil producers—Angola, Chad, Gabon, Nigeria, South Sudan, and Sudan—will see more revenue. For example, Nigeria and Equatorial Guinea have been exporting as much as 3 million barrels of oil a day from the Gulf of Guinea for over four decades. Oil and gas will form most of a third or more African countries' total exports.

African oil producers, on average, are arguably more corrupt than their oil-less counterparts in the continent. The World Bank's Worldwide Governance Indicators show that oil-producing African countries rank in the bottom quintile globally in their ability to control corruption, formulate and implement effective policies, regulate private sector development, and enforce the rule of law. The UN Development Index also ranks those countries in the bottom half in the world.

Plausible Economic Effects of Reform

Until the late 1980s, Africa's only functioning multiparty governments were in Botswana, Senegal, The Gambia, and Mauritius. The first three never managed to produce a change in government. By 2000, however, a Freedom House survey found 32 of 53 African countries were either democratic or at least partially so. In 1999 Thabo Mbeki succeeded Nelson Mandela, and Obsanjo was elected to replace a military dictator in Nigeria. In March 2000, a month after Senegal's High Court decided to prosecute him, Senegal's Abdou Diouf accepted defeat in an election. In oil producing Benin, Thomas Yayi Boni was elected in 2006, when he declared that his cabinet would consist of technocrats from universities and development banks. In Liberia, a former World Bank official, Ellen Johnson-Sirleaf, was elected in 2006.

Perhaps because of democratic development in the continent, poverty is declining, 'Since 1996, the average poverty rate in Sub-Saharan African countries has fallen by about one percentage point a year, and between 2005 and 2008, the portion of Africans in the region living on less than $1.25 a day fell for the first time, from 52 per cent to 48 per cent. If the region's stable countries continue growing at the average rates they have enjoyed for the last decade, most of them will reach a per capita gross national income of $1,000 by 2025, which the World Bank classifies as "middle income".'

For Africa to help itself, it needs to promote peaceful countries with stable government that can provide a steady oil supply. With stability comes economic growth, whether it is founded on the burgeoning industries like banking, Internet communication, or disruptive financial and manufacturing industries. While Hong Kong may not have mineral wealth, it has developed a finely tuned and squeaky clean bureaucracy that Africans would envy, freeing resources up to pursue goals like poverty alleviation.

11

More Accountability Needed to Overcome Resource Curse in African Oil-Producing States

An Indian Minister discusses investments in the oil sector with Gabon's Minister of Mines, Oil and Hydrocarbons.
Source: Wikimedia Commons/Ministry of Petroleum & Natural Gas, GODL-India

This chapter is another look at corruption in Nigeria and Equatorial Guinea, adding to the discussion debates on how to reform governments to become more accountable, and more inductive to economic growth. Hong Kongers can more fully appreciate the predicament countries with a corrupt government can be in.

A Review of Nigeria

As mentioned in the previous chapter, Nigeria, the most populous African country, held elections in 1999, in which the military leader turned politician Olusegun Obasanjo won. At the time, the country was the world's eighth largest oil producer, one of its top exporters (though it imported all of the refined oil products it consumes), and the only African member of OPEC. It was known to have a relatively stable regime. While over 1,800 manufacturing firms closed between 1999 and 2007, contributing to the departure of some multinationals, oil companies stayed unaffected.

The United States supported Nigeria, since the latter supplied 10 per cent of the former's crude oil import, or 1.1 million barrels a day. This decision was independent of the Obasanjo government. The US backed it, despite the President's support for the dictator Charles Taylor, in order to secure its oil supply. There were little opposition to election fraud, for example, as well as aid to a country—riding on almost a decade of record oil revenues in the 1990s—with crumbling infrastructure, lack of access to the medical and educational system for its citizens, and poor economic growth.

During Obasanjo's 8 years in government, Nigeria earned $223 billion, 2.5 times the amount made over the previous 8 years. Kleptocracy and rampant grafting kept the money away from its intended destinations, extending a streak of $400 billion in mismanaged funds since 1960. Nigerians who finally voted Obasanjo out of office were motivated by a frustration stemming from their miserable lives despite the country's riches.

Countries like Nigeria are victims to what Daron Acemoglu, an economist at MIT, and James Robinson, a political scientist at the University of Chicago, termed 'extractive institutions'— which are, according to Shantayanan Devarajan and Wolfgang Fengler of the World Bank, 'policies and practices that are designed to capture the wealth and resources of a society for the benefit of a small but politically powerful elite. One result [of which] is staggering inequality.' Jean Herskovits observed that, as mentioned in the previous chapter, the 'real obstacle to progress is not a lack of resources; it is who controls them and how they are used'. For example, according to Human Rights Watch, oil-producing Rivers State's (population 5.1 million) budget in 2006 was $1.3 billion, but little development occurred there. The governor, meanwhile, owned a private jet and invested heavily in South African real estate. The Economic and Financial Crimes Commission, an anti-corruption agency, in 2006 investigated 31 of Nigeria's 36 governors for corruption.

The general consensus was that the oil money should have been used for improving, infrastructure, economic development, and job creation. People were asking for more accountability, which Herskovits saw as a critical and 'revolutionary' for future regional stability. This calls for a less corrupt government to handle a steady supply of oil, which already declined by 20 per cent in 2006 because of violence in the Niger Delta, as well as distribute oil income equitably.

Equatorial Guinea Revisited

Equatorial Guinea is a bad example of an oil state in Africa. As an oil producer with 1.1 billion barrels of oil in reserves and 120,000 barrels per day in production as of 2019, the country has been plagued by rampant corruption, an unwieldy and unaccountable government, and chronic underdevelopment. As mentioned in the previous chapter, this is sad for a country of 1.3 million people and a per capita GDP that was greater than Japan, France, and the United Kingdom. 76.8 per cent of Equatorial Guineans live in poverty, and it seems that those mostly those connected to the country's president have benefitted from oil.

Oil money is paradoxically an obstacle to development in Africa. Larry Diamond and Jack Mosbacher of Stanford University speculated that it 'fuels inflation, fans waste and massive corruption, distorts exchange rates, undermines the competitiveness of traditional export sectors such as agriculture, and pre-empts the growth of manufacturing. Moreover, as oil prices fluctuate on world markets, oil-rich countries can suddenly become cash poor when booms go bust (since poor countries rarely save any of these revenue windfalls).' Moreover, oil income tends to create oligarchic and authoritarian governments and neglect the civil society, which stifles economic growth.

Not even government accountability is enough in the case of Equatorial Guinea, because the corruption and bad governance have become chronic: 'Although transparency is an integral piece of any country's pursuit of effective and honest governance, transparency alone fails to reverse the underlying incentives afflicting oil-rich countries.' Other oil producers like it include Angola and Sudan, which have ranked in the world's worst 20 per cent in corruption. Oil producers, on average, are more corrupt than those that do not produce the stuff on the continent. The World Bank's Worldwide Governance Indicators show that oil-producing African countries rank in the bottom quintile globally in their ability to control corruption, formulate and implement effective policies, regulate private sector development, and enforce the rule of law. The UN Development Index also ranks those countries in the bottom half in the world.

Diamond and Mosbacher's solution includes direct funneling oil money to the people as taxable income. Originally devised by scholars at Center for Global Development in Washington, D.C., it is a cash-transfer program that needs to be implemented by democratic governments, the foundation of which exist in many countries that will produce oil in the future. The two scholars did not divulge on the exact mechanism, but they were optimistic that such a transfer will create the greatest good for all.

Learning from failed oil states like Equatorial Guinea is relevant for the rest of Africa. 25 billion barrels of exportable oil worth trillions of dollars will come from the East African Rift Valley and West Africa's Gulf of Guinea. They will bring in oil money to Ethiopia, Kenya, Malawi, Mauritius, Tanzania, and Uganda in East Africa and The Gambia, Ghana, Liberia, Sao Tome and Principe, Senegal, and Sierra Leone in West Africa. Some of the reserve estimates were 0.5 billion barrels in Ethiopia, 3 billion barrels in Kenya and Tanzania, and 3.5 billion barrels in Uganda. Countries that are already oil producers like Angola, Chad, Gabon, Nigeria, South Sudan, and Sudan will see more revenue. For example, Nigeria and Equatorial Guinea have been exporting as much as 3 million barrels of oil a day from the Gulf of Guinea for close to 50 years.

This pan-African phenomenon will produce more than one-third these countries' exports and bring in tremendous amounts of money: 'The total annual GDP of the 12 "future" exporters in 2011 was $181 billion. If $3 trillion flows to these countries from oil over a period of 30 to 50 years, then the total annual increase in economic output would amount to $60 billion to $100 billion—an increase of over one third.'

Efforts to Reform

Despite all odds, there seems to be efforts in African countries to keep officials accountable. Until the late 1980s, Africa's only functioning multiparty political systems were in Botswana, Senegal, The Gambia, and Mauritius. The first three never managed to produce a change in government. By 2000, however, 32 of 53 African countries have done so, according to a Freedom House survey. This is following a series of monumental events, such as Thabo Mbeki's succeeding Nelson Mandela in 1999, Obasanjo's replacing a military dictatorship in Nigeria, and Abdou Diouf's defeat in an election in 2000, after Senegal's High Court moved to prosecute him. Nonetheless, the US, the former Soviet Union, and France have long supported dictatorial regimes that served their geopolitical interest. Ethiopia's Mengistu Haile Mariam, Somalia's Mohamed Siad Barre, Rwanda's Juvenal Habyarimana, and the former Zaire's Mobutu Sese Seko were examples of such dictatorships.

Dan Connell, a visiting scholar at Boston University's African Studies Center, and Frank Smyth, a journalist, observed that something is aiding Africa's transition to electoral government. A bloc of African countries—Uganda, Rwanda, Ethiopia, and Eritrea, with Angola and South Africa in the periphery—observed by Tanzania, Zambia, Zimbabwe, and Burundi, tried to topple or influence, politically and militarily, the governments of unstable and/or oligarchic Chad, the Central African Republic, and Somalia. They seek to break the links to Africa's colonial past and the vast patronage system that have undermined economic development. For decades, African leaders did not invest in infrastructure, education, healthcare, and legal and regulatory reform. Countries became aid-dependent, while those who hold power protected themselves with the scant judiciary system they had, at times, violently—as with Idi Amin, Habyarimana, and Mobutu. The dictators were, according to Connell and Smyth, nationalistic, brutal, and self-interested. The people were ready for more accountable leaders.

In comparison, the leaders in this bloc aspires to be responsive to their citizens' welfare, and their fast growing economies proved it. Even Rwanda, which was ravaged by civil war, has seen positive economic growth in the past two decades. In the 1990s, Ethiopia experienced a 3.4 per cent average annual growth in GDP. Uganda grew 6.9 per cent in the same period, at an increasing rate in the second half. Eritrea grew almost 8 per cent annually. The bloc's members, including Uganda, worked hard with the aid of the World Bank to stabilize currencies, privatize the economy, trim government budgets, and create an inviting business environment for investments. Connell and Smyth warned that foreign policy debates are a struggle between what is pragmatic and what is moral. If the new wave of democratically-elected leaders of Africa have their way, it may be possible to have both prosperity and political accountability in the oil-exporting economies.

Economic Effects of Reform

Like with many countries, a major objective of the African oil states is to attain economic growth. There are a variety of opinions as to the actual growth rate, some more optimistic than others. For example, between 2000 and 2011, Africa's GDP averaged a growth rate of 4.7 per cent per year, despite the 2008 financial crisis and its negative global effects. Oil-producing countries, needless to say, were vital to the boom.

Their planning were, according to Devarajan and Fengler, by necessity prescient: 'In early 2008, when the international price of oil rose above $100 a barrel, some oil exporters in the region, such as Angola, Gabon, and Nigeria, planned their budgets as if oil prices were only $65 a barrel. When the price ultimately did fall to that level, in the fall of 2008, those countries were not caught off-guard and had a cushion to fall back on.' Perhaps due to the booming oil sector, $50 billion of private money has been flowing into the continent, surpassing the amount in foreign aid. At the same time, poverty is declining.

How Do Accountable Governments Help the Economy?

Insisting that governments are held accountable for their policies helped in two ways, according to Devarajan and Fengler. Politics became freer and more open after the Cold War. Governments supported by the US or the USSR relinquished control to multiparty politics, and elections followed. Previously, marginalized groups like farmers and rural dwellers (most Africans live in rural areas) found a political voice and benefitted. In countries including oil-producing states, changes took the form of new, competent leaders and technocrats skilled in economics. Exchange rates are adjusted competitively, so farmers and people in rural areas have an incentive to increase their productivity and farm output.

Accountability has also been imposed on certain governments by foreign aid donors. There has been a shift in how aid has been doled out. In the 1980s, aid to African countries were often given with the condition that they consulted with the World Bank and the IMF. Starting in 1999, aid is being given to governments who consult with their own people, civil society groups, businesses, and other community organizations.

Pessimists exist, and for good reasons. Wars and civil or international conflicts still raged on over one-third of Sub-Saharan Africa, including in oil-producing states. Devarajan and Fengler reported that much of Africa 'suffers from rampant corruption, and most of its infrastructure is in poor condition'.

But reforms and 'increased openness of its societies, fueled in part by new information and communications technologies give Africa a good chance of enjoying sustained growth and poverty reduction in the decades to come'. Whether it is infrastructures transforming African societies into higher productivity economies or increasing human capital, accountability gives oil states a reason to develop. As responsible governments implement prudent macroeconomic policies, they deliver 'growth, which created . . . support for further reforms, even during the global economic crisis of recent years'.

12

Alleviating Energy Poverty in Africa Requires a Multilateral Approach

Millions of Africans lack access to electricity.
Source: Wikimedia Commons

Although Africa faces several systemic challenges in energy, providing it to the poor sustainably should be a major concern.

Economic growth, after all, requires reliable energy sources for all. This is something Hong Kong planners should keep in mind, as the poor may be kept out of technological progress in a smart city without energy security. However, investments in the infrastructure are not coming it, and require a multilateral effort to break the impasse. The same may be needed in Hong Kong.

Three Challenges in the Global Energy Sector

There are three major challenges in the global energy sector today: The risk of energy supply disruption, environmental issues caused by energy extraction and consumption, and chronic energy poverty in many parts of the world. Although the metrics for quantifying the number of people who are energy poor, here in reference to the lack of access to electricity only, is still debated on (one method uses the energy expenditure as a percentage of income; another calculates the amount of energy needed for daily needs), only 29 per cent of 1.1 billion Saharan Africans have access to electricity.

A map of the existing and planned power interconnected links in Africa proxies the distribution of power on the continent. The northeast is barren, save a single link from Egypt to the coast of the Democratic Republic of the Congo. So is the Maghreb in general. West Africa is very well-developed, while Southern Africa is in between, neither sparse nor densely connected.

A lack of power and electricity creates myriad inconveniences in Africans' daily lives, in providing adequate healthcare in clinics, hospitals, and surgery rooms, and in conducting lasting businesses. A reliable energy source helps run schools, street lighting, telecommunications, and water systems. There is little argument that economic growth and energy demand go hand in hand. The United Nations, therefore, made the universal access of electricity one of its Sustainable Development Goals by 2030.

Access to sustainable energy services—according to the European Union's Energy Initiative for Poverty Eradication and Sustainable Development (EUEI), a European program to promote the role of energy in development created in 2002— is a precondition for poverty reduction. The extremely poor often suffer from energy poverty and heavily rely on traditional biomass, like wood, agricultural residues, and dung, for cooking and heating.

The Lack of Investments in Electricity

But investments in the electricity industry are not coming in. While $51 billion is needed annually to meet the UN's energy goal, only $36 million was committed into the Sub-Saharan electricity sector in 2019. Only $12.6 billion of that amount will be expected to benefit residential customers, thus making meeting the target all but impossible.

From the beginning, the EUEI did not see market or aid mechanisms by themselves as the solution. It promoted a wide net of coordinated approaches: cooperation between the national and regional governments, between the government and the private sector, foreign countries and supranational groups like the EU with the local governments and companies, and everyone with the local people. Support can take the form of legislative and regulatory, energy policymaking, broad institutional support, and technical help in capacity building. Given how under-developed the electricity industry is on the continent (though many countries are reforming their power sectors), this is as concrete as any pan-African strategy can get.

An example is Nigeria, whose government in 2005 opened its electricity market to competition from private companies (government-private sector cooperation) under the aegis of the government's Poverty Reduction Strategy Papers (national-regional government cooperation), with the help of the IMF's conditional policy support instrument (public and private sector cooperation with a supranational organization). The government worked closely in the privatization process and, is continuing after, to ensure that electricity is affordable to urban and rural citizens alike (government-citizen coordination). One of the main challenges now is to make sure private companies have the incentives to provide power to everyone.

Climate Change and Electricity

But keep in mind that some things are out of human control. The meteorological havoc brought about by climate change has affected power generation as well. In Zambia, the lack of rainfall—the worst in four decades—has halted the amount of water flowing into dams on the Zambezi River and its tributaries. Its government is contemplating diverting water from the Congo River, which is more than 100 kilometres away. Zimbabwe is also having a similar problem. And East Africa—in countries like Ethiopia, Kenya, Mozambique, Tanzania, and Zambia—generates much hydroelectricity on the continent; it remains to be seen if power there will be affected as well.

The energy security of the poor in Hong Kong, in the form of electricity bills, are likewise disproportionately affected by climate change. Stakeholders can take a page from Africa's experience and band together to ensure an affordable and sustainable energy supply for them.

13[2]

To Help Africa's Poor, Fair Trade Movement Must Resist Corporate Interests

The Fair Trade movement tries to help small, poor producers of
commodities like bananas.
Source: Wikimedia Commons

This chapter is about using the tools of trade to influence
business behaviour, towards a socially beneficial goal like

[2]An edited and translated version of this chapter appeared as an op-ed in
Le Monde on September 2, 2020.

poverty alleviation. This is a topic that I will return to in discussing Hong Kong: If the fair trade movement can pressure buyers of bananas to pay African growers a good price for their goods, can and should multinational companies pressure local companies in Hong Kong to hire or sell to the poor? Furthermore, I argue that the Fair Trade movement should resist corporate interests for inclusivity's sake, and that donor money should be spent directly in Africa and not in advocacy in wealthy countries.

What is Fair Trade?

The Fair Trade movement, organized in its current form in the 1960s, has set an ambitious agenda. Its ultimate objective is to right the inequalities between rich and poor countries that were created through trade between the wealthy North and the poorer South. It demands transparency and fairness (however that is defined) before certifying its products, which has expanded from the agricultural, like cotton, rice, fruits, cocoa, tea, and coffee to minerals, such as ruby and diamond.

In Tanzania, as reported by Allison Loconto, of INRA-ENPC in France, and Emmanuel Simbua, of the Tea Research Institute of Tanzania, a tea buyer or blender, to obtain certification from the Fair Trade Labelling Organizations International, must be able to pay a price to producers that covers sustainable production and living costs; a premium that producers can reinvest in development; an monetary advance when producers require; and sign contracts that permit long-term planning and sustainable production.

The Economic Debate of Fair Trade

The economic debate on the Fair Trade movement can be categorized into five issues. Distributive issues question whether Free Trade improves the living conditions of producers, including the poor, and whether it will marginalize non-Free Trade producers. Another is its allocative efficiency: Will free trade distort market signals, like the prices on commodities that indicate their quality—and will Free Trade allow inefficient producers to remain the marketplace? Transfer system efficiency refers to how well Free Trade moves resources between markets. Control system efficiency measures how effectively the Free Trade system identifies and deals with abuses. Finally, a question some pose is whether Free Trade is a viable alternative to existing economic policies.

Skeptics like Gavin Hilson, of the University of Surrey in the UK, argued that even when the source of Fair Trade minerals are known—he used Nyala rubies in Malawi as an example—this traceability may not help poor producers. A lack of agreement over what 'Fair Trade' means is one reason. Another is the distracting melange of agendas that are competing for attention, including poverty, corruption, and human rights abuses.

Some of the problem arose from the labelling organizations themselves. For example, Fair Trade Labelling Organizations International has proposed a reduction in premium to producers in exchange for greater volumes sold under the 'Fair Trade' brand. To create a more mainstream movement, there has long been an effort to include big, profit-maximizing corporations in trading and production. Experts see this as a relegation of the movement's social justice goals.

Catherine Dolan, of Northeastern University in the United States, claimed, using Kenya's Fair Trade tea industry as an example, that the benefits that have supposedly been derived from Fair Trade—direct contracts, empowerment, and higher prices—could have been obtained from pre-existing business relationships between producers and buyers. Loconto and Simbua admitted that it is true in how tea is sold in Kenya and Tanzania.

How to Make Fair Trade Better

Paul Stoddart, an economist at Economic Insight in London, also argued that the Fair Trade movement is missing those poor producers that it alleged was helping. Instead of spending money on campaigns in rich countries, organizations like FINE should use the funds to further empower local liaison officers and poor producers. Indeed, given all the dilemmas that exist in the Fair Trade debate, activists should resist temptations to yield to corporate interests and focus on the poor, whose welfare they want to improve. I will explain how a similar strategy to Fair Trade can bring economic justice to the poor in Hong Kong. However, Robbert Maseland and Albert de Vaal, of the University of Nijmegen in the Netherlands, suggested that Fair Trade is a good alternative to free trade and protections only depending on the goods that are traded. So, even to a Fair Trade activist, free trade can sometimes be good for Africa too.

14

Microfinance Should Be a Bridge, Not a Permanent Solution, for the Poor in Africa

Micro-loans help Africans start and run small businesses in Kenya.
Source: Wikimedia Commons

As introduced earlier, microfinance has become a great tool to combat poverty, with support from a wide range of stakeholders.

Hong Kong's poor should have microfinance services available to them, too, although they need to be guided by the experience of families in Ghana and Nigeria, farmers in Ethiopia, and micro-lenders in Malawi. In any case, one should remember that microcredit is a bridge, not a permanent solution, for the poor graduating to more traditional forms of banking.

How Beneficiaries of Microfinance Behave

Many would agree that microfinance is a blessing to the poor in Africa. For one, it helps poor people build assets. In Ghana, one client welfare program assists those who need to pay medical or funeral bills. Borrowers also use micro-loans to send their children to school, receive better healthcare, and buy household goods. A study by Samuel Annim, of the University of Central Lancashire in the UK, observes that clients of microfinance institutions (MFIs) in Ghana behave quite rationally, as any banking consumer would, given a certain interest rate on the loan and their level of wealth, although there are distinctions. They are risk-averse when they borrow, even though, since they often borrow in groups, they have access to better information than those who do not.

Osaore Aideyan, formerly of Illinois State University in the United States, studied rural Nigeria and found that 57.3 per cent or 84.9 per cent of children, depending of which of the two MFIs their families bank with, went to private schools, compared to a range of 7.4 per cent or 38.9 per cent of those children whose family did not receive micro-loans. Moreover, children are more than four times as likely to afford uniforms and close to 10 times more likely to buy textbooks. There is a drastic difference between those who have food shortage (8.6 per cent or 12.4 per cent versus 33.3 per cent or 51.4 per cent); access to qualified doctors (84.3 per cent or 93 per cent versus 62 per cent or 80.5 per cent); large, well-built and furnished homes; and a steady income (22.5 per cent or 35.4 per cent versus 11.1 per cent or 12.5 per cent). Microfinance seems to benefit Nigerians.

Two Different Stories of Microfinance in Africa

There are a handful of MFIs operating in Ethiopia, beginning with the Amhara Credit and Saving Institution in 1995. The reception was great; from 2001 to 2005, the total portfolio managed jumped 300 per cent. Micro-lenders, however, are constrained by operational factors, like the average amount of loans disbursed to borrowers, the financial revenue ratio, and the cost of borrower ratio. A study in northern Ethiopia showed that MFI is a success there; borrowing from a micro-lender significantly increases farmers' per capita consumption and the likelihood there will be home improvements in the short and long-term, especially when there is repeated borrowing.

The situation in Malawi, however, is much more dire. In one study, the project managers for two MFIs have no university degrees and experience in credit service. Human resource struggles to hire qualified staff; boards of directors are normally non-existent. Some groups lack office space, computer equipment, and cars. Financially, MFIs are so dependent on donors that they have no backup plans to operate without. They lack good procedures for recovering loans if their clients do not pay up. As a result, the performance of these MFIs, except FINCA, a large MFI, is poor.

A Suggestion to Improve Microfinance

Ultimately, another study suggests, MFI clients suffer from diminishing returns, and this is likely the scenario. What a MFI, which lacks the scale and resources of traditional banks, does is to provide financial services to people in ways that commercial banks do not find profitable. That is a reason there is a proliferation of NGOs and non-profit groups in the industry— profit is not the dominant objective. MFIs should help the poor only to the point where commercial banks can take them on as customers. MFIs, supported by informed government regulations, need to make the transition as seamlessly as possible. Possible intermediary steps that will be taken in the meantime include banks entering the micro-lending business, which may put weak MFIs out of business, and MFIs scaling up so that they will be more like commercial banks. This will require qualified workers that many countries lack and risks turning well-intentioned MFIs into high interest-charging moneylenders. In Hong Kong, microfinance will offer opportunities for the poor to borrow under terms that traditional banks will not accept, and job seekers who want to work for micro-lending operations.

15

Education Offers the Best Way to Support Africa's Entrepreneurs

Entrepreneurs meet to learn about online search engine optimization and content development.

Source: Wikimedia Commons

Getting access to credit is one battle for the poor. Starting a business and dealing in a competitive environment that discriminates against certain social groups is another. In Africa, government bureaucracy, political instability, and a lack of networking for women and minorities are challenges. In Hong Kong, training, gender inequality, and lack of access to computers and the Internet obstruct poor entrepreneurs. I argue that education is a great equalizer in Africa, as in Hong Kong and many other places.

Benefits of Entrepreneurship in Africa

Despite having fewer resources than established corporations in the private sector, there is good evidence that entrepreneurship in developing countries and Africa—the street vendors in Lagos, Nigeria, to the hawkers in Nairobi, Kenya—help their economies grow.

This is despite the actual behaviour of traders often observed on the ground, like in Cotonou, Benin's used car market, where buyers and sellers allegedly manipulate social contracts, distrust their business partners, but still expect a big payoff from their business activities.

Entrepreneurship plays two crucial roles in African countries. First, it provides jobs for the millions of workers living in or at the edge of poverty that the formal sector cannot employ. That is 2.3 million people in Egypt in North Africa to over 6.7 million people in South Africa, and many more in between. Included are 140 million young people under 35 years old across the continent. Second, the business activities that entrepreneurs engage in set off a massive economic chain reaction to benefit whole regions. In southern Africa, roaming entrepreneurs were so pervasive that 16 governments were pressured to set up the Southern African Development Community Free Trade Area in 2008, giving millions of people job opportunities that had not existed before.

Obstacles in Starting and Running a Business

The obstacles that small and medium-sized businesses face are the same as large businesses, but because of their size they feel them more acutely and so are thus more vulnerable. Two of them, according to Jonathan Munemo of Salisbury University in the United States, have to do with entry regulations and political instability, the latter of which includes the very real threat of military coups d'état. It does not give too much incentive to an aspiring entrepreneur to wait over two months to start a business, as in Somalia, then have a new government take over and not recognize the business as legitimate.

According to the latest World Bank report on doing business, 7 out of the 10 worst countries for doing business are in Africa. At the bottom of the list is Somalia, a base for pirates without a functional government for the last 20 years. The easiest African country to do business in is Mauritius, an island-country once colonized by the Dutch, French, and British, ranked 20th. The World Bank index uses a range of criteria, covering the ease of registering a business licence and property, obtaining electricity, trading with businesses in other countries, and enforcing contracts and bankruptcy rulings.

Diversity Challenges in African Business

As in western countries, there are challenges for women, who are under-represented in business startups, as well. A study by Reyes Aterido and Mary Hallward-Driemeier at the World Bank blamed this on a productivity gap when women are in positions of authority, as well as possible prejudices against them when they—as opposed to a son—work for their father in a family business. This may be significant in countries like Ghana, where family businesses dominate. All of this adds to the traditional constraints on female entrepreneurship, such as social, cultural, and economic norms, that keep women from borrowing and taking out mortgages.

In South Africa, there also seems to be an under-representation of blacks in entrepreneurship. In interviews, they blame the effects of apartheid, the lack of financial resources and education along with weak social capital and network. Put together, it is hard for them to enter the world of business.

How Can the Government Improve the Business Environment?

But given the challenges that African entrepreneurs face, and the diversity of socio-economic and geographical features in Africa, there are numerous things that an optimistic government can experiment in order to encourage business-building. For example, the late World Bank economist Walter Elkan argued that small businesses, given the right economic environment— think tax holidays for large projects and the removal of ceilings on loan interest rates—can thrive in greater numbers than their large counterparts.

Menemo has a bigger wish list: 'Standardizing incorporation documents; eliminating or reducing the minimum capital requirement to register a business; reducing registration fees and business licence fees; setting up a one-stop shop that makes it possible to complete business start-up procedures at a single location; simplifying the documents needed for registration; and allowing online business registration.'

Aterido and Hallward-Driemeier want governments to ensure gender equality in education, specializing in business skills, and implement measures to provide role models and a network of business contact for women. In post-apartheid South Africa, as it should be elsewhere on the continent, the government should continue to fund promising startups and encourage business training. Social capital and network can be built through socialization in an educational setting. Having to change people's mindset and encouraging them through mentorship seem to be the greatest barrier to entry. Hong Kong's entrepreneurs, facing their own unique challenges, can likewise benefit from government policies that introduce more women and poor residents, many of whom have no technological know-how. Education, if one has to choose a single area to invest in, provides the greatest good to the most people.

16

Continued Public-Private Partnerships in Technology Crucial to Development in Africa

An Internet cafe in rural KwaZulu-Natal, South Africa.
Source: Wikimedia Commons

It seems that everyone wants to be on the Internet and the cell phone. Technologically, they level the playing field between countries, and offer, through electronic payment systems like M-Pesa, the unbanked poor a wide variety of financial services.

Cell phones lower search costs and are used among grain traders in Niger. Such is the excitement surrounding the Internet that that universities and cafes rush to connect students, researchers, and local residents to it. Rwanda's President Paul Kagame promised concessions to software companies and write-offs for bandwidth purchases. But as in Hong Kong, the poor may not receive the bulk of the benefits. A digital divide exists; Internet access and cell phones may be too expensive for the poorest people. There seems to be no evidence to suggest that expanding electronic money systems creates benefits for the economy either.

Internet Pricing in Africa

The Internet is inaccessible, slow, and expensive in Africa. 84.4 per cent of Africans do not use the Internet, according to the International Telecommunication Union. In 2016, Africans in poorer countries had to pay up to 14 per cent of average national income for cell phone Internet connection. Wholesale costs range from $9 per megabit per second—20 times as London—to a whopping $965 per month in Burkina Faso. In Nigeria, the continent's most populous country, there were only a few hundred well trafficked domestically created websites.

Outside of mobile telephony, the countries in East and Central Africa are mostly plagued by unreliable Internet connections. Computer equipment in other countries are reportedly outdated, lack of electricity is an issue, and web contents, when adapted to local tastes, assumes English literacy on the part of the surfer. Video- and script-heavy may not be downloadable due to the slow Internet speed. The situation may be better in West Africa, which uses a more robust undersea cable for its Internet connection.

The Digital Divide in Africa

But access overall is expensive. When the Yeoville branch of the oldest Internet cafe in Africa closed in 2005, it was charging users $2.29 an hour. In Johannesburg, South Africa, there was a large disparity between people who could afford to access the Internet (those making more than $1,310 a month) and those who could not.

The government has encouraged companies to help facilitate the flow of information among all members of the society. But a schism exists, related to race. White South Africans, for example, were most likely to have computers, followed by Indians, other colored people, and blacks. In addition to the technical barriers of surfing the Internet, only 9.6 per cent of the population in this middle-income economy speak English as their first language— English being the lingua franca of commercial computer software and the Internet.

African women, by their race and gender, are doubly excluded from the Internet. All of these observations project to the country level, where richer countries enjoy far more Internet usage than poorer ones. For example, Malawi and Liberia had 96.1 and 81 Internet users per 1,000 people in 2017. Czech Republic and Malaysia had 769.7 and 215.4 Internet users per 1,000 people. There are scholars and policymakers, however, who believe that low Internet penetration rates may lead to low incomes, creating a vicious cycle that can only be broken by injections of computing facilities and technical training.

Unfriendly Internet Regulations

The low Internet usage is exacerbated by unfriendly government regulations. After all, the growth of the Internet industry in the US rose out of the deregulation of telecommunications. Controlling for income, regulation has a significant effect on the diffusion of the Internet.

Countries that required formal approvals for Internet Service Providers (ISPs) before allowing them entry into the Internet market saw the number of Internet hosts, which is probably correlated with the number of Internet cafes, and users fall by half. Those that regulated ISP pricing had their cost of Internet access tripled. Higher scores on competition policy are correlated with higher Internet subscriptions per telephone line.

Why Africa Needs the Internet

Some observers asked a fundamental question: Does Africa need the Internet for economic growth? Some suggest that telecommunication infrastructure for communication services is necessary. But the Internet is not necessary for growth; its development has already been slowed by illiteracy, the lack of access to credit card, and the same factors that have been contributing to the digital divide. Others claim that some people oversold the potential benefits of information technology altogether in developing countries.

But there are several reasons for connecting Africans to the Internet. The World Wide Web and its applications democratize knowledge. Although there is no typical African case in the adoption of the Internet, comparing low-income Burkina Faso to Ghana demonstrates the benefits of connectivity.

In the beginning, Burkina Faso did not have a role for the Internet in its academic institutions at all, judging from the number of Internet connection points. By comparison, the University of Ghana had 65 connection points, though online courses and advanced applications of the Internet were not available. But both countries had ambitious goals of connecting academic, researchers, and health workers to their colleagues in the West.

In academia, the Internet is a necessity. It is a medium not only to access the information of scientists in the West, but also to contribute to creating knowledge. The Internet cafes that have proliferated in African cities can, by default of their existence, act as training centres that enhance computer literacy and skills and promote the concept of the Internet. Kepler, a Rwandan non-profit, uses the Internet to connect uneducated Rwandans to vocational courses.

An underlying motivation for Africans to connect to the Internet is the need to catch up to advanced economies. Fibre-optic cables will continue to be laid. They will permit East Africans to set up back office businesses, like in India and Sri Lanka, that will serve companies in the West. According to Internet World Stats, between 2001 and 2017, the number of Internet users in Kenya, a beneficiary country, grew from 200,000 to 43 million, a 217-time increase.

President Paul Kagame of Rwanda has offered concessions to software companies doing business there. Kenya scrapped sales tax on computers and new cell phones. Bandwidth purchases can be written off, with the effect of making the regional Internet market more price competitive. The same drive that created Africa's first unicorn in 2016 will create a robust Internet network on the continent.

Internet-Enabled Cell Phones

In the meanwhile, Internet connectivity by cell phones seems to offer the greatest promise. One tenth of the continent is covered by mobile Internet. In 2016, cell phone technologies and services generated $110 billion for Sub-Saharan Africa, or 7.7 per cent of GDP, rising to $142 (8.6 per cent of GDP) by 2020—showing the scale of the money that is funneled into the sector and jobs and public money that are produced.

But achieving that objective through public-private partnerships may be the best approach. The government-funded National Science Foundation was crucial in the development of the Internet infrastructure in the US. To rely wholly on private enterprises to deploy a large Internet network would have no historical precedent.

Using the US Internet boom as a model, African governments should collaborate with private enterprises on the continent. That should apply to the ambitious but experimental efforts by American companies to reach a larger geography in Africa, like Google's Project Loon and Facebook's plan to send equipment-laden drones to reach otherwise uncovered places.

By comparison, the adoption of cell phones in Sub-Saharan Africa has been phenomenal. There were ten times as many cell phones as landlines in 2009. In 2016, two-fifths of the people there have cell phones. Morocco's cell phone users increased from nil in 1998 to 41.5 million (122.6 per cent of the population) in 2017; Kenya and South Africa's penetration rates, by comparison, are 87 per cent and 68 per cent.

From 2002 to 2016, subscription rate in Sub-Saharan Africa grew from 3.6 per cent to 73 per cent. In the EU, the rate was 71 per cent to 124.1 per cent. In 2016, there were 754 million cell phone subscribers in Sub-Saharan Africa.

Grain Traders and the Uses for Cell Phones

One of the greatest uses of cell phones is in the commodities market. Because information is costly and asymmetric, there is often excess price dispersion—variations in price—across markets. Cell phones reduce search costs and hence lower price dispersion.

An example is the grain traders of Niger in a study between 2001 and 2006. Instead of travelling to different markets to obtain price information, cell phones allowed them to cover many markets quickly. Unlike perishable commodities, grain is a class of goods that is storable and applicable to many countries in Sub-Saharan Africa. This advantage in gathering information presumably boosts profit. By contrast, entrepreneurs in Rwanda credit their successes with cell phones to the increased frequency of meeting new and existing business contacts.

So applications of cell phones include the dissemination of agricultural price information, monitoring of heath care, and transmission of money in poor countries. Some mobile applications are developed by the telecommunications sector. Some are offered by the public sector. Yet others have been launched through partnerships between the two.

M-Pesa and the Rise of Mobile Money and Banking

Financial applications for cell phones rolled out in 2005 and, as pointed out by a European Investment Bank report in 2018, are increasingly displacing services that are provided by traditional banks. Not only do they help with tasks such as paying bills and transferring money, these apps include m-money systems, like Kenya's M-Pesa, that facilitate international money transfers. Like other apps, m-money systems can be set up by banks or telecom companies, or partnerships between the two. Each of the sectors have their own regulations, which appear to be converging. There are calls for interoperability between m-money systems, for example, MTN in Uganda, Airtel Money and Tigo in Tanzania, and MTN and Airtel Money in Rwanda— using the five-member East African Community.

M-money systems allows people with a cell phone and an account to store money electronically, buy airtime, pay bills, withdraw cash, and transfer funds with a set of text messages, menus, and identification numbers. Even without an account, a person can send and withdraw cash from a cell phone operator or third party, who sets up a pseudo account for them. M-Pesa, launched in 2007 by the British Department for International Development and Vodafone's Safaricom, is the most well-known. In its first 2 years, M-Pesa facilitated $3.7 billion, or 10 per cent of the country's GDP in 2009. As of June 2017, it had 22.6 million subscribers—up from 17.1 the year before— serviced by 287,400 agents in 10 countries. In Kenya, it claims a large share of the 93 per cent of the population who have access to mobile payments.

M-Pesa and other forms of mobile money systems may owe their success to the lack of financial development in Sub-Saharan Africa. Though much improved, only 43 per cent of Sub-Saharan Africans have access to basic financial services, like a bank account. Even in South Africa, the rate hovers around 70 per cent, with only 24 per cent making more than three financial transactions per month. In Rwanda, there were six bank branches per 100,000 people in 2017 (Italy, by comparison, had 44.6 banks). Now there are more M-Pesa customers than bank account holders in the country. Wire transfers are otherwise expensive, unavailable in rural areas, or at high risk of theft.

Economic and Political Weekly, in an article entitled 'Models of Mobile Banking', referred to this effect as the transformational model of mobile banking. That is, previously unbanked people are included and used to affect the socio-economic development of a country. M-Pesa system may even be used as a rudimentary bank account and, due to the higher frequency it is used compared to other money transfer services, an informal insurance network.

After all, M-Pesa allows its users to save more. Reaching beyond traditional banks, it reaches a more diverse clientele. Ultimately, however, it is more of a complementary service to physical banks than a substitute.

Can Mobile Phone Accessible Money Help the Poor?

If M-Pesa is tied to the banking system, its growth can be tied to economic growth and poverty reduction in developing countries, since the expansion of a country's banking system and its connection to growth is well-documented. There may be a reverse causation; the reduction in poverty may have resulted in the growth of e-money. There is little evidence of the connection, beyond statistically weak studies on telecommunication infrastructure's positive impact on growth.

Mobile money systems do not offer interest on savings and access to credit from financial institutions, although Thomas Molony, from the Centre of African Studies at the University of Edinburgh, described M-Pesa as having a 'much better record of getting credit to the rural poor than formal credit systems in low-income countries'. Safaricom does not even allow bank deposit type activities, since it lacks a bank licence. M-money are therefore not banking from a financial or legal standpoint.

But the economic effects of m-money system are potentially enormous. M-money systems can become a new class of currency as its influence grows in international money transfers. Low-income users of e-money in Egypt today view balance transfer not as a substitute for money, but aid to manage cell phone airtime and make cell phone use more cost efficient. Official remittance to Sub-Saharan Africa in 2017 was $37.8 billion; m-money can change the flow of funds and business behaviours at a microeconomic level.

But mobile banking in South Africa has been slow to pick up among poor people in South Africa—and mobile telephony may worsen the increasing gap between the poor and the poorest. While cell phones are still unaffordable for the impoverished, investments in education, energy, roads, and water may even be a priority over communications technology in Africa and arguably in Hong Kong.

Most mobile finance initiatives in Africa ultimately are commercially motivated. Driven by business models, they emphasize profit over social outcome. So one can only hope that positive social and macroeconomic outcome will be derived from electronic finance, through understanding and managing its risks, and empirical evidence will support this initiative.

17

The Economic Challenges of Climate Change in Africa

Droughts have a large economic impact on East Africa.
Source: Wikimedia Commons

Climate change reflects on Hong Kong's poor in economic ways, like higher air-conditioning or heating bills. They may need to be insured if typhoon seasons stretches longer than usual. Their jobs might be affected if they work outdoors in a park. Or they may have to pay more for imported food if erratic weather destroys local crops, grown by the 4,300-odd residents in 2,400 subsidized rural farms. This chapter gives an idea what farmers in agrarian Africa have to endure as the climate becomes more unpredictable. Access to irrigation water, land, and food are main concerns. Homes and physical assets need to be repaired more often. More conflicts may result over scarce resources, leading to economic stagnation. Stakeholders can help the poor by innovating in farming technologies and stepping in to encourage businesses to thrive in an ever uncertain environment.

The Vulnerable Continent

It is an irony that poor people in African countries, which emits far less greenhouse gases than its western and Asian counterparts, are among the most vulnerable from the effects of climate change. The most obvious reason is that Africans are highly agrarian; the agricultural industry makes up 24 per cent of the continent's GDP in 2015. If economic activities that are related to agriculture are included, the proportion would be half of the total economy in Sub-Saharan Africa. So this presents a clear transmission mechanism from changes in the weather to reduced crop yield to lower incomes for farmers and others in the industry (not to mention less nutritional food for the family and children). Other industries are likely to feel the impact, like the eco-tourism in Botswana documented by Wame Hambira and Jarkko Saarinen of Oulu University in Finland.

The Economic Effects of Climate Change

Climate change affects African countries and their poor citizens differently, depending on two factors. First is how exposed they are to the climate flux. One example are the supply of water and irritable land; East Africa is expected to get wetter, while Southern Africa will get drier. Another is the location of the food source, which Thomas Hereto and Stephanie Rosch of Purdue University has pointed out is the single largest item on the poor's budget. Whether the poor is connected to basic utilities and how secure they are is also important. Second is how well they adapt, which is primarily a private-sector response and involves the mobility of families and workers, the management of production, and changes in agricultural output.

Poor countries in Sub-Saharan Africa are likely to be hurt, according to Lucas Bretschger and Simone Valente of ETH Zurich in Switzerland, because of climate change's negative impact on the rate of depreciation of physical assets like factories, storage facilities, and transportation infrastructure. Bad or great variations in weather damage commercial buildings, water tanks, and roads more quickly. Not dealt with because of poverty, this leads to slow economic growth and in fact traps less-developed countries in poverty. Experts at the World Bank, Matteo Lanzafame of the University of Messina in Italy, Melissa Dell of MIT and her colleagues, and Paul Collier of Oxford and his colleagues have not only shown that countries struggle to recover after an environmental shock in terms of having to repair physical assets, but also people's income level and human capital growth.

Conor Devitt, of the University of Chicago, and Richard Tol, of Vrije Universiteit in Amsterdam, also found that climate change slows economic growth. They argue that the human body is simply less productive at higher temperatures. Moreover, climate change decreases crop yield, leading to a smaller choice of nutritious food and possibly malnutrition in workers. Finally, some diseases thrive in warmer climates; workers are less productive when they get sick. Devitt and Tol described a vicious cycle at work in some poor countries: climate change creates scarcity in resources, making civil war more likely. A warring country succumbs to lower economic growth, which makes it more vulnerable to the effects of climate change, which includes armed conflicts.

The Role of Stakeholders in Climate Change

There is a role to play for the private sector and the government. Private companies will have to continue to adapt and innovate in variable climates across the continent. Meanwhile, the government needs to be on top of research that will increase crop yield and resilience. It needs to pick up where companies failed and repair or build new infrastructure—and create a business-friendly environment for the private sector to continue to adapt and innovate. These are advices that are as applicable in Kenya as in Hong Kong, although the scale is obviously much smaller in the latter. After all, it is ultimately through the accumulation of assets that the poor people can increase their wealth. Poverty reduction in the age of climate change, nevertheless, makes it more challenging and expensive.

18

Drier and Headed to War?

Droughts cause conflicts over land use in Kenya.
Source: Wikimedia Commons

In the previous chapter, I wrote about how climate change can lead to war between groups of people sparring over scarce resources. How else can climate change spark conflicts in unexpected ways? A low-income, subsidized farmer in Hong Kong's New Territories might like to know. Neo-Malthusians point to water-related issues, such as the freshwater table and water security. Those living downstream of the Nile River often need to negotiate with those further up, like Egypt. 'Water wars' may start between countries that use the same bodies of water as national boundaries. Finally, the freshwater supply is decreasing in many parts of the continent, the fight over which is also the stuff of wars. However, when the first of such conflicts may occur remains up to speculation.

From Climate Change to War

UNICEF claimed that 40,000 children are dying globally—most of them in Africa—from hunger and diseases brought on by water shortage or dirty water. Achieving the UN objectives of universal primary education and reduction of child and maternal mortality are critically tied to the availability of clean water and sanitation. Diarrhea, guinea worms, which are found only in Africa, and scabies are examples of diseases brought about from a contaminated water supply.

The vulnerability of Africa to 'climatic variability and change,' marked by droughts, famines, floods, and cyclones, leads to water crises. Water and sanitation are not seen as good long-term investments in Sub-Saharan African countries, which did not make them a priority and, compounded by bad credit ratings, could not get the necessary funding from international capital markets. This is apparent even in countries like Egypt, which is 'entirely dependent on the Nile for its wealth'. According to measurements, the Nile provides more than 86 per cent of the water used in the country annually. If there is a drastic shortage in the water supply from the river, tourism, leisure sailing and boating, oil exports, and food production will be halted.

A large amount of neo-Malthusian scholarship in international relations links the lack of access to freshwater and water security to intra- and inter-state violence. Robert Kaplan talked about environmental stress as a 'real strategic danger'. Indeed, in Egypt, the 'only matter that could take [the country] to war again is water,' predicted President Anwar Sadat in 1979. And the target of his comment? Most likely Ethiopia, which lies upstream on the Nile and controls 85 per cent of the inflow.

Former Egyptian Minister Boutros Boutros-Ghali claimed that the 'national security of Egypt is . . . a question of water'. Sudan, he predicted in 1989, would need 5 billion cubic metres of water per year by 2010. Kenya, Tanzania, Uganda, and Rwanda—of the Lake Victoria region—would consume 10 billion cubic metres per year by 2009.

Room for Cooperation

Countries sharing water basins and aquifers, to reinforce cooperation and avert crises, should strengthen and connect national- and international-level institutions to channel pacifist political will into coherent action. This includes synchronizing regional water management with national development goals. These goals may include regional peace and cooperation and can be brought about through 'greater interaction, interdependence, and societal linkages'.

Boutros-Ghali commented, somewhat ambitiously, in 1989 that to get international assistance, they needed 'not only stability, but also a consensus among us' on water sharing issues. The plan he drew up would convert electricity generated in dams in upstream Uganda, Sudan, and the Congo into exchange for cash or capital development funds, which would be utilized for water and irrigation projects in upstream countries. Today, to put things into perspective, less than half of the world's trans boundary basins are under the auspices of any formal agreement for sharing and managing their freshwater. Only 116 of 276 of them belong to a river basin organization. And these agreements and organizations are not enough to deal with conflicts, for lack of crisis management mechanisms.

Furthermore, the UN found that 72 per cent of all major international river basins are in developing countries, including those in Africa. Fewer than 33 per cent of river basin agreements signed between 1948 and 1972 covered those basins. UN Water, which coordinates UN agencies working on water issues, has limited resources and effectiveness as a proactive player in hydro-diplomacy. Informal networks of policy makers must play that role for now.

Will There Be a Water War?

The possibility of water conflicts may be over-estimated. In the 20th century, only seven skirmishes arose over water issues, and no war was fought over water. During that period, 145 treaties on water-related issues were signed. Aaron T. Wolf, of Oregon State University, and his colleagues and Ashok Swain and his colleagues at Uppsala University admitted that there have not been clear-cut 'water wars'.

Indeed, Patrice McMahon, of the University of Nebraska-Lincoln, suggested that there are good theoretical and empirical reasons why water will not be the main cause of interstate conflicts in the future. A whole field of research is focused on water boundaries that are not positioned exactly on national borders and the resultant geopolitical logic that war is inevitable. But scholars often forget that those same regions are already ridden with religious, ethnic, and political problems that are more divisive and agitating than water issues. Moreover, when there are depletions of environmental resources, it is equally likely that the parties involved would cooperate as they are to conflict. There is evidence of this when there were natural disasters among pastoral groups in Kenya.

But there are still concerns that the water-wars hypothesis still holds true. While the region most in danger of war on water has been in the Middle East, geographical factors like desertification, caused by climate change, and man-made ones like demographic pressures, industrialization, and urbanization may make Africa a drier place and a continent that will be at a greater risk for war. Algeria, Egypt, Morocco, and Tunisia, for example, are or will soon be depleting all available fresh surface and groundwater supplies. Despite tremendous efforts, Morocco's population growth rate are causing a declining water supply. Algeria and Tunisia are facing a 'water barrier' that requires more efforts, investments, controls, and regulations. Egypt and Tunisia have already made efforts to curb consumption through taxes on city and industrial water usage.

Scarce water is driven by supply and demand. This is true whether in Ethiopia or in rural Hong Kong. Pandemic water mismanagement (which has relevance to a wide variety of fields like energy generation, food production, health, and even human rights) and climate change decreases the supply, while irrigation and cooling increases the demand for water. This puts tremendous pressure on the water stock.

Dam-building in the 1960s to 1980s in Zambia and Zimbabwe has caused ecological damage as well as social conflict among the Tonga people. In sum, there are good reasons to believe that clean water is in decline in numerous African countries—or in Hong Kong for farming and fishing—and that, along with the bodies of water acting as village or national boundaries and a rationale to build community destroying dams and other construction projects, will cause violence in communities and beyond in the future.

Part III

The Americas

19

Activism Is the First Step to Improving the Health of Poor Canadians

Health outcome for the poor in Canada is markedly different than for the well-off.
Source: Wikimedia Commons

Understanding the health outcome for poor Canadians compared to the general population should be of interest to Hong Kongers. For one thing, Hong Kong's Census Department reveals very little on the health status of low-income residents. So studying a similarly developed healthcare system in which health services are generally access to the public could predict the outcome of poor Hong Kongers.

If that is true, the prognosis of low-income Hong Kong residents are not good. The poor, according to studies, are the sickliest group in society. Poverty is linked to food insecurity, which causes a host of non-communicable diseases. There are various efforts to alleviate poverty in Canada, going back to the 1970s.

A new public health agenda must be drafted, reflecting poverty and economic inequality as the root cause of health inequity. Improving the distribution of social determinants of health (SDOH) is another approach. A success story can be found in Brazil, with its popular Bolsa Família cash transfer program, in which aid is given to individuals only if certain health objectives are met.

Evidence That the Poor Are Less Healthy in Canada

1. André Billette

There is ample evidence that poor people are less healthy in Canada. The late sociologist André Billette wrote a *Canadian Social Work Review* paper in 1979, 'Poor Health and Poor Policies,' in which he mentioned two earlier studies. One, conducted by Philip Enterline and his colleagues, studied sick people in Montreal and found that the poor made the most doctor's visits.

Another academic's work Billette cited was that of Pran Manga, from the University of Ottawa. The statistics Billette drew from was from 1974 to 1975, of a then ongoing study in Ontario on who used medical services. Manga found that the lower the family income, the greater of use of all types of medical services—significantly more for members of families making under $4,000 (in 1976 dollars).

2. Nicholas Vozoris and Valerie Tarasuk

In the *Canadian Journal of Public Health*, Nicholas Vozoris and Valerie Tarasuk, from the Faculty of Medicine at the University of Toronto, observed that welfare recipients were sicker than the average adult in Toronto. In fact, they are sicker than members of other low-income groups, including the working poor. This makes them—there were 1,910,900 people on welfare in 2001—at risk for income-related health issues.

Welfare recipients are considered the extremely poor in industrialized countries like Canada. Using secondary analysis of data from the 1996-1997 National Population Health Survey fitted using a logistic model, Vozoris and Tarasuk tried to find how likely adults on welfare would report poor health. Poor health can be categorized into heart diseases, diabetes, hypertension, obesity, and other ailments.

Adults on welfare are more likely to report diseases in all categories associated with general, mental, and social health. This includes, worryingly, heart diseases, which are preventable by addressing root causes such as financial hardship, food insecurity, and hunger. The investigators cautioned that, nevertheless, the direction is causal relationship between welfare and health, by nature of the logistic model, is unknown. But they suggested that welfare benefit cuts might put recipients at greater health risk.

3. Patricia Collins and Her Colleagues

In 2014, Patricia Collins, of Queen's University, and her colleagues claimed in the *Canadian Journal of Public Health* that there is an established link between poverty and food insecurity and its associated non-communicable diseases. Household food insecurity (HFI) is the inability to consume an acceptably adequate quality or quantity of food, or the uncertainty that one would be able to do so. 3.8 million Canadians—12 per cent of households—were affected in 2014.

Sixty-five per cent of welfare recipients suffer from HFI, 27 per cent with severe forms of it. 37 per cent of those on worker's compensation or employment insurance also experience food insecurity. People suffering from HFI report poorer mental, physical and oral health. They suffer from diabetes, heart disease, hypertension, and depression at a higher rate, and are exacerbated by stagnant or negative income growth in poor households and rising food and basic necessities' costs.

Attacking the Root Cause of Poverty

1. André Billette

Billette and his former research partner found, in a study of social class, that mortality among men in the lowest social class— unskilled workers and farmers—is higher than average. This confirms the work of 19th century British public health pioneers Edwin Chadwick and William Farr. Poverty and illness form a vicious cycle.

Efforts of poverty reduction in the 1970s fall within four groups. Some advocate the redistribution of income to the poor and those on welfare. Others argue for a reduction of regional disparities, such as the establishment of the Department of Regional Economic Expansion. There were local programs, such as the Local Initiative Program, Opportunities for Youth, and New Horizon Programs. Some started housing campaigns for the benefit of low-income groups.

Of the four strategies, Billette believed that redistribution of wealth had the most direct impact on poverty. The government can redistribute through public expenditures on public services, although their effect was inconclusive. Simple transfer payments—towards universal transfers, old age security, and guaranteed income supplement—are also possible. So is taxation, but while absolute poverty decreases, relative poverty increases, according to Billette's analysis.

2. Deanna Williamson

Deanna Williamson, of the University of Alberta, wrote in the *Canadian Journal of Public Health*, that 'efforts to improve the health of Canadians are intricately linked to policies and programs that reduce poverty and its negative influences on health'. In a 2001 study, she collected information about health sector initiatives addressing poverty from Health Canada, 12 provincial and territorial health ministries, and 49 of 137 health regions—including Ontario's district health councils. Specifically, she was identifying policies, programs, and projects that addressed poverty. For example, she dichotomized programs as individual or family, organizational, community, and political strategies.

Williamson found that initiatives are local in nature: 79.9 per cent are regional, 17.9 per cent are provincial or territorial, and 2.2 per cent are federal. 53.1 per cent of the health initiatives focused on poverty and its negative effects on health. 20.5 per cent of the initiatives' objectives are targeted toward poverty: to raise awareness about poverty, to keep people from becoming poor, to enhance skills in people living in poverty, and to change social and economic conditions leading to poverty. Health Canada is employing 'significantly fewer' strategies to address poverty than ministries at lower levels. In addition, 46.9 per cent of the initiatives targeted teen parents and their children, aboriginals, intravenous drug users, and new immigrants.

According to the study, there is an 'ever-growing body of evidence about the detrimental effects that poverty has on health . . . Necessary as individual and family-focused strategies may be in improving the health and quality of life of Canadians in poverty, they do little to reduce the number and proportion of people in poverty. The most effective way to decrease the negative health consequences of poverty is, first and foremost, to reduce poverty.' Some of the causes are changing labour market conditions and insufficient social assistance benefits and minimum wages.

3. Patricia Collins and Her Colleagues

Collins and her colleagues saw a correlation between the risk of HFI and decreasing income. They proposed a model of HFI in which poverty alleviation works alongside charities (like food banks), household improvements and supports (like community food kitchens), and community food systems (like food charters). They are all municipal-level efforts. The investigators expected generous income support programs (like social assistance, child care benefits, and housing supports) from the government to resolve the root causes of poverty in the community.

Towards a New Public Health Agenda

1. *Public Health Problems are an Economic Inequality Issue*

Dennis Raphael, of York University in Toronto, proposed in 1998 in the *Canadian Journal of Public Health* a series of action to attacking poverty in the context of alleviating health inequality. He cited the *Health of Canada's Children Report*, which reported a deep divide between the health of children who are poor and those who are not. Statistics Canada attribute 22 per cent of mortality differences among Canadians to income differentials. According to the retired British epidemiologist Richard Wilkinson, 'increasing economic inequality decreases social cohesion, increases individual malaise, and produces the conditions by which increased mortality and morbidity occur'.

Raphael mentioned in the same piece that the *Ottawa Charter for Health Promotion* included income as a basic prerequisite for health. The public, organizations, and the government should promote public health in the framework of political action, policy development and implementation, and participation.

It is in this framework that impact studies should be conducted on poverty and health. For example, people should study the effect of ending rent controls, instituting drug co-payment plans for seniors, cutting welfare payments alongside income tax cuts for the rich, and eliminating pay equity for women in female-dominated service agencies (provincial level) on poverty. Same at the municipal level for fees in libraries and at parks, as well as on public transportation. Federal changes in transfer grants, unemployment insurance, and pensions can also be studied.

Raphael was not the only one advocating a political solution. Williamson claimed growing scholarly evidence that, despite the possibility of retribution, the health of individual Canadians in poverty and society need concerted efforts to alter the 'fundamental structural conditions contributing to poverty'. She suggested more research in this area.

2. Improving the Distribution of Social Determinants of Health to Decrease Inequalities

In 2015, Raphael published a paper in *Canadian Public Policy* in which he claimed that Canadian public policy, influenced by business, created health inequalities by skewing the distribution of SDOHs, which are, according to the WHO: 'the conditions of daily life—the circumstances in which people are born, grow, live, work, and age'. They are a product of the 'inequitable distribution of power, money, and resources—the structural drivers of those conditions of daily life—globally, nationally, and locally'.

Raphael identified Canada as a liberal welfare state, in which the government 'provides fewer economic and social supports for the population, universal benefits are sparse, and state provision of modest benefits is targeted at the least well off'. The distribution of wages and benefits is skewed, and the labour sector is weak. Income, housing (the affordability of which is a determinant of poverty), and food security are skewed as a result. They are all the symptomatic of the economic dominance of the business sector. These skewed SDOH lead to inequalities in the incidences of adoption of health-threatening behaviours and psycho-social stress.

There are alternative forms of the welfare state, which are social democratic, conservative, and Latin. A social democratic welfare state would eschew the market in favour of the state and would follow the ideological goals of poverty reduction, equality, and employment. It is possible to deviate or replace a welfare state model for another for short periods of time. For example, Canada has swerved from the liberal model when it embraced a universally accessible healthcare system. So Raphael suggested, among in other areas, research in the public's support—through political representation or individually—for a liberal welfare state that produces current distributions of SDOH and health inequalities. There can also be research into how influential health-related charities view SDOH.

3. Does a Food-Based Solution Treat the Causes of Poverty?

Collins and her colleagues' plan of action was predicated on the observation that food-based solutions to food insecurity do not treat the causes of poverty. Food banks, community food kitchens, and food charters do not address the root cause of HFI and will not reduce its prevalence in the long run. Moreover, municipal-level initiatives give provincial and federal governments less incentives to reduce income insecurity using social programs. There is, therefore, a need to study the costs of delivering provincial and federal social benefits compared to food-based initiatives: 'downloading the responsibility and costs of reducing HFI to municipalities and community-based organizations is especially problematic if the initiatives being delivered have limited effectiveness'.

4. A Success Story in Brazil

In practice, such a strategy may culminate in a program like Bolsa Família (Family Grant) in Brazil. Organized in its present form by President Lula in 2003, it is the largest conditional cash transfer program in the world, with a $6.8 billion budget and affecting 13 million families—approximately one quarter of all Brazilian households. The cash transfer to low-income citizens is conditional on educational and health (like prenatal care and vaccinations) requirements.

Due to the Family Grant, healthcare utilization has increased. Pregnant women visited their doctors, on average, 1.5 more times. 12 per cent to 15 per cent more children received all vaccinations required by six months after birth. Their mean body mass index also increased. Another consequence is a decrease in income inequality. According to Davide Rasella and his colleagues at the University of Bahia in Brazil, found from a study of the program that closing the income gap leads to an increase in life expectancy. Family Grant has been widely lauded as a success in poverty alleviation, and, with its positive health implication, should be a great example for the Canadian government to follow.

What Is to Be Done?

The link between being poor and having bad health is grounded in decades-long academic research, from Enterline and Manga's subjects in Montreal and Toronto in the 1970s to Vozoris, and Tarasuk's welfare recipients in 21st century Toronto. Theoretically, poverty and health may form a vicious cycle, as Billette imagined it or as Collins and her colleagues hypothesized through food insecurity. Raphael saw a cause-and-effect reaction, stemming from Canada's choice of political system and its influence on the determinants of wealth in the country. But one should contemplate attacking poverty as though it is the cause of health inequalities in Canada. Possible areas of research in this fight in Canada include the fiscal (Should and how should the government provide more generous federal and provincial social programs?) and political strategies: What is the best way to influence anti-poverty policies? Is the liberal welfare state good for public health? It is certain that both economic and political solutions are necessary to address public health problems, which are grounded in poverty, in Canada.

20

Will Poor Albertans Benefit from Economic Diversification?

Diversifying Alberta's economy will put downward pressure on
Calgary's high housing prices.
Source: Wikimedia Commons

Hong Kong and Alberta have something in common. Each
aspires to be a hub for emerging industries. Hong Kong, at one
time or another, wanted to be a centre for Chinese medicine
and green finance. Alberta is planning to attract software and
artificial intelligence (AI) companies to the Edmonton-Calgary
corridor, despite not gaining any real traction for decades.

I analysed Alberta and concluded that, if the primary goal is job creation, it should stick to what it knows best, which are infrastructure-building, construction, and manufacturing. The lag time between investment in a technology company, including educating a domestic workforce, and its economic payoff will mean not many low-waged, low-skilled Albertans will benefit in the short run.

Economic Diversification in Alberta

Perhaps it has to do with the shale revolution in the US, which drove down heavy crude prices. Or perhaps it has to do with the quest for alternative sources of energy, or responsible government. Diversifying the economy away from the oil sector in Alberta is all but certain. But will it benefit poor Albertans? For economic diversification to be successful, it needs to identify industries that can compete in the Albertan economy for the long haul. Planners select a small, overachieving group of industries, or a large array of industries whose employment growth offsets the future loss of oil and gas jobs.

Is Diversification Good for the Poor? It Depends

So, is this process good for the poor? Of course, it depends on where the money is going to. Today, no one industry dominates the Albertan economy, despite popular conception (former Premier Rachel Notley claimed that no other industries can replace it). Although the province produces 81 per cent of the country's oil and gas, they only contribute to a quarter of the province's GDP. By comparison, Saudi Arabia's oil sector is about 50 per cent of GDP (on the other end of the spectrum, Norway is 19 per cent reliant on oil and gas).

Property and construction are close behind with 18 per cent of Alberta's economy. Manufacturing is approximately one quarter of the energy sector at 7 per cent. Other dominant industries are professional services (including high technology), healthcare, logistics, finance and insurance, and trade.

But the oil industry in the province is not labour intensive. It will not easily absorb the large pool of poor Albertans. Manufacturing (secondary manufacturing specifically), which makes extensive use of processed commodities like oil, are labour intensive and require a large pool of low-cost labourers. This not only helps poor workers from Alberta, but those from outside the province. And, most importantly, manufacturing has scalability and can create many jobs.

What about AI and the high technology industry? Richard Florida, a geographer at the University of Toronto, certainly talks up its prospects in Alberta. But, in short, developing a high tech centre requires extensive training for workers (certificate to associate and bachelor's degrees and beyond), possibly out of the reach for low-income Albertans financially without some serious injection of equipment, mentorship, and funds. These plans will benefit skilled, out-of-province most in the short term and require very optimistic projections with the size of Alberta's AI and high tech industries.

What Do the Poor Want?

For now, the Albertan government needs to develop industries that require a large labour pool and minimal retraining. The population living under the poverty line in Alberta stood at

363,890 people as of the latest census. So AI and high tech fail for two reasons. It would be unrealistic to think that Alberta can be retooled for the knowledge economy on such a scale large and quick enough to constitute a poverty alleviation strategy for so many people. From another perspective, there are already other sectors that require less investments from scratch and time and create more work in the economy for poor Albertans.

Manufacturing, especially if the specific sub-industry is counter-cyclical to the oil industry, is definitely up for the task more than AI and high tech. Investments in transportation infrastructure can as well for the short term (construction constitutes approximately 8 per cent of the Albertan economy). Another consequence of investing in construction is the downward pressure it would put on Edmonton and Calgary housing prices (average sale price of C$322,000 and C$419,600 respectively), which are among the highest in the country. Hong Kong can take note if it wants to lower housing prices, a major concern of the working poor. These forms of economic diversification, furthermore, would be more consistent with the objective of Heritage Savings Trust Fund, Alberta's sovereign fund, to direct money to productive investments in infrastructure. Hong Kong, too, may want to stick to its strengths instead of betting on another new hub status.

21

Resolving Aboriginal Unemployment Would Benefit British Columbia

Political and economic reconciliation between Aboriginals and the Canadian government is an ongoing effort.
Source: Wikimedia Commons

As the saying goes, judge a society by how it treats its weakest members. The aboriginal peoples of Canada, British Columbia in this chapter, have been oppressed since the country's days as a British colony. They are the counterparts to the Vietnamese refugees, the South Asian migrants, and the neglected Africans of Hong Kong—all of whom are more likely to be poor than the general population.

There is good reason to help them integrate into the economy, according to some simple calculations. Imagining their employment situation to be better or at par with the average British Columbian, there would a corresponding (and sizeable) boost to the provincial GDP. If the equivalent statistics were available in Hong Kong, would it tell the same story? If it is true in Hong Kong that the poor are part of the solution, more efforts need to be made to help them gain employment through carefully crafted school-to-work and welfare-to-work programs. And there's an urgency, since the city's GDP growth depends on these workers.

A Model for Aboriginal Employment

Relations between government and First Nations may be at an all-time high. To take reconciliation further, economic integration is crucial. And here's my working theory: fixing the aboriginal people's employment situation can help the economy in British Columbia (B.C.).

Constructing a simple model for economic growth in British Columbia and using data from Statistics Canada, one can relate not only population growth as a factor, but also the aboriginal employment rate and labour force participation rate. At 53.8 per cent, the aboriginal employment rate in the province is below the national aboriginal employment rate (55.2 per cent) and the national employment rate of the total population (61.3 per cent).

Experiments with Different Employment Scenarios

If the employment rate of aboriginals is the same as that of non-aboriginals in the province (59.7 per cent), the model would predict a new provincial gross domestic product of $226.6 billion (in 2007 dollars). That is an increase of 8.3 per cent from the GDP of B.C. in 2015 ($209.1 billion). This represents a world in which aboriginal people face no discrimination in the labour market. It pays off enormously in the economy!

Similar calculations can be done with hypotheticals of a 10 per cent and a 20 per cent increase in aboriginal employment rate, keeping the other explanatory variables constant. This time, I am imagining a world in which the government and stakeholders are trying enormously to get aboriginal people employed. It is a realistic scenario. The model predicts a 16.1 per cent GDP increase to $242.9 billion with a 10 per cent increase in aboriginal employment. With a 20 per cent increase, the provincial GDP should increase a sizable 37.8 per cent to $288.2 billion (again, in 2007 dollars). Again, there is a big pay-off in the amount of income generated for the economy.

What about a full employment situation for Aboriginals? The model predicts a GDP jump of a whopping 115.7 per cent, to $451.0 billion. How about that for benefiting the province in the medium to long-term (since job placement would take some time)? Granted, the direction of the relationship between the provincial GDP and the variables may not be known. It may be that aboriginals getting work spurs the economy, or— equally likely—a booming economy benefits Aboriginals along with other social groups in B.C.

The Main Takeaway

While the model I proffer is for guidance only, the existing data fit very well to it. What is important is the correlation shown between aboriginals getting work—versus looking for work (labour force participation)—and getting paid and the increase in provincial economic development. Aboriginals who work are possibly more likely to contribute to work that form the industrial lifeblood that make up BC's GDP, like manufacturing and construction. This has policy implications.

Policy Implications

First is the need to not only demand Aboriginals on unemployment welfare to look for work (as is required along with many others on government welfare), but to ask them to obtain paying part-time and full-time work ASAP. Participating in the labour force (which includes job seekers) is not good enough according to the model.

Second, the government should help build direct linkages from schools, welfare/unemployment programs, and aboriginal communities to paying work. Formerly that might mean work in the public sector. Knowing that lowering the unemployment rate among First Nations pays off, the government can more aggressively hire people from First Nations and subsidize large-scale internship programs and full-time work placements lasting approximately 2 years with private companies.

Third, the Aboriginal people are crucial part of the solution, as far as the economic well-being of B.C. is concerned. No matter if the provincial budget currently is in surplus. There is $241.9 billion up for grabs.

The relationship between First Nations people and the provincial and federal government has seen steady progress. So have, some may argue, the poor and minorities with Hong Kong society. To witness the former becoming more independent and triumphing over various social maladies and historical burden can only be capped by integrating them into the economic life of B.C. society. The same can be done in Hong Kong, with the statistics to back up the efforts. With economic progress we will see improvements in education, health, housing, political representation, and other standards of living.

22

Increasing Aboriginal Employment in British Columbia Starts with Education and Career Support

Indigenous people parade on Aboriginal Day in Burns Lake, British Columbia. Economic reconciliation and integration is an important objective for government-Indigenous relations in Canada.
Source: Wikimedia Commons

What can the government do to increase Aboriginal job seekers' prospects? The parallel in Hong Kong is: how can the government help minorities and the poor who are looking for work? The chapter draws attention to statistics: university and high school graduates earn more than those who did not complete them. The government can encourage attendance by offering scholarships and grants—a strategy I will return to when discussing vocational training in Hong Kong and the job market in the regional Greater Bay Area. It can signal a clear link between education and a job through internships and short-term work programs. Finally, public money should be spent on career counsellors and affordable transportation to take workers to and from work. All of this is made possible because of careful data collection, which non-profits, universities, and the statistics department in Hong Kong should adhere to.

Economic reconciliation and integration is an important objective for government-Indigenous relations in Canada. A good place to start is the chronically low Indigenous employment rate. After all, the more native people work, the more contributions they make to Canada's GDP, which by many economists' measures makes everyone better off.

The Need to Focus on Education

It is a generally accepted view in Canada that the more education a person receives, the more employable they are. In the western provinces, Indigenous university graduates aged 25 to 54 have a 79.6 per cent employment rate, versus 67.4 per cent for those with a high school diploma and 46.5 per cent for those who did not complete high school. This trend is analogous to the population at large: 86.8 per cent of university graduates have jobs, versus 80.4 per cent for high-school grads and 68.1 per cent for those who do not have a high school education.

Native people, however, historically are less educated than other Canadians. In B.C., only half of all Indigenous people have post-secondary qualifications versus 64 per cent for non-Aboriginals. Close to one quarter of Indigenous people have no academic qualifications—more than twice the national average. It is good to know that Indigenous men and women have almost reached parity in attaining post-secondary qualifications—44 per cent of men versus 52 per cent of women. An integral plan to lower unemployment, therefore, requires that governments continue to promote education as a means of obtaining good-paying work.

The Government's Role in Linking Aboriginals to Jobs

The government can also play a larger role in connecting native people to jobs. According to a 2018 Statistics Canada survey, half of the Indigenous jobseekers between 25 and 54 years old in B.C. contacted companies directly for work; about 65.6 per cent used the Internet. 35 per cent looked for jobs through referrals from friends and relatives. A relatively small portion, 38.9 per cent, currently use government employment agencies.

In another survey in 2018 that asked unemployed B.C. Indigenous people why they could not find work, more than a quarter of respondents said they did not know what kind of work they wanted. In that case, staffing existing employment agencies with competent consultants and advertising their services more aggressively should be a great first step.

To address many unemployed native people who blame unemployment to a lack of education (58.6 per cent) or work experience (54.7 per cent), governments need to give out scholarships and grants for enrolling in professional certificate and degree courses and organize subsidized, short-term work programs at companies and government agencies. This can give a large number of people the qualification to obtain more lucrative jobs.

In the meantime, the government should work with schools, the private sector and wealthy investors to encourage entrepreneurship within Indigenous communities. Finally, half of Indigenous respondents claimed that lack of transportation is a barrier to going to work. The government could experiment with transportation subsidies and shuttle services to work places, in collaboration with various employment agencies and Indigenous community groups.

What Else Can the Government Do?

There are many unique challenges in B.C.'s Indigenous population that may continue to dampen its economy. The government has its role to play, apart from educating, advising and coordinating job seekers. It can encourage universities and think tanks to explore the reasons behind the Indigenous employment gap with the rest of the province and other reasons why Indigenous people have trouble finding work. This may touch on issues like ethnic discrimination, the education gap and the opioid crisis. Completing this task, grounded in careful data collection, is a necessary step toward economic integration and reconciliation. Stakeholders in poverty alleviation in Hong Kong can learn a thing or two from B.C.

23

Why the US Needs to Take Care of Its Illegal Immigrants?

A section of the border wall that separates the United States from Mexico at Tijuana. Dealing with illegal immigrants is a crucial part of America's foreign policy.
Source: Wikimedia Commons

Illegal immigrants have received a lot of attention in the United States in recent years. These poor workers, sometimes with their families in toll, braved hazardous geographies to live in cities across the country. They are like the marginalized migrants to Hong Kong that I mentioned in Chapter 21.

Of course, there are two sides to a debate, and illegal immigration is no exception. Thanks to data compiled by the Los Angeles Times, more information about illegal immigrants and the effect they have on neighbourhood income and crime in a major city can be known. Only then can the appropriate policies be implemented.

This is a continuation of a call for more data on Hong Kong's most vulnerable people—represented by the poor, the Vietnamese refugees, the South Asian migrants, and the neglected Africans. Committed newspapers can gather them. So can think tanks, university research centres, and resourceful charities.

The Debate on Illegal Immigration

Immigration is a crucial part of America's foreign policy. This is especially true at the US-Mexican border, where thousands of Latinos cross illegally each year. Both political parties are interested in a tight border control. During the Clinton Administration Operation Blockade was carried out in El Paso, Texas and Operation Gatekeeper in San Diego, California.

Two camps have emerged. One accepts that illegal immigration cannot be thwarted off completely, either through legislation or enforcement. According to advocates like Jagdish Bhagwati and Francisco Ribera-Batiz, of Columbia University, it is more reasonable to accommodate them, by giving them driver's licences, healthcare, and scholarships. Mexico may bear some of the costs, but the US government is counting on deterring future illegal immigrants. For example, attempts have been made to expand legal immigration and guest workers program.

The other camp favours cracking down on illegal immigrants. Edward Alden, Bernard L. Schwartz Senior Fellow at the Council on Foreign Relations, and Bryan Roberts, an economist, described two kinds of deterrence: before and at the point of border crossing. Current data shows a lot of room for improvement: 90 per cent to 98 per cent of Mexicans are successful in crossing into the US.

Some say the border is more secure than it ever has been. Border Patrol's annual budget rose from $326.2 million in 1992 to $20.7 billion in 2009. In 2019, there were nearly 20,000 border patrol agents at the US-Mexican border, up from 15,000 in 2007. Drones patrol the airspace, while tower-mounted cameras and sensors monitor the ground. The factors that motivate illegal immigrants today—employment, American-born and residing offsprings, deep roots in the US—cannot be deterred by more manpower, technology, or physical barriers (President Donald Trump suggested his proposed wall would cost $10 billion).

After securing its borders, those who favour tough measures against illegal immigrants want to crack down on sanctuary cities. Large cities like San Francisco, Chicago, and New York—more than 300 according to the Center for Immigration Studies—are in this group. To varying degrees, they have refused to comply or cooperate with immigration officials. For example, Los Angeles in 1979 kept its police officers from detaining people for the sole reason of finding out their immigration status.

The Demographics of Illegal Immigrants

Most of the 11 to 12 million illegal immigrants in the US are Latino. While wealthier and more educated legal immigrants gives more than takes from the US economy and society, illegal immigrants often do the opposite. For instance, illegal immigrants paid $2.09 billion in taxes to the Texan and its municipal governments in 2005, but took $2.6 billion in education, health, and other government services.

Data from Los Angeles, provided by the *L.A. Times* Mapping L.A. Project, shows a grim view of illegal immigrants. There were initial assumptions made in the analysis. Since there are no official figures on unauthorized immigrants, statistics on foreign-born residents (which include Asians, Africans, and Europeans) are used as a substitute in the analyses. There are demographic statistics on Latinos in the Mapping L.A. Project as well, and they will be used to corroborate prior observations.

Illegal Migrants and Household Income in Angeleno Neighbourhoods

Plotting the relationship between the percentage of foreign-born population in a neighbourhood and the neighbourhood's median income, one can see that the higher the median income is in a neighbourhood, the lower portion its proportion of foreign-born residents. Hidden Hills, the second wealthiest neighborhood by median income, has 12.7 per cent foreign-born residents. West San Dimas is another wealthy neighbourhood. 22.8 per cent of its residents are foreign-born. By contrast, in downtown Los Angeles, the poorest neighbourhood, 41.9 per cent are foreign-born residents. Mexico is the most represented Latino group among foreign-born Angelenos.

Using a fitted line running through the plot, one can even make predictions about the median income-foreign-born population relationship. To raise Sherman Oaks' median income

20 per cent, the neighbourhood needs to eject 6.8 per cent of its residents. To see Compton's median income rise to that of Southeast Antelope Valley, a middle-class neighbourhood, it needs to have 0.6 per cent fewer foreign-born residents. The model predicts that if a neighbourhood has a median income of $107,050, it would have no foreign-born residents.

Apparently, while the presence of Latinos in a neighbourhood also seems to bring down its median income, they do so to a lesser degree than foreign-born legal immigrants. Calculating a fitted model for Latinos, one can determine that for every percentage increase in Latino residents in a neighbourhood, there would be a corresponding $742 decrease in median income. For foreign-born residents, it is $1207. So the social implication is that if illegal immigrants identify themselves with their Latin communities, including their American-born family members, they tend to be better off economically than if they identify with immigrant communities—which transcend ethnic labels.

It is almost certain that illegal immigrants in LA, based on the data, are poorer than the general population. There is no implication of any causal relationships based on their percentage population and median income in a neighbourhood. The median income may be low because the illegal immigrants moved into it, or illegal immigrants—less possibly—have an affinity for low income neighbourhoods that remind them of home.

Illegal Immigrants and Property Crime

What do the data say about the property crime and violent crime rates, calculated per 10,000 people? If foreign-born residents are used as a proxy for illegal immigrants, there is a positive relationship between the presence of foreign-born residents and property crime rate. For every percentage increase in foreign-born population, there are 0.85 more cases of property crime.

The model has prescriptive powers. Downtown Los Angeles, which has the highest nominal number of property crimes, can reduce 35.6 cases of property crime per capita if all foreign-born residents moved away. Mission Hills can reduce its property crime rate by 10 per cent if the percentage of foreign-born residents decrease by 12.6 per cent.

By contrast, Latinos, faced with the same property crime rates, have different results. The model shows that property crime rate is negatively correlated with the proportion of Latinos in a neighbourhood. In fact, for each one percentage increase, the number of per capita property crimes decrease by 0.16. When there are no Latinos in a neighbourhood, the expected number of property crimes is 82.

Whether the proxy for illegal immigrants is foreign-born or Latinos, the direction of the causal relationship with property crime rates is uncertain. Property crimes can rise or fall because illegal immigrants moved in, or illegal immigrants are attracted to neighbourhoods where property crimes are already rampant.

Illegal Immigrants and Violent Crime

The violent crime rate of illegal immigrants tells a more coherent story. In short, they are more likely to commit violent crimes than the general population. If illegal immigrants are assumed to behave like foreign-born residents of Los Angeles, a percentage increase in immigrant population in any neighbourhood would lead to an increase of 0.31 cases of violent crimes, accounting for at least 10.7 cases of violent crimes when no foreign-born Angelenos live in the neighbourhood.

If Latinos are used as a proxy for illegal immigrants, one would paint a similar picture. The positive relationship is the same. But while a percentage increase in foreign-born residents correlates with 0.31 more cases of violent crimes, a percentage increase in Latinos living in a neighbourhood correlates with 0.24 more cases of violent crimes. When no Latinos live in a Angeleno neighbourhood, the fitted model expects at least 11.5 cases of violent crimes, which is lower than the prediction in the case in which foreign-born residents are used as a proxy for illegal immigrants. According to the data from the Mapping L.A. Project, Latinos are involved in more cases of violent crimes than foreign-born L.A. residents.

As with property crimes, whether illegal immigrants are the perpetrators or victims of these violent crimes is not known. One knows at the least that illegal immigrants did not move into these crime-ridden neighbourhoods because of the high crime rates (although they may have for other related reasons, like lower housing prices due to the high violent crime rates). The data shows that illegal immigrants are disproportionately involved in violent crimes as perpetrators or victims. It is crucial that municipal governments across the country find out which of the two—or both—is the reality.

Policy Implications

This has policy implications. Advocates defending illegal immigrants view them as victims in their country of origin and in their new home. Evidence found, on the balance, to this effect should corroborate their work in providing social, health, and education services to them. If they are not, maybe it is time to defer them off to immigration officials, agencies, and laws that include deportation as a measure.

Hong Kong has faced similar problems with immigrants and refugees from Southeast Asia. The city has welcomed some and turned away many. Maybe a lack of data about them is to blame. After all, it is difficult to craft an effective immigration policy without the hard facts about immigrants and the people they affect.

But as with many social phenomena, the reality of illegal immigration is hampered by imperfect data gathering. The Mapping L.A. Project fortunately provides a new source and presentation of information. Even then, depending on how one categorizes illegal immigrants, definitive conclusions cannot always be drawn. So far, evidence in Los Angeles shows that illegal immigrants are poorer than the average Angeleno and more likely to be involved in property and violent crimes. Unless municipal governments in sanctuary cities are ready to commit to helping vulnerable illegal immigrant communities, they should ensure people's safety and welfare by cooperating with immigration officials.

24³

Veterans Live in Safer Neighbourhoods in Los Angeles

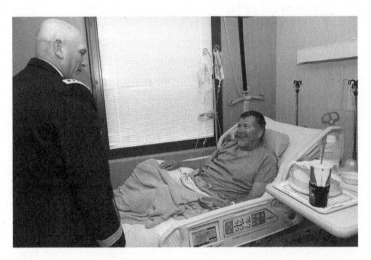

The US Army Chief of Staff meets with veterans in a Los Angeles area hospital.
Source: Wikimedia Commons

In Hong Kong, a close corrolary to the U.S. Armed Services is the Hong Kong Police Force. One would expect the psychological challenges of their jobs and their lives after leaving services to

---

³ This chapter appeared as an op-ed in the *California Political Review* on March 8, 2017.

be congruous. This makes this chapter interesting to Hong Kongers.

In short, veterans live, as the chapter's title suggests, in safer neighborhoods. This may be because of the veterans' presence that they are safe, or because veterans know which neighbourhoods are safe to move into. This is something that, if true for police veterans, would have useful applications in Hong Kong, when data like the Mapping L.A. Project's is eventually made available.

The Challenges of Being a Veteran

National statistics on veterans are grim. As of November 2014, an average of 550 veterans return every day (that is 200,000 troops each year). They have a hard time readjusting. The unemployment rate of veterans since the Iraq and Afghanistan wars is higher (11.1 per cent) than non-veterans (around 8.6 per cent). Twenty per cent of veterans between 18 and 24 years old are unemployed. That is so even with the aggressive recruitment by federal agencies, where almost half of all new employees come from the services. It's estimated that 1.4 million veterans are living below the poverty line.

All of the difficulties take a physical and social toll. Mental illness and substance abuse are widely reported. As of June 2011, 20 per cent of all suicides nationally are veterans. Almost 20 per cent of homeless people are veterans. As of November 2015, more than 10 per cent of the death row are veterans.

The Mapping L.A. Project Dataset

There is cause for optimism. Looking at data from the Mapping L.A. Project, compiled by the *Los Angeles Times*, one can generalize that veterans who live in America's second largest city tend to live in fairly safe neighbourhoods. More so than those who live in neighbourhoods with fewer veterans. For example, the three neighbourhoods identified as having the highest proportion of veterans—Green Valley (19.5 per cent), Elizabeth Lake (18.4 per cent) and Lake Hughes (18.4 per cent)—have no incidences of violent crime in 2017.

The three neighbourhoods accounted for the lowest percentage of veterans—Central-Alameda (1.8 per cent), Chinatown (1.3 per cent) and University Park (1.0 per cent)—have moderate levels of per capita violent crime (61.4, 18.4, and 38.1 incidences per 1,000 residents, respectively). The average violate crime rate in the 207 neighbourhoods is 27.7 incidences per capita. Eight neighbourhoods have over 100 incidences of violent crime per capita. Vermont Vista (155.1 incidences per capita and 6.6 per cent veteran's population) has the highest violent crime crate.

Veterans and Crime

Creating a model using the data, one can observe that the more veterans there are living in a neighbourhood in L.A., the lower the violent crime rate. More specifically, for every 1 per cent increase in the percentage of veterans living in a neighbourhood, there is a decrease of 2.6 incidences of violent crimes.

For example, 101 veterans currently live in Chinatown, the fitted model predicts that 7.1 per cent of the neighbourhood's population need to be veterans (an increase of 448 veterans) for the violent crime rate to be eliminated. Gramercy Park, which has 115.5 incidences of violent crimes, needs 44.4 per cent of its population to be veterans (3,179 veterans, or an increase of

2,240) to eradicate violent crimes. If Hancock Park (violent crime rate 27.2 incidences per capita, close to the city mean), wants to eradicate violent crime, the municipal government would have to see that 10.4 per cent of its residents come from the veteran population. That is 822 veterans, or a 326 increase from the current 496 veterans living in the neighbourhood.

But a note of caution. The causation of the two variables can run in either direction, or in both ways. A neighbourhood's violent crime rate may change because veterans moved into the neighbourhood (street gangs, murderers, etc., may withhold their crime sprees out of fear of the veterans), or veterans moved into a neighbourhood because they saw that it had a low violent crime rate and that it was safe. As with many social phenomena, both scenarios are possible.

Policy Implications

This has policy implications. Veterans, like all people, prefer to live in safe neighbourhoods. In L.A., neighbourhoods with no recorded violent crimes in 2017 have at least 9.6 per cent veterans in their populations. It is good incentive for the municipal government to lower crime rates, for example through gentrification, to create safer homes for veterans readjusting to civilian life.

Another implication is attracting veterans to neighbourhoods with higher crime rates, if it is true that veterans thwart off violent criminals. The municipal government can experiment with tax breaks for veterans who move to neighbourhoods that are traditionally plagued with violent crimes—for example, choosing those neighbourhoods above the mean crime rate.

As with most prescriptions in public policy, introducing veterans (or retired police officers in Hong Kong, if the data exists to support the findings) into a neighbourhood to reduce crimes should not be seen as a silver bullet solution. Crime control requires a blend of preventative measures (for example, education and public campaigns), police mobilization and deterrence in conjunction with the criminal justice system. Veterans, by playing a part in affecting on all three factors, should be rewarded for it.

Neighbourhood Gentrification and Education May Deter Violent Criminals in Los Angeles

Many parts of Compton, California, are in need of repairs. Gentrifying
neighbourhoods in Los Angeles can help reduce crime.
Source: Wikimedia Commons

---

[4] This chapter appeared as an op-ed in the *Daily Caller* on January 23, 2017.

The Mapping L.A. Project, which has already been used to study illegal immigrants and veterans in this book, has another revelation. The higher household incomes are in a neighbourhood, the lower its crime rate. This begs the conclusion: gentrifying neighbourhoods in Los Angeles (or Hong Kong for that matter) lowers crime in the city. This has the added effect of helping the poor, assuming they can afford to stay in the neighbourhood. Again, it remains to be seen if the data holds up if it becomes available in Hong Kong.

People commit violent crimes in Los Angeles for many reasons. Its mayor, Eric Garcetti, wants the city to hire ex-criminals as a remedy. There is certainly an economic aspect to criminality. Now, there is evidence that the frequency of violent crimes is influenced by the income of the people in a neighbourhood.

The Mapping L.A. Project Dataset

The data on median income and the number of incidents of violent crimes per 10,000 in Angeleno neighbourhoods—as compiled by the *L.A. Times* in the Mapping L.A. Project—shows three findings. First, there is a negative correlation between the median income of a neighbourhood and the number of incidents of violent crimes in the city. As a general rule, the higher the median income of a neighbourhood, the fewer incidences of violent crime one would see. For example, Vermont Knolls, which as a median income of $27,730, has 113.6 incidents of violent crimes per 10,000. Rancho Palos Verdes, whose median income is 4.6 times that of Vermont Knolls, has only 4.1 incidents per 10,000.

The data, however, does not explain the direction or more in-depth nature of the relationship. That is, the number of incidents of violent crimes may be lower in a high median income neighbourhood because wealthy people kept criminals at bay by building a strong community, or people in a neighbourhoods became worked harder and earned more because the low incidents of violent crimes. There may also be elements of both, feeding off each other.

A Model of Household Income and Crime

According to a simple model linking the two variables—and using the most recent data—a neighbourhood would be predicted to experience no violent crime (8 neighbourhoods in Los Angeles reported no violent crimes, mostly where people make more money) if its media income is $125,455. 17 out of 265 neighbourhoods (that is the top 6.4 per cent) identified by Mapping L.A. are above this level. Their average violent crime rate is 4.6 incidences per 10,000 (4 neighbourhoods were not included because of missing crime data). Chesterfield Square, which has the highest violent crime rate in Los Angeles and a median income of $37,737, has 175.5 incidences per 10,000.

The model has prescriptive powers. Take Watts for example. Its violent crime rate is 69.2 per 10,000. The model predicts that a small, $5,000 increase in media income in the neighbourhood would lower the crime rate to 52.0 per cent. That is a 24.8 per cent decrease in violent crime rate. Compton, which has the 26th highest violent crime rate in the city, would see less crime if the government can lift the neighbourhood's median income. For a $5,000 increase, the model predicts a violent crime rate of 34.9 per cent—a 31.6 per cent decrease from 51.1 per cent.

Policy Implications

The results show that, if it is true that wealthy people crowd out criminals, the government should consider instituting a program of gentrification in low median income neighbourhoods. 93.6 per cent of the neighbourhood theoretically have room for improvement. New apartment buildings should be built in poorer neighbourhoods. Multi-purpose property development, mixing shopping malls, office buildings, and residences should be encouraged in neighbourhoods with higher incidences of violent crimes (of course with care taken with the need for law enforcement, social services and healthcare, etc.). Parks can encourage people with higher incomes into a neighbourhood.

The data also supports calls for education programs to train poor Angelenos with the skills needed for higher paying jobs. Life in a higher income bracket would possibly deter them from violent crimes.

Like moving veterans into a neighbourhood, raising the median income of a neighbourhoods is not a silver bullet to solving all of Los Angeles' or Hong Kong's crimes. Not all neighbourhoods can have the income level of Malibu. Even the wealthiest one has a handful of cases of violent crimes each year. But there is a strong case for gentrification of Los Angeles and education for lower-income residents. It may be desirable for low-income people in the community, by increasing their home value, living standard, and quality of life.

26

Connecting the Poor and the Elderly to the Internet in New York City Can Create Jobs for Many

New Yorkers should log on to the Internet to take advantage of business opportunities.

Source: Unsplash/NESA by Makers

This chapter is about the digital divide leaving potentially thousands of New Yorkers behind, especially the elderly, the poor, and the technologically challenged. The context is global trade, which is applicable to Hong Kong and will be revisited later in the book.

Americans are perennially losing jobs to India and China through offshoring, to the tune of 40 million workers. An idea popularized 13 years ago, offshoring refers to the loss of jobs from (mostly) richer countries to (mostly) poorer countries. The phenomenon exists mainly in the service sector, as opposed to the manufacturing industry from which industrialized countries have already shifted away.

What is Offshorable?

Offshoring is enabled tremendously by computerization and telecommunications technology, like the Internet. The late Alan Blinder, who was the former vice-chairman of the US Federal Reserve Board, classified what is offshorable and what is not. Impersonally delivered services, which can be delivered electronically with little to no degradation of quality, like keyboard data entry, computer code-writing, or even security monitoring are possibly tradable and offshorable. Personal services, which cannot be delivered electronically or would suffer severe degradation of quality when delivered this way, like surgery, driving a taxi, or lawyering in court are not tradable and offshorable. Whether a service is offshorable is unrelated to whether it is low- or high-skilled. What distinguishes impersonal, or tradable, services from personal ones is that personal services require physical presence or face-to-face contact with end users.

Recovering Offshored Jobs in New York City

The same jobs that Indians or Chinese are getting better at doing than Americans are open to entrepreneurial New Yorkers, too. New Yorkers, including low-income ones and residents who are currently unconnected to the Internet, working at home can, with the right tools, compete for statistical analysis, programming, editing, and security work that are currently being offshored. The range of work available is great: what is personal and impersonal exists on a continuum. There are jobs that are obviously on opposite ends of the spectrum, like data entry and child care. But while the job of a teacher can be delivered electronically over the Internet or videoconferencing, the quality of their service degrades noticeably.

But New York is not keeping many of the jobs that need not be offshored—and is in danger of losing more. After all, offshoring is a large and disruptive force. Information and communications technology will continue to get better and cheaper, and the scope for offshoring will only continue to increase. Yet 1,077,301 New Yorkers have no Internet access.

The Digital Divide

Low-income groups are being left out of the competition for offshorable work. According to the US. Census, the household income group earning under $19,144 make up the largest economic group without any type of Internet access. The group earning between $19,144 and $42,369 is the next largest group.

New Yorkers who are unemployed and not in the labour force have a greater likelihood of not having any type of Internet access—10.6 per cent and 22.3 per cent—than the working population (8.2 per cent). The elderly population, which is an economically vulnerable group, is three times more likely to lack access to the Internet (29.9 per cent) than residents 18 to 64 years old (10 per cent).

There is a large cache of poor and unemployed New Yorkers who stand to gain. The US, as a rich country, always gains from offshoring. How would New York City's urban poor, which include the under-educated and elderly, benefit? First, they need the computer devices. The census data does not give much socio-economic data on cell phone or computer usage, although it should be somewhat reassuring that seven million people own a smartphone and worrying that 682,015 New Yorkers do not own a computer, which can be used for Internet-enabled business transactions with a business partner overseas. For business transactions that empower the poor, after all, acquiring a personal computer should be the primary focus.

Policy Implications

Trade and offshoring are global, their effects can be felt in New York City as well as Hong Kong. The remedy for the latter will be explained in a separate chapter. But in New York City, the government, hopefully along with businesses and non-profit groups, needs to connect the poor to the Internet via computers and smartphones, so that they can take advantage of traditional online methods of connectivity like social media, video telephony, and e-payment. This can be done through the creation of Internet labs that complement government-organized career training centres and programs. Free or low-cost Internet access is definitely something to work on, since only 108,634 people from the under-$42,369 household income group are logging on to the Internet without paying, compared to 703,262 New Yorkers without any type of Internet access in that economic group. Plugged into the web-enabled economy with these tools, the poor can solicit businesses in fields like typing, tele-marketing, and code-writing. The statistics, after all, shows that a large domestic pool of workers is waiting to be tapped.

27

Businesses Need to Protect Themselves against Failing Partners, Clients in Economic Downturn

Enron owned two buildings in downtown Houston before its collapse in 2001. Businesses should practice good credit risk management to avoid bankruptcy.
Source: Wikimedia Commons

Credit risk refers to the probability that a business partner or client goes bankrupt. In the worst-case scenario, the partner is a major source of income and, lacking a replacement, brings down one's company. This chapter is a cautionary tale for micro-entrepreneurs in Hong Kong, dealing with megalithic companies with enormous balance sheets.

The global economy is not expected to recover to its pre-pandemic level until 2022, according to the National Association for Business Economics. The decrease in Federal Reserve rate—the closely-watched, government-set rate at which commercial banks lend to each other—to close to zero hinted at overall worries in an otherwise long-expanding economy that cannot sustain indefinitely. In the meanwhile, America's trading partners have been economically hurt in prolonged trade wars.

Without doubt, there will be imminent bankruptcies, from small businesses to some with the notoriety and the massive scale of Enron, Worldcom and Lehman Brothers. For businesses to ready itself for this type of risk, lest they take the whole economy down with them, they need to toughen up on their internal control and credit risk management.

Credit Risk Management

Credit risk reflects macro conditions, for example, the strength of the economy and terrorism, and company operations. Scholars have suggested that counterparty default risk contributes to financial contagions, like that following the Lehman Brothers collapse. At Enron, the credit risk department worked closely with the market risk department, divisions representing the company's products, and a team of quantitative analysts.

To analyse a business partner's default risk, a company needs to gauge the risk assumed compared to the cost of risk transfer and the effect of an event like bankruptcy has from the point of view of the company. To do this, it can simply—though not so simple in execution—assume a portion of its accounts receivable to be bad debt. The onus is on the company to monitor the credit rating of counterparties through strong internal control. A company can also protect itself from credit risk by demanding collateral, in the form of cash, a letter of credit, or lien, collecting money through legal channels if necessary.

Another way are surety bonds, which provide off-balance sheet loans, are contingent on the occurrence of an event, and have high requirements for those companies with low credit ratings. Credit derivatives, a class of risk-mitigating financial instrument that includes credit default swaps (CDS), have clearly defined event triggers and provide companies with an exposure of up to 5 years. Credit insurance is a flexible form of protection that covers losses from unpaid receivables. Credit insurers can cover the risk, which can vary dramatically in size.

The Case of Enron

The initial estimates of credit risk exposed to Enron by its trading partners at the time of its bankruptcy in 2001 were $70 million at Dynegy, $50 million at Mirant, and $50 million at El Paso. Triggered CDS on Enron was estimated to be up to $6 billion. The efficiency of the credit derivatives market was obvious within 30 days after the company's bankruptcy, when nearly all credit derivatives trades on Enron were settled. But credit risk management requires accounting accuracy, which was notably absent at Enron. Financial misreporting, one can say, was at the heart of the crisis. And according to academics at Caltech and Columbia University, accounting distortions influenced credit risk models by exaggerating asset volatility—swings in the asset's price, the more volatile the less predictable it is—a hypothesis which can be backed up with data from Parmalat, whose collapse was the largest bankruptcy in Europe.

In the exuberance of the stock market, many in the United States may have already forgotten the underperforming days of the Great Recession. But they must rely on credit risk management and transparent and accurate accounting standards to ensure that internal control is as strong as possible. These are good lessons to heed, even for micro-entrepreneurs in Hong Kong. Moreover, there are positive externalities, like investment opportunities linked to future credit ratings, $9.4 trillion worth of CDS, and surety bonds.

28[5]

Why the Shale Revolution Is Beneficial for the World's Poor?

Output in the Permian Basin benefitted greatly from the Shale Revolution.
Source: Wikimedia Commons

One of the requirements for a successful anti-poverty scheme is scalability. The economists whom I named in Chapter 4 do.

---

[5] This chapter appeared as an op-ed in *Red Alert Politics* on February 8, 2017.

Jeffrey Sachs has his experimental Millennium Villages across Africa. Hernando de Soto's legal property reform has been replicated on many continents. Muhammad Yunus' microfinance bred innumerable MFIs and subsidiaries in commercial banks around the world. Bolsa Família (Family Grant) has the potential to become another scalable success, benefitting millions of Brazilians. It will be revisited in the next chapter, and serves only as a foil to yet another candidate, shale oil and gas. Despite concerns with their environmental impact, the shale revolution has lowered energy cost and transferred new drilling know-how to Saudi Arabia and China, among other countries. Maybe economically vulnerable people in Hong Kong will feel its effects, too.

Family Grant: A Big Idea in Poverty Fighting

Fighting poverty requires big ideas and the implementation of those big ideas. Brazil, noted by journalist Jonathan Tepperman for its poverty-fighting successes, certainly had one in Family Grant. Central to former President Lula's social welfare campaign, Family Grant was simply a cash-giving program. Most development programs offered goods and services.

The predecessor to this program began in Campinas and Brasília in 1995, leading to 100 other cities to do the same. Lula's predecessor, Fernando Cardoso tried a flimsy version nationally. It would not be until Lula's administration that the program was implemented on a grander and more ambitious scale.

Three key ideas contributed to Family Grant's success, which should be replicable in other low-income countries. First, distributing food and other goods is 'complicated, costly, and inefficient,' necessitating a bureaucracy that is a problem in itself in badly governed and often corrupt societies. Second, Lula's initiative assumed that the poor knew best what the poor needed. This has since been supported by academic studies. Third—in the context of the privatizations of government-run companies in the 1980s and 1990s that marginalized millions economically— Lula gave money directly to Brazilians to re-enter to market economy.

Energy Poverty as a Symptom of Extreme Poverty

Meanwhile, another effort is made to combat energy poverty, a symptom of extreme poverty. 50 per cent of the world's population lack energy security; 2 billion people have bad to no access to electricity at all. 90 per cent of those suffering from energy poverty live in South Asia and Sub-Saharan Africa.

Governments are not inclined to help. So much so that foreign companies and non-profits are expected to alleviate the lack of access to the modern lifestyle, which allows for water pumps, ovens, medical equipment in hospitals—all that is taken for granted. Alphabet, the parent company of Google, set up an initiative called Project Loon to launch high-altitude balloons that will cover the world with Internet access.

Morgan D. Bazilian, lead energy specialist at the World Bank, reported that 2 per cent of Liberians have regular access to electricity, and 50 per cent of Tanzanian companies have trouble conducting business because of energy insecurity. Obstacles like these keep poor people in poverty, because energy is intertwined with improvements in health, education, and employment. And like Lula's program, an effective solution to energy poverty requires big ideas.

'People have gained access to electricity . . . thanks to concerted government leadership, massive public investments in infrastructure, good planning, well-trained work forces, supportive regulations, and financially viable institutions,' according to Bazilian.

Shale Oil: Another Big Idea?

The shale revolution in oil and gas is good news for the poor, benefitting them through lower energy costs. By 2014, efficiency gains in the shale sector have been approximately 25 per cent per year, and 'increases in capital expenditures are triggering even more potential production growth,' writes Citi Global Head of Commodities Research Edward L. Morse. Although shale oil and gas extraction is originally an American development, the technology for it is transferable outside of the US.

Saudi Arabia, for example, wants to explore shale oil and gas to free up more oil for exports and increase the country's revenues. So does Russia. Other foreign countries would want to engage in shale drilling to reduce dependence on imports, increase export earnings, and enable domestic economic development. That would all put downward pressure on energy prices in the global markets.

There are potential problems that affect shale oil and gas exploration that would have an effect on oil and gas-producing low-income countries. One is the environmental externalities; the fracking process pollutes underground aquifers and creates waste above ground. This would come down to the potency of local regulations. Another is the question of whether the surge in production in the beginning of the fracking process is sustainable. This concern seems to be unfounded. Finally, the economics of fracking may not be lasting; in 2012, the shale exploration industry spent $60 billion more than it generated in revenue. But the high costs associated with the shale revolution were mostly attributed to land acquisition, which is high in the early years.

The lack of energy for poor people is still a great challenge. As true in Hong Kong as it is in Africa, poor people need a cheap, sustainable source of energy. It has led to non-government entities, including foreign companies, to generate their own solutions. In all likelihood, the shale oil industry will end up doing more good than harm.

29

When Conditional Cash Transfer Programs Work

Brazil's Family Grant is the largest and most well-known conditional cash transfer program in the world.
Source: Wikimedia Commons

Cash handouts are popular in Hong Kong as a form of government transfer. Some argue that there is a better form of assistance, made popular by Brazil's President Lula. It is inexpensive, as a percentage of GDP. It exults preventive healthcare and school attendance. It is replicable in New York City, Memphis, Tennessee, as well as rural Brazil. In Hong Kong, it can be used as a vehicle to better the health status and vocational skills of the poor. Wealthier residents should have a say in where their tax money goes, too.

Conditional cash transfer programs (CCTs) are popular in low- and middle-income countries. They are popular in Latin America, where the first one began in Mexico under Ernesto Zedillo's administration as Progresa, now called Prospera. Used primarily to coax the poor into getting medical checkups and their children to get vaccinated and to school, CCTs have since been implemented in Bangladesh, Cambodia, and Pakistan to increase school attendance for girls. The critics have been proven wrong; families with extra cash have less incentive to send their children to work rather than to school.

Brazil's Family Grant Revisited

CCTs are superior to other anti-poverty programs, partly because they are inexpensive. Brazil's Family Grant program cost the government about 0.4 per cent of its GDP. By comparison, the World Bank reports that developing countries spend on average 1.5 per cent of their GDP on social safety net programs. Consolidating myriad CCTs in various ministries when he took office, with foreign aid, President Lula created the current Family Grant that reaches 11.1 million families and over 46 million people today.

CCTs in Asia

Asian countries are showing an interest in CCTs. Indonesia's program reached 9 per cent of the population in 2016, up from 2 per cent in 2012. In the Philippines, 20 per cent of the population received cash transfers in 2015, up from 4 per cent in 2009. Contrary to critics, there is no evidence that beneficiaries of CCTs work less—the 'crutch economy' argument—according to research at the World Bank in 2018.

CCTs in the Americas

CCT has mixed results when applied to wealthy countries and cities. It was first implemented in New York City in 2010, as the Family Reward program, by MDRC, a non-profit group. While immediate hardship was alleviated, Family Reward, which through private sources gave $8,700 to 4,800 families and 11,000 children, did not create the income stream that would allow people to acquire shelter and food sustainably after the program ended. Although more children graduated from high school and entered university as a result of the program, it did not affect primary and lower secondary school enrollment or graduation rate. There was no impact on medical outcomes, except dental care.

A modified Family Reward program was conducted in the Bronx, New York, and Memphis, Tennessee in 2011 and was inconclusive as well. Within the 4 years of the trial, economic hardship was alleviated. Participants, of which there were approximately 1,200 families in each city, reported better health and more preventive dental visits. Likewise, cash transfers did not affect the enrollment or graduation rate of primary school children.

It seems that the dynamics of poverty is very different in the big cities the United States than low- and middle-income countries where CCTs succeed. Even there, enrollment is greater in rural areas than within large cities. For example, 41 per cent of rural households Brazil participate in Family Grant, versus 17 per cent of households in cities. The cause of this disparity needs to be examined and resolved, if CCTs are to be used as an anti-poverty tool in more communities. 55 per cent of the world's population lived in cities in 2018, which the United Nations projects will reach 68 per cent by 2050. 416 million people will live in Indian cities, 444 million will live in Chinese and Nigerian cities, and there will be many poor people for which there is an effective anti-poverty strategy.

Why Do CCTs Work?

For now, CCTs work in many parts of the world, because they go beyond handing out money. It is a good alternative to direct cash transfers, like the cash handouts that Hong Kong policymakers prefer. CCTs put a value on education and health and give people a reason to invest in them in communities where not everyone gets routine medical examinations and a high school or university education, in other words, the fact of live in the developing world. CCTs also work through lifting whole countries to a higher educational level and reassure wealthier, taxpaying citizens that the poor are not getting money for doing nothing.

Part IV

Asia and the Pacific

30

Australia's Dutch Disease

If managed properly, income from gold, like those found in Western
Australia, can benefit the country's poor.
Source: Wikimedia Commons

In Chapters 10 and 11, I talked about how incompetent
governments in Africa squandered the greatest natural wealth
through corruption and financial mismanagement, leaving few
resources available to help the poor. Australia in the Asia-Pacific

is well-known for its own version, called the Dutch disease. There are other historical examples of it—Hong Kong's development as a financial hub may be considered one—but Australia is said to have handled the sudden influx of gold and mineral wealth very well. W. Max Corden and J. Peter Neary, two academics, offer a view of the decisions Australia's policymakers might have had to make to deal with the Dutch disease. Australia's poverty rate is below that of Hong Kong, so there might be something to learn from the country.

Examples of the Dutch Disease

Some countries, like Australia, suffer from a generalized form of the resource curse, called the Dutch disease. Dutch disease are the harmful consequences of a large increase in a country's income, normally associated with a natural resource discovery but in fact any large inflow of foreign currency—for example, from natural resource prices, foreign aid, and foreign direct investments. There are many examples of the Dutch disease in recent history. Oil discoveries in Indonesia in 1974 and 1979 greatly increased revenue, so did the North Sea for Norway between 1970 and 1990, Russia, Venezuela, Canada's Athabasca oil sands, and Azerbaijan in the 2000s. The Philip-pines' influx of foreign exchange in the 1990s, as well as London's development as a financial centre—the latter now threatened by the repercussions of Brexit—can be said to be symptomatic of the Dutch disease. Hong Kong, too, can fit into this last category, having risen dramatically as a hub for raising international capital for startup companies. Countries affected by the Asian tsunami in 2004 have to deal with a great deluge of foreign assistance money. Somalian pirates, in their small way, are discovering a large source of income for their country. Textbook cases of the Dutch disease can be found in Chilean commodities in the 2000s and New World gold in 16th century Spain and Portugal.

Australia's Dutch Disease

In Australia, gold was discovered in the 1850s and various minerals in the past two decades. In 2016, four of the five main exports to Japan are natural resources. In Western Australia, eight out of 10 sources of exports are metals, minerals, or natural resources; the lagging sector, which includes wheat, is quite small, and there is virtually no manufacturing or service industry in the region. They bring tremendous wealth to Australians; they have a per capita GDP of US$51,430, and economic growth in the past decade ranged from 2.1 per cent to 3.7 per cent. The inflation rate is at a healthy 3 per cent to 1.3 per cent. Granted, unemployment hovered between 5 per cent and 5.9 per cent, and the country is a net importer. Far from squander its wealth, Australia arguably handled its Dutch disease very well.

W. Max Corden and J. Peter Neary

W. Max Corden and J. Peter Neary, professors at Johns Hopkins University and Oxford University, showed that the Dutch disease permits the traditional export sector to get crowded out by the two other sectors of the economy (the three sectors are the booming and lagging export, traded-goods sectors and the non-traded-goods sector that supplies domestic residents), in what is called the resource movement effect.

While some say that the Dutch disease is actually a self-correcting mechanism for domestic demand to adapt as production shifts from the tradable to the non-tradable sector, there are economists who see the industry foreclosures and lost employment as economically and politically painful, not to forget that the shift away from manufacturing prevents human capital development.

Policymakers need to determine if the gain in natural resources is temporary or permanent. If it is temporary, the government might want to protect the vulnerable sectors—for example, through foreign exchange intervention—or spend the windfall wisely—as through an oil fund. For permanent resource gains, governments need to prepare for structural changes—for example, by boosting productivity in the non-traded goods sector—and retrain workers. They need to diversify exports, for fear of external shocks.

Hong Kong's rapid rise as an international financial centre in the twenty-first century, on par in some respects with New York City and London, attracted a huge flow of foreign currency. This may be its own case of the Dutch disease. Will Hong Kong squander its wealth, or use it for social good? Corden has talked about the effects of a real exchange rate appreciation of a resource boom. He considered four scenarios: doing nothing, running a fiscal surplus, lowering the interest rate, and establishing a sovereign wealth fund. But the costs of exchange rate protection are great. Doing nothing is the option to choose if industries cannot distinguish between the lagging traceable sector and the non-tradable sector.

31

It's India's Moment to Bloom in
the US-China Trade War

A ship is being built in Gujarat, India. If the US-China trade war lingers on, India's role in regional and global commerce will likely increase.
Source: Wikimedia Commons

India's economic growth story is intertwined with China's, which should be of interest to Hong Kong workers eyeing work in the reintegrated regional economy. There are many debates as to the cause, including the role of reforms in the 1980s and

1990s and post-colonial policies. The fact is, regionally, China today dwarfs India in manufacturing exports, a fact that may be shaken by China's recent refocus on domestic markets. Hong Kong, which has a small manufacturing sector, probably needs to retrain ambitious workers for work in the mainland.

India's economic story, which lifted 271 million people out of poverty from 2005 to 2017, is unique in three ways. First, it did not experience 8 per cent to 10 per cent per annum growth like East Asian countries, and it did not stagnate for long periods like Africa or Latin America. Second, India had a substantial private sector, but pursued near-autarkic trade policies and highly interventionist domestic policies for more than three decades. Third, India is one of four developing countries with an effective democracy since the 1940s—and among them, it is the most diverse on many socio-political levels.

The Rise of the Modern Indian Economy

The country's growth story from 1951 to the present can be described in four phases, distinguished primarily by their growth rates. Current growth, which started in 1988, represents a shift in the trend growth into a new phase. There are four reasons. First, from 2003 to 2006, India integrated into the world economy like in no prior period. Total trade in goods and services was 43 per cent of GDP by 2006, while merchandise trade was 31 per cent of GDP. Added to that were billions more in remittance and FDI. Second, given the large stock of foreign exchange reserves of $430 billion in September, India would unlikely face a large rupee depreciation; the dollar value of the achieved GDP would be preserved. Third, the savings and investment rates in India have been rising and will continue to rise in the near future. Fourth, the GDP growth in the current phase has no sign of slowing down (6.6 per cent in 2017, versus 6.3 per cent average from 1988-2006).

Due to four features of its economy, India has managed to avoid complete stagnation. With the exception of short stints, India has maintained a stable macroeconomic environment. Second, policy changes in India have been gradual and largely predictable. Third, apart from a brief period of emergency rule, India has shown remarkable political stability. Fourth, India has generally exhibited the capacity to carry out government policies through setting up institutions and mechanisms.

Explanations for India's Economic Growth

J. Bradford DeLong, an economic historian at the University of California at Berkeley, did not deny the contribution of India's 1980s liberalization was due to faster growth or the role of the 1990s reform to sustain it. But he cannot find incontrovertible evidence establishing the positive role of the second wave of reforms in sustaining rapid growth. Dani Rodrik, an economist at Harvard University, argued that those liberalizing reforms in the 1990s failed to make a significant contribution to India's growth. There is economic literature that questioned the sustainability of the growth acceleration following the 1980s reform, and the 1990s and early 2000s must be relevant in the subsequent growth.

The late Deena Khatkhate of the IMF responded to a 'fatuous and facetious' suggestion that the shift from 1 per cent growth, pre-independence, to 3 per cent to 4 per cent during 1951 to 1980 was greater than the shifts after the 1980s, and it could be attributed to socialist politics. He stated that the difference between the two periods is that one is colonial and the other politically independent; a non-colonial policy is always preferred to a colonial policy. This assertion has been supported by the work of others, including that of the late British economic historian Angus Maddison.

India's and China's Evolving Roles in the Global Economy

Manufacturing trade has accounted for the bulk of the international trade activities of Greater China, and has continued to grow, while South Asia—which includes India— has relied less on manufacturing. From 1990 to 2010, China and South Asia increased their global share in manufacturing exports, although China ultimately attained a 21.6 per cent share while South Asia managed only 1.7 per cent. China's export destination is primarily East Asia and Pacific, while South Asia's major markets are in East Asia, the EU, and NAFTA countries. Intra-China manufacturing was significant from 1990 to 2010, but insignificant compared to South Asia by trade share. This will change as China recently turned to its domestic market for growth. Hong Kong's workers, as the city re-integrates into the Greater Chinese economy, will need to retrain to compete in the regional economy (see Chapter 45). As for China, its comparative advantage is, according to the Relative Comparative Advantage Index, in processing and not assembly. If it continues to refocus its efforts to its home economy, India's businesses will only find themselves taking a greater role in the regional supply chain.

32

Abenomics Will Be Slow, But Methodical

Former Japanese Prime Minister Shinzo Abe speaks at a press conference.
Source: Government of Japan

Shinzo Abe may have stepped down as Prime Minister of Japan, but Abenomics will live on in one form or another. It was conceptualized to support the economy, especially the low-waged workers, so there is obviously something to gain in studying its strategies for Hong Kong. Wage bargaining benefits the part-time worker, who subsist on low wages and traditionally has little negotiating power. Tax credits were given to businesses that raise wages, which is also beneficial to the poor. Gains from sound monetary policies are expected trickle down to subcontractors and workers. One of the policies is including more women and the elderly in the workplace—all good lessons to apply in Hong Kong, where they are poorer as a group.

Before the pandemic led to a severe contraction in Japan's economy, sustained periods of GDP growth gave hope that economic recovery was imminent. Most people credit the rebound to the government's policy of the three-pronged Abenomics. But what is it and how does it work?

The Three Arrows of Abenomics

The three 'arrows' of Abenomics, proposed by Shinzo Abe, the Prime Minister since December 2012, are monetary stimulus (massive quantitative easing), fiscal 'flexibility' (timely fiscal stimulus), and (pro-growth) structural reform. Joseph Stiglitz, in a 2013 blog for *The New York Times*, wanted the US to emulate Abenomics. Structural policies include increasing labour force participation (for example, women and the 'older old') by changing social mores and enforcing anti-discrimination laws, transforming the manufacturing economy to a service-sector economy, and adapting to the dramatic changes in global comparative advantages, to climate change, and to the demographic challenges.

Fiscal policies affect the aggregate demand, the stimulus of which can help structural transformation. Japan's debt would be an obstacle. Monetary policies include quantitative easing; the attention is focused on reversing deflation. 'Weakening the yen's exchange rate will make Japanese goods more competitive and thus stimulate the economy's growth . . . It is equally true that the Federal Reserve's policy of "quantitative easing" weakens the dollar.' Stiglitz observed that 'monetary policy can only go so far. One needs to have coordinated monetary, fiscal, and structural policies.'

Was Abenomics Successful?

By many standards, Abenomics has not been successful. While the Bank of Japan (BOJ) has, reported *The Economist*, 'more than doubled the size of its balance sheet since April 2013 and imposed a sub-zero interest rate in February 2016, still more easing' was seen to be necessary, with the 2 per cent inflation rate target unmet. When pay did not rise before the price of goods, reflating the economy has proven painful.

IMF's Dennis Botman and Zoltan Jakab made the observation that wage-bargaining in Japan had not led to wage increases at small and medium-sized enterprises (SME) and with non-regular workers. With higher inflation, this was hardly reform. They believed that higher wages were needed to break the deflationary spiral and establish a virtuous growth cycle (for example, large paychecks can support aggregate demand and favourable conditions for firms to raise investments). There were factors that kept wages from rising: the emergence of non-regular workers (who pushed down aggregate basic wage growth), competitiveness concerns (due to exchange rate appreciation), a weak SME sector (which is 70 per cent of employment), and coordination problems (firms wanted to free-ride on wage increases by other firms).

Of the obstacles, Abenomics' third arrow (structural reform) could, apart from introducing a model of labour market flexibility and security, improve coordination. Abe had tried moral suasion, setting up the Tripartite Commission to be more involved in wage negotiations, kept from extending a cut in national public servants' wages, introduced tax credit to firms that raised wages, and contemplated increasing the minimum wage, which was among the lowest in the OECD.

It was a hint that Abenomics was inadequate when two other IMF staffers advocated for an additional arrow. Luc Everaert and Giovanni Ganelli observed that debt could be burdensome when prices and income failed to grow. Public debt in Japan rose to nearly 2.5 times GDP, while nominal GDP fell during the decades of deflation. Their work showed that life-time contracts and non-regular contracts (37 per cent of the total share) kept wages low and led to deflation. Abenomics, through its monetary policies, boosted corporate profits that were expected to trickle down to subcontractors and workers.

But while nominal GDP increased and fewer people were unemployed, wages grew less than the BOJ's inflation target. Everaert and Ganelli argued that raising wages and social security benefits would leave people better off (not to mention the decrease in real interest rate) without firms losing competitiveness and profitability. There are coordination problems despite Abe's minimum wage and relying on moral suasion to achieve the wage increase.

So a fourth arrow would be necessary: a 'comply or explain' mechanism for profitable companies to raise wages by 2 per cent or more; strengthening tax incentives to raise wages; penalties for companies that do not raise wages; and raising public sector wages in a forward looking manner. This arrow can be reinforced by the creation of new labour contracts that are a middle ground between life-time and non-regular contracts that give more bargaining power to workers.

The Japanese government is reported to have run budget deficits for over 20 years. While Abe wanted to rein in public finances, a 2014 recession blamed on a consumption tax increase has deterred him from doing so again. As of the article's publication, the Prime Minister introduced a new fiscal stimulus package worth ¥28 trillion, or 6 per cent of GDP. The gross domestic debt, according to OECD in 2015, rose to 226 per cent of GDP, with some suggesting a debt crisis is impending.

In structural reform, Abe's 'womenomics' policy—among which is to increase women's labour force participation—has suffered numerous setbacks. A scheme giving ¥300,000 to small companies that promoted women to management positions was shot down. The current labour participation rate of women is around 63 per cent. They hold 70 per cent of non-regular work. Only 38 per cent of women remain in labour force after having a child. Goldman Sachs noted two demographic trends: by 2060, Japan will lose 40 million people, and the number of aged people is slated to double. In Japan's traditional and immigrant-adverse society, there is little plan to increase immigration to make up for the lost labour.

The Future of Abenomics

But many believe Abenomics, in whatever form it may take, will ultimately be successful. *The Economist* suggested that 'as long as monetary and fiscal policy work in tandem, demand [which is crucial in reflating the economy] should be resilient . . . Abe's bold macroeconomic efforts may then achieve some of what his structural reforms have so far fallen short of achieving'. Japan's net interest payments on its debts are among the lowest in the G7. And structural reform, which Stiglitz has said concerns Japan's social mores, will take time. In a 2014 blog for East Asia Forum, Naohiro Yashiro discussed one aspect of Shinzo Abe's structural reform—the third arrow in Abenomics—especially as it related to labour regulation. While structural reform had been difficult to take hold, the Strategic Special Zones policy had been implemented quickly in six metropolitan areas. A combination of regulatory reform and fiscal incentives, the policy allowed higher buildings to be built, as well as schools and hospitals by private (possibly foreign) firms. It also set legal requirements for firing employees, increased the time that workers must work for a company before they were guaranteed a 'life-time' contract, and introduced official guidelines for dismissing employees with severance pay. These zones are necessary in Japan's consensus-based society and which offer an agreeable environment for foreigners to do business. The talks were described to take place in three stages, showing the slow pace at which structural reforms needed to get done in Japan. Abenomics, nevertheless, offers a guide for inspired poverty alleviation for Hong Kong.

33

Can Hong Kong Prevent a Japanese-Style 'Lost Decades?'

A homeless man sleeping on the streets of Tokyo. Epic economic events probably need to take place before a game-changing anti-poverty strategy can be implemented.
Source: Wikimedia Commons

Behind every gutsy economic policy like Abenomics are years of experience and turbulent times. Without the 'lost decades' of Japan, there may not have been the will to abolish lifetime employment. The three arrows, along with the fourth suggested, called for a devolution of wage bargaining power from business owners to the subcontractors, part-timers, and workers. That might well have been a reflection of the hardship employees faced during the economic stagnation.

This chapter explains some of the events during Japan's malaise. Hopefully, Hong Kongers can appreciate that, in their own society, it takes time to design and implement macroeconomic and anti-poverty policies.

The Lost Decades

In the years following Japan's economic downturn in the late 1980s, the relative poverty rate of Japan rose from 13.2 per cent in 1988 to 15.7 per cent in 2015. The reasons behind the 'lost decades' of Japan are real estate and stock market bubbles that burst in the 1990s, followed by a series of unfortunate events in the economy, including an overall sluggish growth rate (less than 1 per cent for the past 15 years) and deflation (1999-2003 and 2009-2010). The bubbles existed due to loose monetary policy, tax distortion, and financial deregulation. These events were juxtaposed with the US forcing Japan to appreciate the yen in the late 1980s, possibly in an effort to increase the supply of yen. At the end, liquidity was cut off, bursting the bubbles. Deregulation included opening up the capital account, which put stress on regional (medium sized) banks. This led banks to make more risky loans and precipitate the *jusen* crisis of the early 1990s.

From 1991 to 1996, money was tight in the Japanese economy, and real estate and stock prices dropped. Banks understated their problem with bad loans, while seeing their credit rating decline. The Ministry of Finance and BOJ were too slow to react. They saw a large number of large banks become insolvent. They needed public money, though the *jusen* crisis hindered them from doing so. Bureaucrats, especially high officials rotated and created inefficiencies. Other reasons were plainly political ones and a falsely optimistic attitude that real estate prices would recover soon.

Since 1997, when Yamaichi Securities and Sanyo Securities—the former was Japan's oldest brokerage and the other a medium-sized firm in the same industry—went bust, due to the crash of the stock market and housing markets and the loss of confidence in accounting and auditing. At the end of 1997, the Emergency Economic Package, worth ¥17 trillion, was established (most of whose fund would not be used). Long-Term Credit Bank of Japan (LTCB) almost went bankrupt, and Sumitomo refused to merge. In October 1998, the Diet enacted the Financial Revitalization Act and Bank Recapitalization Act, offering ¥60 trillion for assistance. By the end of that year, LTCB and Nippon Credit Bank were nationalized. From March 1992 to March 2000, bad loans loss amounted to ¥66 trillion, or 13 per cent of GDP in 2000. Land prices in 2014 were about 80 per cent of their value in 1980, while stock prices have recovered and outperformed their 1980 value, appreciating 250 per cent.

There are opportunities to regain economic growth, namely from capital, labour, and productivity. Japan, according to K.C. Fung, of UC Santa Cruz, has great infrastructure; the labour supply is declining due to demographic changes and can be replenished through immigration; and productivity is dependent on R&D spending (which Japan has a healthy dose of) and can be enhanced through collaboration between the private sector and universities.

What Caused the Lost Decades?

Mitsuhiro Fukao, of Musashino University in Tokyo, explained the cause of the 'lost decades' using the concept of Japanese-style management, which is characterized by lifetime employment, a bank system with long-term cross-shareholding, and borrowing relationships with banks, and keiretsu. These relationships are maintained by 'credible commitment' backed up by large latent profit in stocks and real estate. When the bubble burst at the end of the 1980s, coupled with new, often foreign, shareholding, management could keep less 'pocket' of rescue funds. The government used to have this 'pocket' as well: deposit interest and branching controls for failed banks, rent for Fiscal Invest and Loan Program projects, and government-sponsored financial institutions (GSFIs) that can distribute the gap between the regulated deposit-interest rate and the on-going lending rate as a subsidy. In the late 1980s and early 1990s, the Ministry of Finance lost the power to give out the first 'pocket'. GSFIs now need taxpayer money to provide low interest loans, which found it hard to make a profit. In response, banks raised lending interest rates to small and medium-sized firms, which could not afford the rates despite the zero-interest policy of the BOJ. Fukao suggested a mild inflation and monetary expansion to counteract a higher nominal or lending interest rate with a lower real borrowing rate.

The cause of the lost decades in Japan was due to a difficulty transitioning from the traditional Japanese governance system to a new one, exacerbated by policies that created a deflationary environment. The result was that the corporate sector was left without a traditional governance structure, banking and insurance sectors that were losing money, and a national debt that was rapidly mounting. Companies with negative equity continued to operate because of extremely low interest rates; banks with little or no capital did not foreclose them because they might go bankrupt themselves. Banks, with the deflation and zero-interest rate policy, had to be heavily subsidized and possibly nationalized; life insurance companies would not be able to back their policies' high returns with long-term, high-yielding assets. So the current problems in the Japanese economy were an accelerating deflation and an unsustainable budget deficit, and a loss-making banking sector troubled by bad loans and large GSFIs. Both macro- and micro-economic policy solutions are required. The inflation target should be set at 0-3 per cent on the core-consumer price index inflation rate, so as to halt deflation and raise nominal lending rates without raising real interest rates. GSFIs, which are supported by lobbies, should be abolished. All of this may bankrupt many banks and insolvent firms.

There are few similarities between Hong Kong and Japan in this discussion, apart from the time frame one should expect to see changes like Abenomics or a push in poverty alleviation. Certainly Hong Kong is a mature economy, but it is centred on the service industries. The city's debt reached an all-time high in 2016, but it is still at a modest 38.4 per cent of GDP. Japan's real mistake was not that it allowed the yen to rise [after the 1985 Plaza Accord between five major powers], but that it had previously resisted an appreciation for too long, so that when it did happen the yen soared. But Hong Kong's has little control over its monetary policy, since its currency is pegged to the US dollar.

The city, however, can learn from Japan's demographic shift. In the words of one Chinese expert, 'We learned from Japan how quickly growth can stop when demography changes.' Moreover, with real estate prices, the BOJ apparently burst the bubble in 1989 to trigger the Nikkei's collapse. Hong Kong does not want that to happen at home.

34

What Will Become of the Japanese Firm?

A masked train employee on standby at a station in Japan. Japanese workers'
special relationship with their employers may explain the country's low
unemployment rate.
Source: Wikimedia Commons

Labour is another area in which big changes took time. Workers
in Japan have made great strides in wage-bargaining despite
of its corporate environment, which can be very conservative.
There are five features, which the UC Santa Cruz economist
K.C. Fung referred to as: production, workers within those

companies, the labour unions, the J-firm's relationship with its group bank, and the Japanese government's policy related to industries.

The Japanese firms (J-firms, made famous by the late Masahiko Aoki, formerly of Stanford University) are proud of their innovations in production techniques. Lifetime employment was considered the norm. Labour unions often bargain for workers of a specific company instead of the whole industry. Large, possibly anti-competitive business groups run the economy. The iron triangle formed by the ruling party, ministries, and businesses also makes Japanese business mysterious. Lifetime employment's demise seems to coincide with the rise of non-regular workers and quasi lifetime employment, a trend that will benefit many low-waged Japanese. Hong Kong has its own version of the part-timer, the slasher, whose becoming a part of economic life there must have evolved in a similar way as the Japanese.

The Production System in Japan

The first feature, production, deals with the way Japanese manufacturers implement coordination and has served as a model for foreigners. Terms like zero inventory and just-in-time manufacturing (JIT) have become commonplace concepts in management. The story goes that the genesis of Toyota's JIT system came from a trip that a group of executives took to the US. After visiting the car-manufacturing centre of Detroit, they happened upon a supermarket, where a missing store item on the shelf gave them the inspiration for the process. The customers, they concluded, should determine when and what should be produced. Zero inventory is now used in many industries outside the automobile sector. JIT has been applied to global suppliers, like Dell Computers, using online sales and specifications.

The kanban system, according to the *Encyclopedia Britannica*, refers to an inventory control technique that 'permits Japanese firms to schedule production and manage inventories more effectively'. Kanban literally means 'card,' and refers to the tickets that are attached to parts in the manufacturing process. It is related to the zero inventory and JIT systems, though more market and demand driven. An overarching theme is *kaizen*, which is central to total quality control and refers to 'the notion that improvement must involve all members of a company'. One might even say that the continuousness of the improvement process is relentless.

The Worker-Firm Relationship in Japan

The second feature of the Japanese economy has to do with the workers within J-firms. Compared to specialized jobs, Japanese firms use job rotation with employees. This is consistent with the JIT technique. Everyone knows one another's job; the style needs more independent decision making, better intellectual work, and more contextual skills. Job rotation is also consistent with white-collarization.

Japanese workers are also used to quasi-lifetime employment, although it exists only in large companies. These 'regular' or 'incumbent' employees are hired straight out of a tertiary-level institution. As salarymen who went to the right prep or high school and right university, they would acclimatize to a specific company culture and become a senpai to future recruits. According to Masataka Maeda's article on Japan Center for

Economic Research's website, whether a person lands a job in a large company makes a large difference in their lifetime earnings. To note, these employment bonds are implicit, not guaranteed, contracts. Nevertheless, there have been questions raised about how quasi-lifetime employment can be efficient for companies, which lack flexibility to terminate workers.

Another equally puzzling fact of the worker-firm relationship in Japan is wage seniority. That is, more experienced employees in a job position, regardless of relative skills, get paid more. This is a paradox because the firm is not seeking to maximize share prices—a weighted sum of the interests of its workers and owners—yet successful Japanese companies follow the practice. It is a question for defenders of lifetime employment. Possibly, workers are viewed as shareholders, and they are paid more for their time at the company. Additionally, firms may be focused more on capital gains than dividend payouts—or expansion and diversification than core competence, giving more opportunities for regular employees.

On a firm level, to maintain market share and employment, J-firms would even accept a drop in export price in yen and profits (or perhaps alternatively, keen on market share and less on profits). Fung sought to understand the adjustment behaviour of J-firms by comparing Aoki's model to the neoclassical firm under three disturbances: a yen shock, a tariff, and an import quota. When the yen appreciates, the export price rises, and the total organizational rent would decrease for J-firms. In A-firms, exchange rate changes would not affect the firm's growth rate. When there is a tariff, the organizational rent decreases, but the export price and growth rate remain unchanged in J-firms. The export price rises in A-firms. When there is an import quota, the J-firm would see export price and growth rate rise, and the total organizational rent would decrease. A-firms would experience the same effect.

There is also a bonus system or profit sharing with workers (both are related in regression studies). Profit sharing extends to blue-collar workers, unlike in American firms outside of the high-tech industry, where only top managers receive bonuses. This ensures that the interests of the firm and its workers are in sync. The late Havard economist Martin Weitzman proposed using profit-sharing as a tool to combat unemployment. Fung used a duopoly model in a microeconomic context to show profit-sharing decreases unemployment (versus a macroeconomic model) in an oligopolistic industry. The results showed that profit-sharing causes an industry-wide wage reduction, leading to a decline in product price and an expansion of the total industry production. The latter leads to a rise in employment in the industry. Another result was that the wage rate of the profit-sharing firm declined more than one that was not profit-sharing. The market share and employment of the profit-sharing firm increased while those of the non-profit-sharing firm were reduced. So the total industry economic rent of the profit-sharing firm and union increased, leading to beneficial effects. This can explain the success of the Japanese economy, which featured a profit-sharing bonus system in firms that has been neglected in economic studies.

Labour Unions in Japan

The third feature of the Japanese economy is connected to the labour unions. In Japan, there exist enterprise unions, specific to a company, rather than an industrial union like the UAW in the US. A question with these unions is whether they are real labour unions or co-opted by companies. The history of labour unions breaks the stereotypes of passive and cooperative Japanese workers. Think the militant workers strikers and movements in the 1950s and 1960s. Some academics draw comparisons between Japanese labour unions and unions in other countries, for example Germany (which comprise of board of directors and workers who have a say in the union, or co-determination). There were the Employer Federation and the National Labor Union and Government.

Keiretsu in Japan

The fourth feature of the Japanese economy are the keiretsu. Before the war, great, family-owned zaibatsu were created, like Mitsubishi, which was comprised of a network of more than 100 loosely connected splinter companies. Zaibatsu anticipated foreign money, so they took over companies through cross-shareholding and formed keiretsu, or a group of companies enmeshed in economic relationships. There are two kinds of keiretsu: horizontal and vertical. Horizontal keiretsu are financial groups centred on a main bank. By law, the bank can only hold up to 5 per cent of each member company, though through cross-shareholding between member companies, the bank can control more. Perhaps because of this, it is hard to buy out a Japanese company (with a notable exception of Nissan by Renault). Japanese, therefore, has a significantly lower FDI compared to other rich countries. The bank acts as the main lender for financing projects and, non-contractually, the rescuer of last rescuer (for instance, Sumitomo's rescue of Mazda). The member firms, which are typically not in the same business, have a non-contractual relationship that can be best described by ships being tied together to weather rough waters. This view is not shared by everyone any more.

Vertical keiretsu, like Toyota and Panasonic, would include a manufacturer that provides capital and work for layers of suppliers (in long-term relationships with few entries and exits). Firms at the higher echelons can conduct R&D; those at the lower rung have less technological expertise. Benefits of cost reductions are shared in this efficiency-enhancing exercise. Toyota, for example, occasionally buys from outside suppliers to put pressure on costly keiretsu members.

There are criticisms of how a keiretsu operates. The main bank charges higher interest rates than the average financial institutions, although one can argue that it is an insurance premium for when a member firm needs to be rescued. Member firms also have lower profits than they otherwise would, although their profits are more stable. A keiretsu's firms coordinate in the President's club, which is not transparent. There are people who argue that financial keiretsu are anti-competitive and oligopolistic and point to the banking crisis in Japan and the US for support (that is, keiretsu inhibit imports). Mechanisms for dealing with these issues include SII, the WTO, and bilateral talks.

Government-Industrial Relations

The fifth feature of the Japanese economy is the government's relationship with industry. There exist an 'iron triangle' of the LDP, businesses, the *kasumigaseki* (ministerial district) bureaucracy. The government comprises of the Diet, which has two elected houses. The Prime Minister, currently Shinzo Abe, is normally the majority leader in the House of Representatives.

Important ministries are METI, the Ministry of Finance and
the Ministry of Foreign Affairs.

What Will Stay? The Sturdy Keiretsu

The feature that will likely continue in the future are the
horizontal and vertical keiretsu. Sandra Dow, of Middlebury
College, and Jean McGuire, of Louisiana State University, looked
at the strength of ties of keiretsu in three periods (economic
growth from 1987 to 1991; economic decline from 1992 to
1996; and economic decline with regulatory changes from
1997 to 2001) and found that while horizontal keiretsu mostly
displayed strong ties throughout, vertical keiretsu maintained
weaker ties. They reasoned that a change in affiliation is due to
the greater use of short-term debt, the P/E ratio (the higher the
ratio, the stronger the tie), and foreign of significant (greater
than 5 per cent) ownership stake. Despite regulations and
economic malaise, keiretsu to various degrees have found closer
ties between member firms.

Keiretsu in Japan thrived and turned into a tool for
innovating faster while radically cutting costs when Western-
style management became in vogue. The vertical keiretsu
is exemplified at Toyota, which built up suppliers' stores of
knowledge by being on the lookout for problems, anomalies,
and opportunities through the development and production
of parts. The company developed keiretsu-like relationships
overseas, replicating the qualities of the successful parent: cost,
quality, innovation, and a 'peace of mind'. The process, as
well as the associated feature of the Japanese economy, became
a prototype for foreign companies, like Scania and Ikea in
Sweden.

What Will Go? The Future of Employment in Japan

Of the five features of the Japanese economy, the one that is most likely to disappear is the second feature, the current worker-firm relationship, which has repercussions with the salaryman's job stability. The first feature (the unique Japanese production processes) and the fourth (the keiretsu) have survived the recession and become a model for companies in other countries, including integrated business groups in China and Taiwan. The fifth feature, the government, will remain relevant and democratic despite questions about the tenure of the constitutional monarch. The third feature, Japan's enterprise unions, will remain with the help of the government and its Tripartite Commission (which engages businesses and trade unions in wage talks). This goes on while facing the challenge of a shrinking labour union, according to Wikipedia, since non-regular workers cannot join labour unions. Because of the economic situation, major unions in steel, electronics and automobile industries had to restrict their demands or receive no offers at all from the management.

Wikipedia states that *shushin koyo* (permanent employment) is gone. During and after the recession and the most recent financial crisis, firms have suspended lifetime employment and have instead implemented mass layoffs. Naohiro Yashiro, in a 2014 blog for East Asia Forum, described a set of labour regulation reforms that set legal requirements for firing employees, increased the time that workers must work for a company before they are guaranteed a 'life-time' contract, and introduced official guidelines for dismissing employees with severance pay—in an effort to offer an agreeable environment for foreigners to do business.

A related topic is the rise of non-regular workers, which are 37.9 per cent—more than one-third—of the work force in the fourth quarter of 2015. They are a symptom of a prolonged recession, along with statistics describing hiring freeze, work hour reduction, transfers, the reduction or elimination of bonuses, and the suspension of pay raises. Dennis Botman and Zoltan Jakab, on a blog at IMF, blamed the emergence of non-regular workers for price stagnation, because they push down aggregate basic wage growth.

Perhaps it takes an economic shock for employers in Hong Kong to offer better terms for part-time employees and slashers. Anything that puts downward pressure on wages is good for low-income workers. The lesson from Japan is that change takes time.

The current employment system—quasi life-time employment, wage seniority, and such—keeps firms from increasing wages and leads to deflation, according to Luc Everaert and Giovanni Ganelli on a 2016 IMF blog entry. Wages need to beat the BOJ's inflation target. To do that requires a fourth arrow to Abenomics' traditional three: a 'comply or explain' mechanism for profitable companies to raise wages by 2 per cent or more; strengthening tax incentives to raise wages; penalties for companies that do not raise wages; and raising public sector wages in a forward looking manner. This arrow can be reinforced by the creation of new labour contracts that are a middle ground between life-time and non-regular contracts that give more bargaining power to workers, including in matters relating to wages.

35[6]

Should China Buy American Shale Oil and Gas to Support the Belt and Road Initiative?

The KazMunayGaz building in Astana, Kazakhstan. The energy producing country is a crucial partner in China's Belt and Road Initiative.
Source: Wikimedia Commons

In Africa (see Chapter 12), we learn that alleviating energy poverty requires a multilateral approach. We also learn that the

---

[6] A version of this chapter appeared as an op-ed in *The News Lens (International)* on February 10, 2017.

countries should be optimistic about shale oil and gas (Chapter 28) for energy security. So it is quite logical that China, who initiated the massive Belt and Road Initiative (BRI), should include the US, which has become a major player in shale oil and gas production. After all, the BRI countries have a voracious appetite for energy for its infrastructure projects, and the US seems to be a great business partner. BRI countries should, in fact, involve more energy suppliers to lower costs. Hong Kong, a BRI partner, should also diversify its energy sources so that its residents can enjoy cheaper heating, electricity, and transportation.

China's Interest in the Belt and Road Initiative

China has been experiencing a bout of industrial overcapacity. To deal with it, its government established the BRI to establish or re-establish land and maritime trade routes from Shanghai to Venice, crossing a vast expanse of land. A total of 64 countries (many of which are low-income) are involved in the Eurasian portion. Three economic corridors on land will be constructed through it. The 'Twenty-First Century Maritime Silk Road' will involve oceans and bodies of water touching and separating South Asia, East Africa, the Arabian Peninsula, and Mediterranean Europe. As a result of the 900 projects, 4.4 billion people will be affected, costing US$890 billion. China is committing US$4 trillion to BRI countries.

China needs the BRI furthermore because it needs to secure natural resources, like oil, and promote the RMB as an international currency. Strategically, infrastructure work will extend to neglected areas of the country. It helps to showcase the economic achievements of the country. The BRI also sets the stage for China to exert geopolitical influence over the countries it touches.

What Does the United States Think of BRI?

The US seemed to be indifferent to dismissive. In official meetings and conferences in Washington and at international venues, the BRI was never formally acknowledged. But the US will almost certainly see the benefits of collaborating with China. Many of the BRI countries need development aid, less than 10 per cent of which could be met with existing commitments from China and various agencies. The BRI may become 'the biggest economic development project in history'. The US can become a direct or indirect business partner on many fronts.

That is to say, if the US remains diffident or antagonistic, it suffers when its allies in Europe fail to grow economically to their potential and join the BRI if they have not. An effective collaboration, moreover, would allow US contractors to secure BRI projects and bolster its presence in militarily unstable regions of the world—benefitting many countries.

Why the US Would Make a Good Energy Supplier?

Therefore, it will become apparent that cooperating with China is a good deal for the US, and vice versa. Is buying energy from the US to support BRI projects one of those good deals? The US is the world's largest combined producer of oil and natural gas. China imports 75 per cent of its oil and will consume 60 per cent of the world's petroleum in 2030. As a large consumer of coal (75 per cent of its energy consumption is from the dirty stuff), China is definitely looking for a cleaner energy supply.

Barring nuclear and hydroelectric energy, which alongside other non-fossil fuel supplies make up less than 20 per cent of energy consumption, natural gas seems to be the best alternative. By 2030, the demand for natural gas in the country is expected to increase 1.5 times to 510 billion cubic metres (bcm) per year. Current domestic supply is 175 bcm per year, and—taking into account domestic production, shale gas, and imports from Russia—132 bcm per year will be needed. An import of 1.1 per cent of American production in natural gas can make up for 25 per cent of the remaining demand. Adjusting the amount will yield the optimal level China should purchase.

Buying a wide array of energy—solar, wind, or nuclear—is better than betting on any single one. In principle, buying shale oil and gas from the US and other trusted countries will give China a source of diversification. Many of the countries that China currently purchases energy from come from unstable parts of the world, whether it's Eurasia or the Middle East. The US seems to be a trustworthy partner, who adheres to the rules of international trade. China and its BRI partners should consider buying American shale oil and gas in a multilateral deal as a way to support BRI projects. They will gain cheaper energy, and the millions of people, including poor Hong Kongers looking for less expensive heating, electricity, and transportation costs, will become more energy secure.

Can Former Soviet Union Oil Replace Saudi Arabia?

The OPEC cartel meets regularly at its Vienna headquarters.
Source: Wikimedia Commons

If I want to procure a cheap source of oil for the energy poor in Hong Kong, so that they can enjoy lowering transportation costs, I would pick any of the Southeast Asian countries or China, which is right next door, over the Middle East and its conflict-

---

[7] This chapter has been condensed and translated for an op-ed in *The Stand News* on February 23, 2018.

prone producers. But can the city really escape the influence of Arab suppliers? Relevant data is scant in Hong Kong, so I looked to China, which has tried to become less dependent on oil from the Middle East by signing deals and constructing pipelines with the former Soviet Union States (FSU). The FSU is the term the energy industry currently uses in reference to Russia and its now 14 independent states, the Commonwealth of Independent States (CIS). But Saudi Arabia and the Organization of Petroleum Exporting Countries (OPEC) producers have a much greater reserve of oil. As a cartel, they exert great pricing power in the interconnected global energy market. Their influence can only be minimized, not neutralized.

Sharon Cho of Bloomberg reported in April 2017 that Russia surpassed Saudi Arabia as the top oil supplier to China. Imports increased 9.3 per cent from February to 4.7 million metric tons. Angola, an OPEC member, was second with 4.67 million tons, while Saudi Arabia, another major OPEC producer, fell to third. A month later, Reuters repeated the same pronouncement.

It was not the first time Russia has accomplished this feat. In June 2015, Anjli Raval of the Financial Times reported that Russia overtook Saudi Arabia as the number one Chinese supplier for the first time on record. The FSU particularly those countries situated on the Caspian shelf, have shown that they have a major role in China's growing need for secure oil supplies abroad.

This essay will argue that an increasing level of oil consumption in China is accompanied by an increase in oil import. There is a lack of alternatives for oil in critical sectors, making the country's reliance on Persian Gulf and African oil an issue of energy security. Factors such as the 'Malacca dilemma' and China's apolitical, economically focused energy policy abroad are considered.

Russia and other FSU countries hold great potential to counterbalance Saudi Arabia as an oil supply in the long-term. But there are limits. The size of the Saudi oil reserve, the economics of cartels in OPEC's favour, and the unwillingness of Russian government and other FSU governments and their oil firms to challenge OPEC will ensure that China will depend on Saudi Arabia's petroleum for a long time.

China's Need for a Secure Oil Supply

1. *Consumption*

China's search for a secure oil supply requires an appreciation of the country's need for the black stuff. Oil constituted 40 per cent of China's energy consumption in 2002. From 2000 to 2019, oil consumption increased from 226.9 million tons to 620 million tons, with a 6.37 per cent average annual growth rate between 1995 and 2017 (the world growth rate was 1.36 per cent). In 2018, China's demand for oil was 12.7 million barrels per day (b/d), growing 0.35 million b/d year-on-year. OPEC foresaw an increase of 0.35 million b/d in the last quarter of 2019.

In 2007, China became the world's second largest oil consumer, with foreign oil dependency increasing from 54.2 per cent in 2009 to 69.8 per cent in 2018. 60 per cent of China's oil may possibly be imported by 2030. According to the International Energy Agency (IEA), China's demand in oil will overtake Europe in 2020 and the US, currently the largest market, by 2035. 57.7 per cent of the oil consumption is in transportation—not surprising given 12.7 million cars were sold in 2019 and the total number domestic flights increased 2.5 times between 2009 and 2018.

2. *Import Statistics*

Because of China's appetite for oil, it has increasingly relied on foreign sources. In 1993, China became a net oil importer. In 2009, imports reached 200 million tons for the first time, and China became the largest net oil importer in the world in 2014.

Bloomberg reported that total crude imports reached 10.7 million b/d in April 2019, compared to April 2011, when China's net oil imports was 5.2 million b/d. That year, the IEA estimated the country's petroleum import will increase to 12.8 million b/d by 2035. This imposes a great expense for China. If oil prices reach US$113 in 2035, the total cost of crude oil imports will be US$525 billion.

What Makes China Energy Insecure?

1. *Lack of Alternative Sources of Energy*

China's lack of security with oil is plagued by several factors, one of which is the lack of alternatives for petroleum. Unlike natural gas, there is no ready substitute for oil as a transport fuel, which is arguably the lifeblood of industries. As a result, China remains far more dependent on foreign sources for oil than for any other energy source, which will remain so with the advent of shale gas.

2. *Reliance on the Persian Gulf and the Asia Pacific*

The reliance on oil has been coupled with China's dependence on its Persian Gulf and Asian Pacific suppliers. In 1995, the two regions were the source of 88 per cent of China's crude oil imports, with Indonesia—the largest Asian exporter to China—making up one-third of total imports. The Middle East is home to political unstable regimes and radical Islamists who may disrupt China's oil supply. By 2010, the percentage of imported oil from Africa and the Persian Gulf have been reduced to 77 per cent. Today, despite further diversification into Africa and Russia, 46 per cent of the country's petroleum imports still come from the Persian Gulf.

3. *The Malacca Dilemma*

Another reason China needs to diversify from these regions is the 'Malacca dilemma,' named after one of the most trafficked bodies of water in the world. There exists a chokepoint at the Strait of Malacca, possibly blocking off oil tankers from Africa and the Persian Gulf. In fact, 80 per cent of China's oil imports pass through the strait. Louise Merrington, a former analyst at the Australian Department of Defense, and Lirong Wang, of Zhejiang Normal University in China, even suggested that the situation is worsening, with piracy and potential terrorism threatening the seas, including the Strait of Hormuz that links the Persian Gulf to the Gulf of Oman and the Indian Ocean.

4. *China's Current Energy Strategy*

Considering the challenges China faces in securing its oil supply abroad, the country's ambitions should not be viewed in the political framework proposed by Brock Tessman, of the University of Montana, and Wojtek Wolfe, of Rutgers University. Rather, the Energy Policy Trilemma framework is used—appreciating the balance between the need for energy security with cost and environmental impact. This is supported by China's routine dealings with Western sanctioned regimes—like Angola, Russia, Iran, Iraq, Venezuela, and Congo (totalling 14 per cent of petroleum imports in 2013)—leading to criticisms for complicity in Sudan and colonialism in South America and Africa (China insisted that those constitute South-South cooperation).

The tools that China has used, therefore, is primarily economic, in the form of the National Oil Companies (NOC) (CNPC, Sinopec, and CNOOC), which have spent US$18.2 billion in M&A activities with upstream oil and gas companies, accounting for 13 per cent of all oil and gas acquisitions. These deals have grown to more than 200 projects in 50 countries. They also produce so-called equity oil that totaled 45 million tons in 2008. Columbia University's Erica Downs, however, questioned whether Chinese oil companies make good investment decisions in equity oil and Shaofeng Chen, of Peking University, asked whether equity oil can help buffer oil shocks.

FSU Oil as a Possible Alternative

Financiers Edward L. Morse and James Richard argued that 'the revival of the Russian oil industry had geopolitical implications that could be ignored neither by Saudi Arabia [one of the major foreign suppliers of oil to China] and other oil exporters'. Jan Kalicki, public policy fellow at the Wilson Center in Washington, D.C., calculated that the vast reserve of oil in the Caspian region, combined with Russia's production capacity, could counterbalance Middle Eastern oil. CIA data shows that the combined production capacity of Russia and other

FSU countries in the Caspian region can convincingly displace Saudi production.

1. *Oil Capacity in the FSU*

The story of Russia's increase in oil capacity (which, according to OPEC, topped 11.4 million b/d as of September 2019, compared to Saudi Arabia's 9.8 million b/d) is one of the most solid growth. In May 2004, Yukos signed a deal to build pipelines to China and with Russian National Railways that would transport 170,000 b/d. That was an increase from 2002, when the company was preparing to export a total of 500,000 b/d from Eastern Siberia to China. NOCs made a deal with Russia to provide a 300,000 b/d supply over 20 years through the Eastern Siberia-Pacific Ocean pipeline and its spur line, starting in 2011. President Vladimir Putin recently announced a 4,000 km pipeline, called the biggest construction project in the world. The transport system expanded from the relatively small rail shipments via a pipeline into Heilongjiang, which may help transport oil from anticipated major finds off the eastern coast on Sakhalin Island and the Northern seas of the Arctic Circle.

2. *Caspian Oil*

What is interesting were the tremendous amounts of petroleum discovered in the region around the Caspian Sea. New York University's Carolyn Kissane reported 30 billion barrels in Kazakhstan, 7 billion barrels of oil in Azerbaijan, 6 billion barrels in Turkmenistan, 0.6 billion barrels in Uzbekistan, and 12 million barrels in Tajikistan. Conservative estimates show that the Caspian shelf holds 75 billion barrels, 115 per cent of what BP Amoco credit[ed.] to the entire [FSU] in 2000, and estimates go up to 115 billion barrels of oil—many time greater than the amount found in the North Sea.

Kazakhstan is a useful partner in China's search for energy diversification, with its capacity representing 5 per cent of China's demand for oil. In 2014, China's share of equity in Kazakhstan's oil sector was significantly larger than that of the US and Russia. The Kazakhstan-China pipeline carries 400,000 b/d to China over 2,880 kilometres. The idea for the Kazakhstan-Xinjiang pipeline was conceived as early as 1993.

China entered the fields in 1997, when CNPC acquired the rights to the Aktobe field, which includes the Zhanazhol oil and gas condensate field and the Keniyak oil blocks. China is making up for its late entry, and missed opportunities (for example, the 50 billion-barrel Kashagan field) through long-term regional financial commitments for exploration, production, and pipelines, buttressed by a vast currency reserve. An initial 60 per cent stake in the Aktyubinsk oil company was increased by an additional 25 per cent stake in May 2003.

3. *What do FSU Countries and China Have in Common?*

An alliance between Russia and major FSU producers and China would be bolstered by geo-political similarities. Territorial depth is one factor. The combined land area of the countries would cover a large portion of Eurasia. The shared landmass would facilitate oil transport by bypassing the geo-politically unstable and navigationally dangerous Strait of Malacca.

The large populations in the countries would provide possibly cheap and educated labour for building infrastructure and operating the extraction machinery and pipeline. This ensures a continuity of oil supply. Russia, the rest of FSU, and China also have significant military presence in Eurasia, and have a large arsenal of weapon, including nuclear weapons. But it would certainly provide security to pipelines and workers in the oil fields, preventing supply disruption. Finally, the triumvirate has a fast growing economic capability with a large share of the world's natural resources. That is to say, the size of those countries' economies offers an incentive for the oil supply to continue and new infrastructure to be built. Their large oil reserves will provide a long-term, secure supply to China.

Is FSU Oil Secure?

1. *A Comparison of Major Oil Producers' Reserves*

Is there security in FSU oil? The answer is no, because of the inherent limits of the suppliers' reserves and infrastructure and the economics of the OPEC cartel. According to CIA data, Russia has 80 billion barrels of oil in its proven reserves (the quantity of oil that is, with reasonable certainty, recoverable) in 2016. In fact, seven countries have greater proven reserves than Russia, including Iran (157.8 billion barrels), Saudi Arabia (269 billion barrels), and warring Iraq (143 billion barrels). None of the FSU members other than Russia came in the top 10 (Kazakhstan ranks twelfth). It does not help that pipelines between FSU countries and China are sometimes deficient; as of 2001, most of Kazakhstan's oil exports are transported through Russian pipelines.

2. *The Economics of OPEC*

But nothing is more certain than the power of OPEC in the oil industry. Put simply, the OPEC cartel can and will exert great influence on the market prices of oil if China deviates from Persian Gulf and OPEC suppliers. Noam Scheiber—in an essay in the *New York Times Magazine*—called it the 'iron law of economics'. Oil trades in a global market, with prices determined by world supply and demand. Robert Kaufmann, of Boston University, and his colleagues showed in a Granger statistical analysis that OPEC capacity utilization, production quotas, and adherence to those quotas—among other factors—influenced oil prices (although not the other way around).

A large producer can affect the oil supply and prices. Saudi Arabia and the Persian Gulf, with 600 billion-plus barrels of oil, are such an influencer. 63 per cent of all proven oil reserves are in the Middle East; 25 per cent are in Saudi Arabia. According to data from OPEC, the share of proven oil reserves is dominated by its members. An example of OPEC exerting its power was in September 2004, when Russian oil companies in the country's Ural area were frustrated by OPEC, led by Saudi Arabia, selling oil to Western Europe and the US at a lower price to keep its market dominance in the West.

A defining feature of Saudi Arabia's oil policy is its 3 million b/d of spare capacity (in 2002, when its production was 7.4 million b/d), which is enough to displace the production of another large oil-exporting country (though importantly not Russia) if there is disruption in the oil supply. It is the 'energy equivalent of nuclear weapons'. China, possibly in response, established its own strategic petroleum reserve in 2001. By 2020, the projected capacity will be 475 million barrels, or 90 days of import, taking into account the increase in consumption.

OPEC has, most importantly, been successful. OPEC solves the three problems—coordination, cheating, and entry. It is therefore able to raise oil prices. OPEC has somewhat put a stranglehold on China. Three of China's top four oil suppliers (Saudi Arabia, Iraq, and Angola), accounting for 36.5 per cent of its supply in 2019, are OPEC members. Pierre Noël, Senior Fellow at the International Institute of Strategic Studies in London, alluded to the success of the cartel, despite of the price of oil reaching US$100 a barrel in the last decade, the shift of Saudi Arabia to a less oil-dependent economy, a distrust of the Iraqi government, and the US shale revolution driving down the price of the oil supply.

The post-WWII history of oil has truly been intricately linked to OPEC. From 1945 until the 1973-4 oil crisis, global demand for oil grew strongly, although the real prices were low and stable—at times even falling. After WWII, oil supply capacity expanded rapidly. Uncertainty led to rapid depletion of known reserves, even when prices were lower than future expected prices. The oil crisis was initiated by OPEC's action to constrain supply growth and higher prices, leading to lower demand growth. Some, like the Russians, may see the 1980s as a period of price war initiated by Saudi Arabia on all other oil producers.

From the mid-1990s and from 2005 Chinese showed great demand growth that was met by imports. This in turn gave China great influence on the world oil market, as alluded to by increases in oil price in 2005 and early 2006. The influence is expected to continue. But China will face the 'Persian Gulf dilemma,' which is an increasing dependence on oil from the region as the country continues to diversify away from it. Today, China also pays market price for many, if not all, of the recent deals. Like the world's major oil importers, the country sees itself and the others as 'all part of a single, seamless oil market driven by supply and demand'. As for Russia, it has a cooperative, rather than antagonistic, relationship with OPEC, despite historical examples to the contrary. This makes attempts to displace Saudi Arabia or any OPEC member as a supplier to China unlikely.

The Future of China's Oil Supply

Andrew B. Kennedy, of Australian National University, claimed that diversifying its supply portfolio since the 1990s will not keep China from relying on the Persian Gulf and Africa for a 'high percentage of its imports' in the future. In the meantime, Angola, a major Chinese supplier, joined OPEC in 2007, showing the organization's efforts to stay relevant as a price fixer. Countries like Saudi Arabia and Kuwait sought to build closer ties with China by building oil refineries. For example, Saudi Aramco built an oil refinery in Qingdao that went into operation in 2008, and has since been asked to develop another refinery with Sinopec in Fujian. There is also evidence of greater geopolitical engagement by China in the Persian Gulf to increase energy security. But there is an undeniable drop in import from Persian Gulf countries. Joseph Mann, of Bar Ilan University in Israel, reported that non-OPEC countries' contributions rose 'significantly'.

While FSU oil cannot truly supplant Saudi and OPEC petroleum sources—due to the size of their proven reserves and the strength of the OPEC cartel and Saudi Arabia's important place in it—their import, which is becoming more significant in recent years, should help China 'diversify, secure, and stabilize' prices. Groups such as the Shanghai Cooperation Organization, with Russia and four Central Asia states (Kazakhstan, Kyrgyzstan, Tajikistan, and Uzbekistan) as its members, are creating a forum on energy-related issues. They can form the basis for greater multilateral cooperation in the initial stages of the BRI, due to the need for a stable oil supply in the Asian countries connected to China. Hong Kong, as a BRI partner, should also diversify, and not replace OPEC oil to solve its energy poverty problems.

Part V

Hong Kong

Hong Kong's Education System Has Room to Improve on Gender Equality

The education system in Hong Kong can improve on gender equality.
Source: Wikimedia Commons

Women are fundamentally a crucial part of poverty alleviation. The microfinance movement would not have begun without

---

[8] This chapter appeared as an op-ed in the *Hong Kong Free Press* on July 31, 2016.

them (see Chapter 4). HIV/AIDS and malaria control (see Chapters 6 and 7) must consider transmission in pregnant women. They need to build networks, if they want to become entrepreneurs in Africa and elsewhere (see Chapter 15). A successful rebound in the Japanese economy also depend on their joining the workforce (see Chapter 32). They are no different in Hong Kong, where there are disparities between men and women—and between poor men and poor women. An analysis similar to the ones I did for Aboriginal employment in Canada shows that educating women and encouraging them to work is economically beneficial for the whole city. Just to be sure, however, gender inequality is only one of many disparities that exist in Hong Kong.

Women and Economic Development

Gender equality and economic development go hand in hand. The former Secretary-General of the UN Kofi Annan suggested that gender equality was a pre-requisite to achieving the Millennium Development Goals. Esther Duflo, a renowned economist, proffered a connection between the two, but gender equality should be strived for its own sake.

Hong Kong treats women well by many standards. Women are offered similar opportunities as men in education. If women want to, they can work. Female politicians occupy top positions in government, even though not at the same frequencies as men.

One of the city's shortcomings is its education system. Hong Kong—despite its government's free, 12-year education curriculum—enrolled only 87.8 per cent of all possible girls in secondary schools in 2014. The US had a female enrollment rate of 92.0 per cent in 2014. France had an enrollment rate of 94.6 per cent in 2004. The UK had a better enrollment rate for girls in secondary schools of 98.8 per cent.

A Model of Gender and Economic Growth

Suppose the government learns from other countries and the city attains better numbers. If Hong Kong's net enrollment rate in secondary schools for girls is at France's level—and if it has a female labour force participation rate (another measure of gender equality) at Switzerland's level (61.8 per cent versus Hong Kong's 51.1 per cent, which is a decent number for an industrialized economy)—its GDP, according to my analysis, would be US$435 billion (HK$3.4 trillion). That is a 40.3 per cent increase from the city's 2015 GDP of US$310 billion (HK$2.4 trillion).

If Hong Kong's government does not want to learn from other countries' policies, it could still improve on its gender policies. The net enrollment rate in secondary schools for girls may increase a reasonable 5 per cent and Hong Kong's female labour force participation rate increases 5 per cent. Using numbers from 2014, Hong Kong's GDP will still improve 21.9 per cent from US$291.2 billion (HK$2.3 trillion) to US$354.9 billion (HK$2.8 trillion).

This is important in these tough economic times. There is a very strong link between education for women and a boost in national income in Hong Kong. The challenge for policymakers is to find out what keeps 12.2 per cent of girls who should be in school absent. Maybe they could not afford auxiliary costs to education—books, stationary, food, and transportation, etc. This calls for innovative funding programs, including vouchers, grants, and family assistance.

Policy Implications

Maybe girls are missing school because of their families. They may be taking on a job, which requires the government reassess social welfare programs to low income families. Girls also need to know that they have greater career opportunities if they finish secondary and tertiary education with greater income associated with it. Finally, they may be suffering from abuse, which requires the aid of social workers.

In modern Hong Kong, education is not kept to the privileged or to the male gender. Given the numbers to show its correlation to economic growth, educating girls in secondary schools—and reaching full attainment—should definitely be a priority for the government. It would be a good step towards eradicating the different forms of disparities in the city.

The Road Out of Poverty and to Gender Equality in Hong Kong Starts at School

Hong Kong SAR Chief Executive Carrie Lam Cheng Yuet-ngor speaks at a technology conference in 2018. Remedies for gender inequality include encouraging women to run for public office. *Source*: Wikimedia Commons

Continuing our discussion in the previous chapter on gender inequality, I highlight areas that need to be addressed. Girls need

---

[9] This chapter appeared in the *South China Morning Post* on February 10, 2019.

to be introduced to female role models. Anti-discrimination laws need to be refined. Ways to keep girls safe from criminals have to be developed. Even in a developed economy like Hong Kong, education is seen as the most effective way to right societal wrongs.

Gender Disparity in Hong Kong

Hong Kong is a society full of disparities, and children's access to education is one of them. Secondary school enrollments rose from 89.3 per cent in 2012 to 92.9 per cent in 2017, ahead of the East Asia and Pacific average of 79.5 per cent. But that still means 24,008 children who should be in secondary school are not.

At the same time, 92.8 per cent of girls of school age are in secondary education in Hong Kong, lower than the 93.1 per cent for boys. Despite reaching gender parity, the Hong Kong government does not give literacy data for its elderly and adult population, alongside their gender breakdown. These missing statistics would likely show a stark difference between men and women.

This has implications for poverty in Hong Kong. There is a large gap between low-income Hong Kong men and women. According to the 2017 census, there were 80,800 men who earned less than HK$6,000 (US$765) per month (HK$4,000 is the official poverty line), but 451,700 women. Fighting poverty in this city must address the variables that disproportionately affect women and girls.

How Should Hong Kong Address Gender Inequality?

1. *Political and Legal Efforts*

There are three fronts: political, legal, and public. Hong Kong's female politicians can provide better role models for young girls, advocate for female causes and transform the ability of women to enter politics by running for public office. LegCo is currently made up of 15.7 per cent women—far from gender equity.

Legal issues include changes to the 1995 Sex Discrimination Ordinance proposed in 2018, which should make the white-collar workplace more welcoming to women.

2. *Education*

Arguably, the most attention should be given to public efforts to remedy gender disparity. The government spent 3.3 per cent of GDP on education in 2018. The average in the OECD, a club of mostly rich countries, was 5.2 per cent in 2015. Of the recurrent expenditure of HK$80.1 billion, the government spent 22.8 per cent on primary education and 33.2 per cent on secondary education. Hong Kong should increase its spending, and use the money to fund unique education programs for girls, with the goal of keeping them healthy and increasing their autonomy.

To educate and nourish girls, it is essential that the government help keep them safe. There is probably not a finer example of a vicious circle in Hong Kong society than the domestic violence that propagates poverty, and vice versa. Disturbances in young women's lives disrupt their studies, push them into bad social circles and ultimately lead to many quitting school prematurely. The psychological toll of a financially unsatisfying life breeds tension at home, and the vicious cycle continues.

In fact, seven districts—North, Kwun Tong, Sham Shui Po, Yuen Long, Wong Tai Sin, Tuen Mun and Kwai Tsing—have an average poverty rate of 14.7 per cent and accounted for 56.7 per cent of newly reported cases of child abuse,

52.7 per cent of newly reported cases of spousal or partner abuse and 32.6 per cent of newly reported sex crimes. In short, violence exists cosily in the poorest neighbourhoods. Law enforcement should definitely not become complacent, given the general decline in crime in Hong Kong in all categories, including violence, property, and drug offenses. The government should promote economic development in poor districts to sever crime's ties to destitution.

The overarching theme is to enhance the security of women and girls by reducing their vulnerability to economic shocks, bad health, disability and personal violence. All of this is intrinsic to improving their well-being and encouraging investment in additional education and higher-risk, higher-reward activities. The government has its role to play, by managing the economy wisely and providing health and social services when they are needed. It is in this way that the assets of the poor can slowly be built up.

39

How to Increase Socio-Economic Mobility in Hong Kong?

The Li Ka Shing Faculty of Medicine at the University of Hong Kong was endowed by the city's wealthiest man. Both of his sons are wealthy businessmen.
Source: Wikimedia Commons

From my experience around the world, education can help remedy many problems in society. Knowledge is power, as the saying goes. It may even offer people hope, when so many in

Hong Kong are obstructed by the persistence of intergenerational wealth, which entraps them in poverty while rich people and their children become richer. This is a study of the wealth gap in the city.

Intergenerational Earnings Elasticity

Economists and policy makers sometimes use the concept of intergenerational earnings elasticity (IEE)—a measure of how much people's income depends on their parents' income—to study inequality and income distribution. An IEE of zero means that there is no correlation, while a value of one signifies that how much one generation makes is totally dependent on the level of their parents' earnings. The most recent estimates of Hong Kong's IEE range from 0.23 to 0.42—a low to average level. (the US has an elasticity of about 0.5, while the OECD average is 0.38). This means an American millionaire's children are more likely to earn millions of dollars than a Hong Kong millionaire's children.

The Great Gatsby Curve and IEE

Another useful tool in the study of inequality is the Great Gatsby curve, which says that the more unequal a society gets, the greater the IEE. So in Hong Kong, where income inequality has been increasing for the past 40 years, more children of rich people will become rich, and more children of the poor will stay poor.

How the Wealth Gap Persists: The Data

The critical pathway for climbing the socio-economic ladder in Hong Kong is higher education. A recent survey of 22 to

47 year olds found that a man who finished university will have children who are 10 and 3.5 times more likely to finish high school and university, respectively. Similar differentials were found for women.

How far a person goes academically determines the kind of work and salary Hong Kongers take. Generally, a good education leads to high-paying managerial and professional work, while those with little education get jobs with titles like craftsmen, retail salesmen, plant workers, and entry-level office employees. The survey found that university graduates are four to five times more likely to become managers and professionals compared to primary and secondary school graduates. Those with even some non-degree studies are more than three times more likely to become professionals.

As a result, the lower a Hong Konger's education attainment, the less they will make. 2.3 per cent of people surveyed who have only a secondary school education or below have an income close to or below the poverty level ($4,000 per month), compared to 0.3 per cent for university graduates. 9.8 per cent earn less than $10,000 per month, seven times more than university graduates. Of course, workers can trade up from their low-paying jobs for managerial or professional work, In fact, 31 per cent of the respondents did so, although a large portion stayed at their original jobs.

Education and a More Equal Society

To create a more equal and generationally mobile society—where the occupation and income of a person should not be dictated by their parents' career choices and earnings—the government must commit more resources to education. Education is already key in developing entrepreneurs in Africa, helping low-waged Albertans transition the new economy, and increasing career prospects for Aboriginals in British Columbia. In Los Angeles, educating poor residents may help reduce crime. Some New Yorkers need to be educated to take advantage of the Internet economy. In Hong Kong, enrolling girls in school may boost economic growth.

There is currently no universal grant and loan scheme to cover all tuition and fees of under-educated Hong Kongers in vocational and certificate programs. One-fifth of the people surveyed who attained only a secondary school education found vocational training useful for career advancement. But 68.5 per cent of those respondents received no financial aid, meaning professional training seems to benefit mostly those can afford to pay their own way. This would only increase the wealth gap between the well-off who have access to education and those who do not.

There are also those early school leavers (pre-primary school) that the government has systematically written off. This group needs to be advised and nurtured. Part of the process should be to use work programs that ensure a smooth transition from schools to the work force. Both fresh graduates in their twenties and workers who have been out of work for a period of time should be included to encompass a large age range.

40

Free Transport a Crucial Step in Alleviating Elderly Poverty

Following the example of Estonia and Luxembourg, Hong Kong should offer free public transport to the elderly.
Source: Wikimedia Commons

We remember from Japan that the 'lost decades' might have been worsened by demographic shifts. As the average life expectancy of people increases, there are calls for the elderly to be more socially engaged, even returning to the workforce. In New York City, this may be as simple as teaching them to use the computer and the Internet. Abenomics hinges on getting older citizens back to work. Looking at available studies and data, Hong Kong's elderly population can become more involved in their community. We can support the poorest by keeping them healthy and enabling them to travel outside their districts to seek career network and companionship.

Hong Kong's life expectancy, already the highest in the world, is bound to rise, and the population aged 65 or above is expected to reach 34.5 per cent of the total in 2048—almost twice the current proportion. Poverty among the elderly is correspondingly rising as well, from approximately 28 per cent in 1991 to 44.4 per cent in 2017. The trend in the poverty rate plateaued at around 45 per cent since 2009, although the situation may be worse. According to Hung Wong, of the Chinese University of Hong Kong, the average monthly household income of the elderly was $4,450 in 2011, which in nominal terms is barely above the poverty line today and would put many at risk of poverty.

Who and Where Are the Elderly?

According to a study by Lih-Shing Chan and Kee-Lee Chou, of the Education University of Hong Kong, the elderly poor tend to be female and widowed or single. They are more likely to have less than a primary school education and be financially dependent on welfare or family.

The elderly poor often cannot afford to live in the city, so they are move to remote places—in the New Territories,

Tuen Mun, Yuen Long, Tin Shui Wai, Sheung Shui, Fan Ling, and Tai Po. There they face enormous challenges finding work. They are excluded from the labour market for their age and lack of education, and can only take on unskilled jobs. In their free time, they cannot afford a social life. Wong reported that the elderly in remote areas find transportation to social gatherings too expensive; they have no money for social activities; and socializing takes too much time. Added to these are other reasons that further isolate older people from the population.

Public Health under Strain

Because of the size of the elderly population, they are projected to put a strain on public health spending, as pointed out in the 2019 Chief Executive's policy address. This is not an insurmountable problem. The government has already advocated measures to prevent illnesses through setting up District Health Centers that, via 'medical-social collaboration and public-private partnership,' promote health, consult patients, and manage chronic illnesses.

Solutions: Fitness Trackers, Free Public Transport, and CCT

More creative solutions can be sought to manage healthcare costs for the elderly that do not require building medical facilities and staffing them with workers. Something as simple as arming the elderly with a fitness tracker to ensure daily exercise can help lower incidents of cardiovascular diseases, among other ailments. Hospitals can hire more gerontologists, who are better suited to deal with the diverse needs of poor elderly patients. Medical centres should be encouraged to import up-to-date technologies from abroad, keeping in mind that the best elderly care is to minimize costly surgeries and lengthy treatments. An example are minimally invasive surgical equipment, which when competently manned can reduce human errors (hospitals themselves must share the blame on burdening Hong Kong's healthcare system, since they pay a sizable amount to settle doctor complaints, to the tune of HK$49 million between 2012 and 2017).

The savings can then be used in schemes to help those who want to work or participate more actively in Hong Kong life. This includes providing free public transportation to the elderly, which will connect them to offices and other places of business activity that offer them higher wages and to people like them in the city for social and emotional support. Free public transportation has existed for the general public in Tallinn, Estonia, since 2013 and in 11 of the country's 15 counties today. Wealthy Luxembourg, which is dealing with a rising poverty rate, is expected to offer the same benefit in 2020, and other countries are showing interest.

Money saved can also be redistributed in CCT programs, made famous by Brazil's Family Grant program. The elderly poor, for example, may be given a certain sum biannually, in addition to the allowance and assistance that they already receive, conditional on undergoing routine medical checkups or skills training.

41[10]

Hong Kong's Poor Need to Be Logged on to the Internet

Many Hong Kongers do not have access to Internet-enabled computers.
Source: Wikimedia Commons

---

[10] This chapter appeared in the *South China Morning Post* on July 8, 2018.

This chapter revisits offshoring, which has been a big idea in international trade over the last few years—especially in the US. That 40 million Americans could lose their jobs to other countries should shocking not only to Americans, but also to Hong Kongers. Many low-waged workers in the city are probably missing out on the business opportunities. A big factor is the digital divide, which exists everywhere: in Johannesburg, where many cannot afford to access the Internet, in Kenya where the poor cannot afford cell phones to use M-Pesa, and in New York City, where out-of-work residents have no computers to take up online work. Public and private money can be used to set up cell phone accounts and Internet cafes, which will prepare Hong Kong for a 'smart' future.

Offshoring

Offshoring is the migration of jobs from (mostly) richer countries to (mostly) poorer countries. As industrialized economies have increasingly moved away from manufacturing, the offshoring debate has increasingly come to focus on services. Two factors behind this are rise of computerization and telecommunications technologies like the Internet, which enabled it; and the entry into the global economy of India and China, which benefited from it.

So what is offshorable? To recap what was said in Chapter 26, Alan Blinder made a distinction between those impersonal services—which can be delivered electronically with little to no degradation of quality, and so are tradable and potentially offshorable—and personal services which cannot be delivered electronically, or which suffer severe degradation of quality when delivered in such a way, and are hence non-tradable.

By this definition, keyboard data entry and manuscript editing are offshorable, but surgery is non-tradable. Writing computer code is also an impersonal service that can be delivered electronically with ease, while driving a taxi or lawyering in court cannot. It should be noted that what is offshorable is unrelated to whether the job is low- or high-skilled.

What distinguishes impersonal, or tradable, services from personal ones is that personal services require physical presence or face-to-face contact with end users. Typing services as well as financial security analysis are already being delivered electronically from India. Radiologists should be concerned for their jobs, although most doctors should not. While the police's work generally isn't offshorable, the work of security guards, consisting of monitoring cameras, may be.

Offshorable jobs are not, as some have suggested, necessarily confined to rule-based tasks: Blinder pointed out that many complex tasks that require refined skills and human intervention are routinely offshored, with the aid of telecommunication facilities. This includes statistical analysis, programming, editing, and security work.

Finally, what is personal and impersonal exists on a continuum. To summarize Chapter 26 again, there are jobs that are obviously on opposite ends of the spectrum: data entry and child care, for example. But there are others in between, and while the job of an architect or professor can be delivered electronically over the Internet or videoconferencing, the quality of their service degrades noticeably.

Are Hong Kong's Poor Benefitting from Offshoring? The Digital Divide in the City

Are Hong Kong's poor benefitting from offshoring? After all, offshoring is a large and disruptive force in the services sector. Since information and communications technology will continue to get better and cheaper, the scope for offshoring will increase substantially. As a developed economy, Hong Kong has a large services sector.

But Hong Kong's digital divide will keep the poor from benefitting from offshoring. Some 98.9 per cent of Hong Kong residents with an income of $50,000 or more have a computer, compared to 72.2 per cent of those who make $10,000 to $19,999 and a meagre 37.9 per cent of those making less than $10,000.

Internet penetration in Hong Kong is among the highest in the world—92.6 per cent of households have broadband connection and there are 51,914 public Wi-Fi access points in the city, according to 2018 figures. But again, the poor are under-represented. Only 69.3 per cent of residents in public rental housing own computers that are connected to any form of Internet. By income, only 36.7 per cent of households with an income of under $10,000 own an Internet-enabled computer. In families that make more than $50,000, the penetration rate is 98.6 per cent. Along the age divide, the elderly are also markedly less web-enabled, with only 37.4 per cent knowing how to use the Internet.

What Does the Data Mean? And Some Policy Implications

The question is whether these figures will prevent Hong Kong, and its urban poor, from benefitting from the offshoring craze. The census data does not give much information on mobile Internet usage, although the functions on a cell phone that can be using for offshoring with a business partner overseas, as of now, are somewhat limited. So if Hong Kong is to benefit from offshored jobs, computers will be necessary. And Hong Kong's urban poor, with their low rate of Internet connectivity, will not benefit from the deluge of jobs that could theoretically move from the rich world.

To change that, the city's government needs to connect the poor to the Internet and 3G and 4G mobile networks: that way, they can take advantage of traditional online methods of connectivity like social media and video telephony, as well as newer services like e-payment. This can be done through subsidies or through the creation of 'Internet labs' that complement government-organized career training centres and programs.

Plugged into the international economy with these electronic tools, the poor can solicit businesses from abroad in fields like typing, translation, and language tuition. The statistics, after all, shows that a large pool of labour is waiting to be used in an age of global offshoring.

42[11]

A 'Smart' Hong Kong Must First Figure Out How to Bridge Its Digital Divide

Many poor and undereducated Hong Kongers do not have access to personal computers and smartphones.
Source: Unsplash/Austin Poon

---

[11] This chapter appeared as an op-ed in the *South China Morning Post* on May 19, 2019.

In Chapter 16, I explained how—for all the interesting technologies that are available to Africa, like various systems for delivering the Internet and electronic money—it still takes extra effort, perhaps from the private as well as the public sector, to distribute the service equally to everyone on the continent. In Chapter 26, I have shown that the digital divide is not a problem indigenous to Hong Kong, but in large cities like New York. If it is solved, job opportunities abound for the poor. In this chapter, I suggest how Internet equality and equal access to technology can help a city become 'smart'.

Hong Kong should aspire to be a smart city, that is, one in which advanced information technologies are integrated into government, work, and everyday lives. There are many prerequisites for creating a smart city, one of which is a strong digital economy. The odds are good for Hong Kong, if Mainland China's enthusiasm for adopting e-payment is any indication.

Hong Kong as a Smart City

According to McKinsey and PricewaterhouseCoopers, the penetration rate of mobile payments in China has grown from 25 per cent in 2013 to 86 per cent in 2019. The year before, the value of mobile payments in China, in terms of amount consumed, was US$41.51 trillion, 43 times the transaction value of digital payments in the United States.

In a digital economy, there is an ever-increasing need for mobile phones. With 1.58 billion subscribers in the mainland, they link various elements of the smart city. For example, there have been tremendous venture capital investments in big data, artificial intelligence (AI), financial technologies (fintech), virtual reality (VR), autonomous driving, and wearables in China that rival or surpass those in the United States. The products and inventions from these financial injections, totaling more than US$105 billion, are sure to spill over into Hong Kong as it develops into a technologically integrated city with new ways of conducting logistics, city planning, healthcare, other professional activities and e-commerce.

The Digital Divide

There are, however, challenges to Hong Kong's becoming a smart city. One is inclusion; many poor and undereducated Hong Kongers do not have access to the technologies like personal computers and smartphones that most take for granted. According to latest census, 80.9 per cent of Hong Kongers have a computer at home, and 80.2 per cent of all households have computers that are connected to the Internet. So the city cannot be fully dependent on digital devices and communication without a sizeable portion of the city being left out.

As mentioned in the previous chapter, there exists a digital divide. Only 37.9 per cent of people making less than HK$10,000 per month have a computer at home, and not all are Internet-enabled (36.7 per cent). By comparison, 98.9 per cent of those earning more than HK$50,000 per month have a computer and 98.6 per cent of them have computers with Internet access. Data also shows that Hong Kongers with only a primary education are half as likely to have the basic digital literacy to use a computer. In Hong Kong, education and income are directly correlated—for example, the median salary of a woman with only a primary education is HK$8,300, while a female university graduate has a median salary of HK$15,000.

So the statistics show that undereducated, poorer people are less likely to know how to use a computer. Retirees and the elderly, among whom the poverty rate is 44.4 per cent, have a very low computer usage rate compared to the general population—44.2 per cent versus 84 per cent.

The Role of Mobile Devices

An important part of Hong Kong's digital transformation are mobile devices. In the city, 88.6 per cent of residents have smartphones, more than Japan and South Korea. But this hides the fact that low-income residents do not have the same access. The smartphone penetration rate among those with a primary education or below—representing those who, on average, make the least money in the city—was 58.1 per cent in 2018, or around 1.5 times lower than university graduates. Retirees and the elderly have a low penetration rate as well, at 57.6 per cent.

How Can Hong Kong Become a Smart City?

To create a smart city of the future, Hong Kong must nurture a tech-savvy population that is ready to adopt new innovations. But underlying region-leading statistics in how and how much residents are using computers, smartphones and the Internet are indications that certain groups—the poor and the undereducated—are not benefiting from new technologies at the same rate. Africans found themselves with the same problem when they tried to leapfrog technologies with cell phones; many could not afford them. This unequal access to technological gains, already substantial, may not only represent missed business opportunities online, but accumulate and turn into an economic chasm if creative solutions, perhaps involving public-private partnerships, are not found.

Hong Kong Must Tend to the Unique Challenges of the Poor under COVID-19

A bottle of hand sanitizer for customers of a taxi in Hong Kong. Stringent public health measures, including temporarily closing shops and keeping workers home, have become common during the COVID-19 pandemic.
Source: Wikimedia Commons

---

[12] An edited version of this chapter appeared as an op-ed in the *South China Morning Post* on June 10, 2020.

COVID-19 brought out the challenges that the poor face in Hong Kong. While children from better-off families stay at home and study using a variety of smart devices and online learning tools, their poor peers would be lucky to have access to a smart phone with which they can complete coursework. Their parents, staying at home more than usual, do not have the luxury of electronic gadgets for socializing and making extra money.

This digital divide requires drastic action, or the socio-economic gap between the rich and the poor may widen into something that is difficult to mend. A universal computer and Internet plan for income groups that traditionally have little access to computers is one. Stay-at-home workers need to be insured, too. Public-private partnerships, as I have previously recommended for poor Africans and Hong Kongers, may accomplish both tasks well.

31.9 per cent of Hong Kongers suffer from a wide range of chronic illnesses, led by hypertension (46.6 per cent), high cholesterol (23.6 per cent), and diabetes (21.2 per cent), which make COVID-19 a particularly nasty ailment to deal with if contracted. But helping the poor in the city at this time is more than handing out masks to long queues of people. The pandemic poses unique challenges that require creative solutions.

The Challenges of the Poor under COVID-19

1. *Internet Inequality*

Internet inequality is a case in point. Confined to their homes, the poor are doubly constrained by their lack of computers and high-speed Internet connection. The government's 2020 Thematic Household Survey on personal computer and Internet penetration still shows a large gap between the poor and the better-off. While 96.5 per cent of Hong Kongers making HK$50,000 or more per month have a computer with Internet connection at home, only 65.5 per cent of those making between HK$10,000 and $20,000 do—and a horrific 33.8 per cent of those making HK$10,000 per month. Most of the access to computing by the poor is likely through a cell phone, which has a 91.5 per cent penetration rate. But a palm-sized device is totally inadequate for the most basic computing tasks at work, like word processing, spreadsheet work, and database entry.

This Internet inequality manifests itself in a learning divide in education. It is well documented among schoolchildren, who are falling behind their peers in education. As an institution that equalizes the socio-economic playing field, schools provide students with libraries, computing facilities, face-to-face counselling from school staff, social opportunities with children their own age, and time away from the problems at home. Having equal access to these resources gives poor children a well-trodden pathway to middle-class jobs and higher earnings. But while it is hard enough for well-equipped students to replicate the school environment at home with their notebook computers, videoconferencing and collaborative software, and various multimedia websites, for the poor, the scholastic experience may be much more limited without them.

2. *Adults at Home*

Adults from low-income households, who now have fewer opportunities to socialize and network outside their homes, are likewise disadvantaged at home. As the unemployment rate spiked, poor people with work cannot congregate with others to learn new skills or attend workshops to enhance their employability. This amounts to a large number of Hong Kongers, spanning industries that include construction, manufacturing, retail, and personal service and job functions that include clerks, sales and service workers, craftsmen, factory, and non-technical workers.

In a 2019 government survey, 20.4 per cent of the respondents have undertaken some kind of job training course, because their employers requested it or out of their own initiative, in the past year. Even 18 per cent of those from the construction industry were sent by their companies for professional upgrading. Main reasons that were stated for taking these classes include meeting current job requirements and staying competitive in the labour market.

Those without work, without the technologies available to the middle class, cannot stay productive at home during the pandemic. According to the same survey, the main considerations of the unemployed willing to take up work are flexible working hours (63.6 per cent of the respondents), reasonable salary (38.9 per cent), proximity to home (37.3 per cent), and comfort and safety (28.2 per cent). Although working from home over the Internet can open up a host of opportunities for many, poor households' lack of computers and Internet connection keep them from benefitting.

Policy Suggestions

1. *A Universal Internet Plan*

Expert opinions seem to suggest that COVID-19 will be around for some time and debilitating Hong Kongers' way of life, until an effective vaccine is developed and herd immunity is reached. Meanwhile, the government should think beyond the usual remedies of cash payouts and macroeconomic stimuli. The poor are hampered by a lack of income, education, and professional network, whose effects can be greatly lessened by a universal high-speed Internet and computer plan for all low-income families making less than HK$20,000 per month. This would be welcomed by those who believe that Internet access is a human right and make Hong Kong's economic recovery much quicker when it comes. The strategy also complements the city's goal of becoming a technologically-advanced, Greater Bay Area-integrated smart city, by ensuring inclusive computer ownership.

2. *Medical Coverage for Stay-at-Home Workers*

To fortify this leap, policies should be reconfigured to encourage greater medical coverage for stay-at-home workers from employers. Currently, 51.1 per cent of Hong Kongers are medically insured by their employers; the lowest rate is in the construction industry (28.2 per cent). This would help the poor afford hospital care in future pandemics as well as economic shocks.

44

How Stakeholders Can Raise the Standard for Helping Poor Hong Kongers?

Oxfam, a British anti-poverty group, publishes an annual report on poverty in Hong Kong.
Source: Wikimedia Commons

As I explained in Chapter 13, the Fair Trade movement has been effective in pressuring buyers of foodstuff and minerals in Africa to set reasonable prices. Is it reasonable to say that pressure groups can influence the behaviour of businesses in Hong Kong, compelling them to do good by labelling their products and service 'poverty friendly?'

Corporate Social Responsibility in Hong Kong

The city has sophisticated legal and financial systems, as well as developed corporate social responsibility (CSR) programs. Stakeholders in poverty alleviation can work together to develop standards for including low-income people in their businesses. They include international and local clients of banks, non-profits, and companies. Hong Kongers' willingness to conform to multilaterally-determined standards will ultimately help its poor residents.

The most recent World Bank figures show that Hong Kong's trade (import and export) as a percentage of GDP—a measure of its economy's openness—is 375 per cent, which is the second highest in the world. The city has no tariffs and ranks very high on trade, investment, and financial freedom by the Heritage Foundation, which named it the world's freest economy in 2019. According to the Hong Kong government, 1,530 foreign companies have regional headquarters here. This is, of course, no coincidence. Hong Kong is also represented at multilateral trade organizations such as APEC, the Asian Development Bank, and the Bank of International Settlement.

'Poverty Friendly' Labelling

As a consequence, one would think that the business community has developed a CSR framework to help low-income Hong Kongers. After all, foreign corporations routinely demand that its local clients and regulators meet or alter rules and standards in labour, wage, accounting, and intellectual rights protection. They would threaten to freeze job hires or move their office elsewhere. There can be a HK GAAP or HKFRS-style standard for the treatment of low-income clients. Stakeholders can require employees of a company to obtain sensitivity training before certifying it 'poverty friendly'—the way Big Four accounting firms require all of its accountants to have professional licences.

Then companies may choose to only deal with firms who are also 'poverty friendly'. If multinationals are involved, they may choose to do business in Hong Kong only if the subsidiaries comply with the accepted standards towards the poor. To ignore these standards is to risk prestige or lose access to capital, technology, and consumer goods.

So instead of Tanzanian tea farmers, the target of 'poverty friendly' certification include poor Sham Tsui Po and North Point residents. If a large bank requires its branches to offer specialized loans and investment products to low-income people as they do other customers, other banks may follow suit. The same goes for insurance companies and universities offering medical plans and educational assistance.

The success of Hong Kong as a highly developed financial, legal, and CSR-minded centre comes from its need to conform to high standards. Taking its cue from the Fair Trade movement, stakeholders everywhere can develop a set of goals and guidelines to certify companies, organizations, and individuals as 'poverty friendly'. By raising the standards in doing business and dealing with the poor and setting them the same everywhere in the city, people will be respected and given the dignity they deserve.

45[13]

Hong Kong's Poorer Workers Can Profit from the Greater Bay Area, with the Right Skills

Fufan Tooling is a maker of plastic injection molds in Shenzhen, in the
Guangdong-Hong Kong-Macau Greater Bay Area.
Source: Wikimedia Commons

---

[13] An edited version of this chapter appeared as an op-ed in the South China
Morning Post on November 3, 2017.

Hong Kong also aims to be a Greater Bay Area city. It is a dynamic region, full of potential as a place for Chinese investments, great infrastructures, automation, and innovation. There is a place for the poorest Hong Kongers, provided that they are willing to retrain and relocate. This marks another instance where education is key to solving what can be a major employment issue in Hong Kong in the future.

Given the tremendous promise in the development of the Pearl River Delta—or the Guangdong-Hong Kong-Macau 'Greater Bay Area'—there is certainly something in it for the poor people of Hong Kong, if not the rest of the delta. Right? Not quite.

Covering less than 1 per cent of China and comprising only 5 per cent of its population, the Pearl River Delta produces more than 10 per cent of the country's gross domestic product, exports more than 25 per cent of the total, and has attracted over US$1 trillion of foreign direct investment since 1980. The region has a higher per capita GDP than the Bohai Economic Rim and the Yangtze River Delta and serves as an important link between China and the world.

Yet, the factors that are prompting great shifts in the economy for the better are also keeping the poor and under-educated from sharing in the windfall.

How Will the Pearl River Delta Adapt to the New Economy?

1. *Diversification*

First, the labour pool in the Pearl River Delta is shrinking and, as a result, wages are rising. Therefore, factory owners are moving their plants to cities—not necessarily within the delta—with better labour conditions. This would require job-seeking workers to be as mobile as these factories. This is not reasonable to assume for poor people, especially when they may have *hukou* (household registration) restrictions.

Companies, in order to diversify, are also redirecting their exports to the Chinese market. At best, this phenomenon is a wash for labourers, if they do not need to retrain for this market shift. At worst, poor labourers are unable to acquire the new skills at work and lose their jobs.

2. *Integration: Infrastructure-Building*

Second, the Pearl River Delta will see a massive investment in infrastructure. Goldman Sachs calls advanced infrastructure building with continuous upgrades a 'mega trend' in the region. Greater integration is necessary for many reasons, such as political fragmentation, internal trade barriers, market separation and inadequate coordination with the urban sprawl, spatial mismatch, environment degradation, and an excessive use of scarce resources. These may cause a decline in regional competitiveness and keep regional blocs from becoming important domestic economic engines and global players.

As the Pearl River Delta retools its infrastructure, originally built for exports for logistics networks in the domestic market, it is building great projects like 6,000 km of highway in Guangdong, 1,400 million tons of cargo capacity in five major ports by 2020, three airports: in Foshan, Huizhou, and Guangzhou, several 'one to two hours commuting circles,' and the well-known Hong Kong-Zhuhai-Macau and Shenzhen-Zhongshan bridges.

These will improve industry delineation by driving cities into industrial clusters that synergize through the division of labour. But the Pearl River Delta has highly dispersed cities with equally dispersed human, physical, and educational resources, which do not benefit the poor people. They would again need to move where the projects go for low-paying work and/or retrain for new jobs.

3. *Automation*

Third, the Pearl River Delta is set on a path to automation. Migrant inflow to the delta is decreasing, and the low birth rate means the cheap labour pool is not being replenished. To make up for the deficit in productivity—now increasing at 7 per cent per year compared to 8.5 per cent in 1996—factories will have to introduce robotics in the manufacturing process. This is now at an early stage, with China currently using 10 times fewer robots in manufacturing than a country like South Korea.

Dongguan has set aside 200 million yuan (HK\$236 million) for this, Guangdong has committed 943 billion yuan to eliminate 80 per cent of its industrial workforce in 3 years. This is not good news for poor and under-educated people, many of whom work in plants.

The process of phasing in automation through a market-driven process, furthermore, would require knowledge in manufacturing techniques like Six Sigma, lean manufacturing, and smart automation. This would require additional education.

4. *Innovation*

Finally, innovation seems to be an important trend in the delta. Cities like Shenzhen have evolved from sweatshops to advanced manufacturing, robotics, and genomics—attracting companies like Huawei, Tencent and Apple. All of this requires a highly educated workforce.

To private companies, innovation means manufacturing higher-value-added products with more advanced technologies, while to the government, innovation is a long-term strategy to produce more competitive, internationally-oriented Chinese companies, whose traditional advantage was cheap labour and the economies of scale.

The government, however, recently announced its support for innovation through creating a one-stop investment and financing information service for small and medium-sized enterprises and a one-stop intellectual property rights service for patent examination, rights protection and verification, and an innovation-oriented evaluation and incentive scheme within state-owned enterprises. These may be opportunities for the under-educated in the Pearl River Delta.

How to Succeed in the Pearl River Delta?

The ultimate success of globalization depends, among other factors, on the mobility and flexibility of the labour force.

If world conditions change so that an agrarian society transforms into an industrial economy, its labour force must adapt through retraining—or be ready to be displaced by foreign workers with the requisite skills.

The poor in Hong Kong and the rest of the delta are under-educated and often unable to move for work. A sizeable cache of scholarship and grant money for vocational training should be a good start for Hong Kong's poor labourers.

The Lok Ma Chau Loop, an innovation and technology park jointly developed by Hong Kong and Shenzhen, is a prime example of what the poor need in the coming years.

Shenzhen, in this venture, is expected to contribute its start-ups and capital, while Hong Kong will contribute its professional expertise in scaling, branding and managing companies at a global level. Many economic activities in the Pearl River Delta—from reconfiguring the logistics from an international market to a domestic one, to building infrastructure, introducing automation, and innovating—require greater training and education. It is a good place to start to make sure that no one gets left behind.

46

Businesses and Stakeholders are Committing to the Greater Bay Area to Drive towards Innovation and Growth

The Hong Kong-Zhuhai-Macau Bridge took 8 years to build.
Source: Wikimedia Commons

The future of the Greater Bay Area is, in all likelihood, the future of Hong Kong. Out of economic necessity, the city will need to further integrate with the nine other cities in the mainland and Macau. Those looking to live, work, and do business there probably want to know whether the region is all that it is hyped up to be. So it is good to know, again, that not only the Greater Bay Area is an up-and-coming demographic and economic force in the world, it adapts to the shifting investment trends through integration, diversification, automation, and innovation. Most importantly, it has the backing of businesses and those in power. Hong Kong residents, even the poor, should be comfortable moving, working, and doing business there.

Many observers in the Guangdong-Hong Kong-Macau Greater Bay Area—originally the Pearl River Delta—may question if this regional bloc, created politically to match the likes of San Francisco and Tokyo Bay Areas—will succeed, with repercussions for millions of workers. The management guru Kenichi Ohmae predicted that the rise of the region state need not be the enemies of central governments. The Greater Bay Area, as the data show so far, is an engine of the country's growth.

The Rise of the Greater Bay Area

By now, the region has surpassed New York City and Tokyo as the world's largest megacity. With foreign direct FDI at US$23.6 billion in 2012, foreign investments is slowing, prompting regional governments and firms to adopt measures in diversification, integration, automation, and innovation. Integration, which includes grand infrastructure and far-reaching inter-city projects, is arguably done at the greatest scale.

These developments have relevance beyond the region. The GBA has and is expected to continue to be leading the country in innovation and the power of the market force. As China's BRI takes shape, there will be opportunities for ASEAN member countries to benefit from the development of major infrastructure projects in the greater bay area, such as the Hong Kong-Zhuhai-Macau Bridge and the Shenzhen-Zhongshan Bridge. Through development in the Greater Bay Area, the region bloc will lead innovation in China and provide a template for the rest of the country to advance technologically.

Economic Trends

Other countries are catching up to China. As other countries are becoming more competitive, FDI into the Greater Bay Area will eventually slow down. This is despite a dramatic increase from $1.5 billion in 1990 to $23.6 billion in 2012. Academic studies in Chinese provinces show the negative impact of declining FDI on Chinese economic growth.

Coupled with domestic firms' productivity, FDI has a positive effect through technology transfers, management knowledge and export marketing, competition and demonstration effects, and labour mobility. FDI may spur the growth of cities within the Greater Bay Area, implying that public investments should be directed at infrastructure and facilities to better take advantage of economic growth.

How Will the Greater Bay Area Adapt?

1. *Diversification Revisited*

As of now, the Greater Bay Area is facing demographic and macroeconomic challenges. An aging population is one problem, so are cheaper wages that companies outside Guangdong are willing to pay workers to leave. But the Greater Bay Area seems ready to adapt. Firms are diversifying their labour force to other parts of the country and markets for their finished goods. There has been greater integration within and outside the region, with regard to infrastructure, in response to the changing marketplace. This strategy will turn out to have the biggest ramification, since everyone—including industries and workers—depend on transportation for the movement of goods, for leisure, and for work.

2. *Integration Revisited*

It is important, since—compared to the other bay areas of the world—cities in the Greater Bay Area are separated by great distances, leading to highly dispersed human, physical, and education resources. The spatially and politically fragmenting effects of urban entrepreneurialism and local protectionism (a product of urban and regional politics in post-reform China) may lead to competition between regions for mobile and market capital—and a decline in overall regional competitiveness. There have been other reasons for integration: pre-existing internal trade barriers, market separation and inadequate coordination to urban sprawl, spatial mismatch, environmental degradation, and the excessive use of scarce resources.

A Goldman Sachs report in 2016 stated that tighter inter-city cooperation and integration help lift the Greater Bay Area to greater efficiency and competitiveness. The good news is that there are enormous ongoing construction projects, spanning from bridges and roads to deep-water ports. The regional and central governments are definitely committed to solidifying this regional bloc. Cooperative initiatives, like the Pan-PRD Forum, which were criticized for being too informal and badly organized, are now developing into a powerful platform for broad, multi-functional coordination that includes Hong Kong and Macau.

3. *Automation and Innovation*

Another way to deal with changes in the Greater Bay Area is the adoption of automation and innovation. The municipal governments in the region have tried, collectively for some time, to attract world-class technology companies and talent. To companies, it means a commitment to making higher added value, technologically advanced products. To the government, which intervenes intermittently with industrial upgrading policy measures, innovation requires a longer term, competitive strategy to incubate internationally oriented Chinese companies. The Greater Bay Area's traditional advantage—even when cheap labour is going elsewhere—is scale economy, or a reduction in the average cost of products when companies increase output.

There is, as a result, a virtuous cycle. When firms notch up successes in creating and producing new products, investors are more eager to support new ventures. As mentioned in the previous chapter, the state supports those small- and medium-sized enterprises and micro-enterprises, calling for a one-stop investment and financing information service and intellectual property rights protection and services. When Greater Bay Area firms do well, investments will come in. And Hong Kong, along with the private and public sector in the mainland, want this massive project to succeed.

47^{14}

As Industries Shift, Retraining Hong Kong's Workers Is Key to Staying Competitive

Dock workers attend a strike in Hong Kong.
Source: Wikimedia Commons

As economies mature, they transition from an industrial society to a service-oriented one. This is also true in Hong Kong, which has transformed from a manufacturing city to a financial and professional services hub. It may even be argued that the city has

---

[14] An edited version of this chapter appeared as an op-ed in the South China Morning Post on January 19, 2019.

been suffering from a case of the Dutch disease, gaining from a sudden influx of money for its capital markets in the twenty-first century. Economists say that if the shift is permanent, people need to be prepared for job retraining. Like elsewhere in the industrialized world, there are government programs in Hong Kong for that purpose, although they may be run better. Empowering local vocational schools help, too, as we will discuss later in the book. The rise of the Greater Bay Area, it seems, offers a new world of possibilities for low-waged workers.

The Current State of the Industrial Shift

Hong Kong's economy has been changing fundamentally for many years. That the city's dependence on manufacturing is tapering off is well documented: the sector employed 4.8 per cent of all workers aged 15 and over—or 167,400 people—in 2008, but 2.6 per cent—or 100,000—in 2018, according to November 2019's 'Quarterly Report on General Household Survey'. Less often discussed is the decline in the share of employment of the import/export trade and the wholesale industry (by 5.3 per cent) and the transport, storage, postal and courier services, information and communications industries (by 0.4 per cent) in the same period. These have been replaced by the likes of construction, hospitality and professional and business services.

No one should be surprised. The rise of the 'Greater Bay Area' scheme and the US-China trade war highlight Hong Kong's shift to a service-oriented economy. That means many jobs at all economic levels are at stake, but instead of waiting around to see what damage may be done, the government should take the opportunity to create a better worker adjustment program.

Worker Adjustment Programs in the US and EU

Many major economies have some sort of worker adjustment program that can help those displaced by shifts in industry patterns to retrain. For example there is the Trade Adjustment Assistance (TAA) scheme in the US. Created in 1962, TAA's benefits include relocation assistance, subsidized healthcare insurance and extended unemployment benefits—provided recipients are enrolled in job training programs. Originally targeting factory workers, farmers and fishermen, the TAA was revised in 2009 and 2011 to cover workers in service sectors such as information technology, insurance, banking and legal services.

In a similar vein, the European Union offers the European Globalization Adjustment Fund (EGF), which supports economically displaced workers in finding work, gives career advice, offers mentoring and coaching, helps with starting businesses and organizes classes and retraining opportunities.

Government Assistance Programs in Hong Kong

In Hong Kong, the government offers a certain level of support to workers along the lines of the TAA and the EGF. But the authorities should first consolidate all these services into a formal worker adjustment program and place these services in a physical location.

The Work Incentive Transport Subsidy Scheme meanwhile reimburses low-income Hong Kongers for their commuting costs. This could easily be expanded to cover all workers who become unemployed by shifts in industries.

At the same time, the government currently offers no relocation assistance to skilled Hong Kongers with the ability to speak the right dialect who want to work in the Greater Bay Area or elsewhere in Mainland China.

The government should also consider funding more courses to educate and retrain workers. Although bodies like the Employees Retraining Board and the Continuing Education Fund work with educational groups to teach and upgrade skills, the number of spots in vocational courses does not meet the demand from thousands of unemployed and low-income people.

Government websites and job boards, moreover, are inaccessible to the many poor people and elderly jobseekers who disproportionately have no access to smartphones or computers in their homes. This is a great opportunity for public-private partnerships to step in. More cafes can be built where Internet time can be purchased cheaply, so that people can check up on new jobs. Tax concessions can be given to companies for equipping low-income Hong Kongers with Internet-enabled cell phones, tablet computers, and laptops. Businesses can also fund charities that hand out used smart devices to the poor.

Career counseling for unemployed workers should also be accessible to the poor. This means staffing counseling centres with enough advisers and minimizing the waiting times for consultations.

What Needs to Be Done?

We have already discussed how, in the era of offshoring, manufacturing jobs are being displaced by those in tradable and non-tradable services. There are winners and losers in Hong Kong's ongoing industrial shift, which experts of the Dutch disease say prevent human capital development, such as job specialization. Even so, job retraining, and relocation along the lines of the TAA and EGF, should be the natural responses to make sure local workers stay competitive, and the government must polish its worker adjustment program so that it is tailored to meet the unique challenges of China-Hong Kong trade, including those in the large Greater Bay Area job market.

How Can China and Hong Kong Combat Inequality through Education?

Visitors attend an open house at Sai Ying Pun's St. Louis School. The government should make sure that all children complete school and are free from domestic violence and drugs. *Source*: Wikimedia Commons

In this book, I have mentioned certain groups of people who, on average, make less than the general population. Aboriginal

---

[15] This chapter appeared as an op-ed in *Hong Kong Free Press* on December 9, 2017.

people in British Columbia consistently earn less than non-Aboriginals. Illegal immigrants in Los Angeles bring down the median household income of a neighbourhood with their low wages. Women in Hong Kong make less than men. The children of poor Hong Kongers tend to make less money, compared to their wealthier friends, as measured by intergenerational earnings elasticity.

Hong Kong can learn from China, whose economy it is integrating into. Before the 2010s, there was already an increase in income inequality in rural areas and the cities. After 2010, the concentration of wealth among the richest increased substantially. The government promised to bring down the Gini coefficient, a popular measure of inequality.

In fact, there have been admirable efforts to increase access to education, in the belief that greater economic opportunities available to poor but smart people can end the intergenerational transmission of inequality. Hong Kong can take some lessons from China's playbook, and prioritize education in its own anti-poverty efforts.

An Issue of Wealth in China

Inequality is a growing problem in China, not only in rural but also in urban parts of the country. People recognize it as a social problem that needs to be addressed. In a 2012 national survey, income inequality was ranked a greater problem than corruption and unemployment.

There are problems associated with the concentration of revenue, wealth, and power, including the creation of too-big-to-fail entities in the economy and the resulting systemic instability, which require market-based solutions along with state intervention.

The history of income inequality in China can be described in two distinct periods: before and after the 2010s. Reforms that started in 1978 have dramatically reduced poverty, yet increased income inequality. Income inequality is steadily rising in urban and rural China, although inequality remains higher in rural areas than in urban areas.

Before the 2010s

In the meanwhile, China's Human Development Index, as reported in a new paper by Barry Naughton in 2017, has improved from the 'low human development' of 0.42 in 1980 to the 'high human development' level of 0.73 in 2014. As measured by the Gini coefficient, inequality increased from 0.327 to 0.508 from 1980 to 2008, as Macquarie University's Pundarik Mukhopadhaya reported; rural inequality increased from 0.275 to 0.371, while urban inequality increased from 0.162 to 0.328. Income disparities rose along urban-rural as well as the east-west and the coastal-interior divide.

Thomas Piketty, of the Paris School of Economics, plotted data from the tax records of emerging economies and found that inequality in China increased at an extraordinary rate from 1990 to 2000. From 2000 to 2010, the upper 1 per cent's share of total national income was 10-11 per cent, less than the 12-14 per cent of India, Indonesia, Britain, and Canada. Moreover, China's top centile's share of total income was much lower than the 16-18 per cent held in South Africa, Argentina, and the US.

Inequality in the 2010s

In the 2010s, the consensus is that income inequality in China has become greater than that in the US. China's Gini coefficient hovered above 0.5, versus 0.45 in the US in 2010 (Hong Kong's Gini coefficient in 2016 was 0.539, according to the Census and Statistics Department).

As China's GDP converges towards the US, inequality is also increasing to its level. As Facundo Alvaredo and his colleagues at the National Bureau of Economic Research found in 2017. The share of pre-tax income going to the poorest half of the population has decreased to 15 per cent, which is close to the US figure. 10 per cent of the wealthiest in China own 70 per cent of private wealth, up from 40 per cent in 1995. The private wealth-income ratio was over 450 per cent in 2015, approaching the US's 500 per cent and 550-600 per cent in the UK and France.

Despite the meritocratic nature of formal schooling, the IMF found that education is a significant driver of the increase in income inequality in China, alongside structural factors like the rural-urban divide and differences between provinces.

There are different views on how education leads to income inequality. One view presumes an intergenerational transmission of education, the magnification of the advantages gained through education in terms of earnings, and the reinforcement of those economic gains by the formation of barriers to entry into the labour market. Another possibility is through unearned privilege and corruption.

The Chinese government, recognizing income inequality as a major social problem, has addressed the issue, and the Hong

Kong government should follow. Chongqing's government integrated the Gini coefficient in its 12th Five-Year Plan by promising to bring it down from 0.42 to 0.35.

Addressing Inequality with Education

China has also increased access to higher education by building universities at an increasing rate, and allowing foreign universities to operate in partnership with domestic schools.

The number of universities in China increased from 1,022 to 2,263 between 2001 and 2011. The government allowed private companies abroad to set up campuses in the country, like the AKC Group, which currently serves 135,000 students in India and other countries.

The Hong Kong government, too, can encourage a stronger private sector presence in higher education, which is currently dominated by public universities with weak ties to privately-run and weakly-connected vocational schools in the city. It should aim to raise spending on education in the direction of the central government, which raised spending on a portfolio of projects that included education from 30 per cent of the budget in 2008 to 36 per cent in 2013.

Monitoring Progress in China and Hong Kong

The Chinese government should continue to monitor the Compulsory Education Law to ensure all citizen have access to lower levels of education. The law requires 9 years of compulsory schooling. Children cannot be charged for school, and they cannot work during their compulsory education.

While Hong Kong's schoolchildren have a high primary and secondary school attainment rate, the government and its various agencies should make sure that all school-aged children complete school and are free from distractions like domestic violence and drugs.

The Chinese government also needs to give secondary school students from rural areas greater access to the sort of National Higher Education Entrance Examination preparation enjoyed by their urban counterparts. Hong Kong's government, likewise, can sponsor remedial as well as supplementary classes for students from low-income families.

In Shanghai municipality, spending on students in rural areas is only 50-60 per cent of those in urban areas. This is reinforced by the *hukou* household registration system, which restricts the mobility of rural citizens who might wish to pursue educational, job training or work opportunities in the cities. Ameliorating this situation may require reform, which we know— from earlier chapters on Abenomics, the 'lost decades,' and the features of the Japanese firm—may take a long time. But it is necessary if income equality is an ultimate objective.

How to Reform Public Vocational Schools to Benefit Poor People?

The Vocational Training Council (VTC) offers a diverse range of professional courses. Its course offerings need to be expanded to accommodate the needs of low-income Hong Kongers.
Source: Wikimedia Commons

The Vocational Training Council (VTC) is an important educational institution responsible for training thousands of students for a variety of careers. If not for its lack of courses and seats, it should be the centrepiece of the government's poverty-fighting efforts, since education is crucial to eliminating most forms of inequality described so far. As part of the fix, VTC-affiliated schools should lower the admission requirements for its courses and make courses more affordable by, for example, allowing students to pay tuition with their future earnings.

What is the VTC?

The VTC is the biggest provider of vocation training in Hong Kong, overseeing an array of publicly-funded schools, institutes, and centres. Compared to universities, they are very comprehensive. Industry specific schools include the Chinese Culinary Institute, the Hotel and Tourism Institute, Maritime Services Training Institute, Technological and Higher Education Institute of Hong Kong, and Hong Kong Design Institute. The Shine Skills Centres, which according to VTC's website 'provides industry-specific skills training, rehabilitation, and support services for people with disabilities,' serve students as young as 15 years old. Prospects are generally good for those who attend, with success rate at finding work at around 90 per cent for eight of the nine schools that released employment data.

The Number of Students Who Need the VTC

But the VTC is not living up to its potential. In 2018, 1.37 million people live below the poverty line, defined for a one-person household as an income of $4,000 per month. VTC has around 200,000 students, so the number of poor Hong Kongers that can benefit from vocational training is almost seven times greater than what current capacity allows.

Moreover, approximately 70 per cent of the poor population—close to one million people—are working. Despite their vocational nature, many of these VTC-managed schools do not cater primarily to working Hong Kongers. Of the 47,975 students enrolled in four of the schools (Hong Kong Institute of Vocational Education, Hong Kong Design Institute, School of Business Information Systems, Youth College) this academic year, only a quarter are part-time enrollees. A vocational school that effectively helps the poor must take into account their inability, for professional and financial reasons, to commit to school full-time.

The Subjects that are Taught at VTC

Despite its dominance in vocational training, VTC-managed schools seem to lack sufficient spots in foundational computer and technology courses to educate all low-income Hong Kongers for the marketplace. The Faculty of Science and Technology of the Technological and Higher Education Institute of Hong Kong enrolled only 1,374 students this academic year.

The School for Higher and Professional Education (SHAPE) offers technology and engineering programs, but they are prohibitive to all but those with good high school grades and a superior science and English background. The Institute of Professional Education and Knowledge (PEAK), whose courses host more students than any other school under VTC, offers few programming courses. There are only seven certificate courses, five professional diploma courses and two professional certificate courses. Although course offering includes artificial intelligence, machine learning, and 3D printing, there seems to be a dearth of the essential stuff—the Python, the C++, networking, and database management classes—that would allow Hong Kong workers greater mobility within their industries and in the Greater Bay Area.

What Needs to be Done at the VTC?

A reform of the VTC would require the creation of a more inclusive and practical vocational training network. This can be achieved by cutting down on degree programs and increasing the number of certificate and diploma courses—programs of study that offer the greatest return on investment. At the same time, VTC-managed schools should lower the entry requirements, like high school diplomas and work experience, so that motivated but under-educated and low-income people will have fewer barriers to education.

To meet demand, the VTC should work with local and overseas universities to share facilities, professors, and classrooms. The government can increase scholarship and grants, especially for local students, to lessen enrollees' financial burden. Another strategy is to eliminate student debt through an 'income-share agreement,' a sort of income-based loan repayment scheme suggested in the United States, where enormous university debts are a serious problem. In simple terms, instead of paying a portion or all of a student's tuition, they would agree to pay a percentage of their future earnings for a fixed period of time.

In a rapidly changing economy—its rise as a hyper-charged centre for raising financial capital, offshoring, the creation of a smart city, the pandemic-induced slump, integration into the Greater Bay Area, the shift away from manufacturing and other sectors—hundreds of thousands of Hong Kongers need to be professionally retrained and upgraded. Vocational education remains the best way for workers to remain competitive quickly. Low-income workers are more vulnerable than the average labourer, but, with the help of an improved institution like the VTC, the government can definitely offer them a fighting chance.

50[16]

Should University Be Free?

A panel discussion on inequality at the University of Hong Kong.
Source: Gary Lai

---

[16] This chapter has been adapted for an op-ed in the *Toronto Star* on August 20, 2019.

Free universities have been in the public debate in many countries for some time, because it is a financial burden on students, and many countries have already been charging no tuition. Universities are essential not only in Hong Kong, but in Africa, where doctors are in shortage, competent technocrats are needed to run oil-producing countries, entrepreneurs need business literacy skills, and engineers are essential to run Internet and communications projects.

In Alberta, university graduates are certainly needed to work in a diversified economy. In British Columbia, Aboriginals with a university degree earn more than high school graduates; economic reconciliation almost requires them to receive some post-secondary education.

In Hong Kong, some students have moved to cities in the Greater Bay Area to attend cheaper universities. Post-secondary institutions provide a wider range of social, athletic, and academic experiences than vocational schools, like those offered by VTC-affiliated schools. There are several arguments for charging no tuition: schools should be part of the social safety net, Hong Kong is better off with as many college-educated citizens as possible, and they improve the quality of education. The goal of free universities is to create a more equal society.

The controversy surrounding university tuition has been multi-faceted. Some argue for a lower rate, stating that it is a right to obtain a university education and the government or private institution has an obligation to make it accessible to all who are qualified. Others point to the increasing funding that is necessary to carry on research that has to be levied from students attending them. One fact stands out. Public universities in more egalitarian countries, like those in Scandinavia, charge much less, if any, than countries like the United States and the UK. If Hong Kong has any aspirations to close its wealth gap and lower its Gini coefficient, its universities should follow suit and scrap their tuitions.

Many Universities in the World Charge No Tuition

It should be noted that charging no tuition at public universities is not such a radical idea. Many leading economies of the world charge none, like Germany, France, Sweden, and Denmark. According to Statista, in the 2018/2019 winter semester, 2.9 million students studied, tuition-free, at various universities, technical colleges, and other schools of higher education. Although the policy has changed in France for non-European students, those who benefit from the policy pay only €170 to €601 per year in public universities, depending on the course. In Sweden and Denmark, domestic and European students do not have to pay tuition.

University as Part of the Social Safety Net

University should be free, above all because it is an important component of the social safety net, like healthcare. Tertiary education may not be for everyone, but they should be accessible to all who need it. To achieve this, countries like Indonesia commit a sizable portion of their social safety net programs to education, specifically to scholarships. A tuition-free policy, however, would be more flexible and inclusive than government bursaries and loans, which often require applicants to ask for money before or soon after graduating from secondary school and sometimes with a guarantor.

Free Universities Produce Better-Informed Citizens

Furthermore, free university helps the Hong Kong population become better informed citizens, and there are social benefits to it. Major academic studies have already linked education to good health. Studies have shown that people who are more educated are less likely to be poor, have children out of wedlock, and abuse and neglect their offspring. Education even has some unintentional effect on crime reduction. In this politically charged city, having free access to the top scholars on legal and government matters would be very useful to exercising one's civic duties. Or if one believes that business is the defining characteristic of Hong Kong, citizens who have tutelage in university-level management and economics can better engage in dialogues at the highest level.

Free Universities Make Better Universities

Finally, offering university education for free leads to a larger number of socially relevant classes and student organizations. At the University of Bielefeld in Germany, a student can major in Aesthetic Education, Informatics for the Natural Sciences, and Text Technology and Computer Linguistics. At Uppsala University in Sweden, a student can minor in Kurdish, Saami, and Special Education. The Sorbonne in Paris has student clubs for entrepreneurs, an improv troupe, and a group for people who understand sign language. No doubt this diversity of student life reflects the market demand of the cities these schools are located in that would not have existed if the tuition was not low or non-existent. In the universities of Hong Kong, attracting a more diverse student body—which may mean older students as well as the poor and people with disabilities—may lead to courses and student organizations that are more practical and innovative. Students may start a working business consultancy for nearby small businesses. And a university may create a Legal Studies major for non-law students for dealing with Hong Kong's intricate legal system.

As an egalitarian statement—which means to strive for an ever more inclusive society—Hong Kong should follow the successes in Germany, Sweden, and Denmark, among other countries and implement a no-tuition policy in its public universities, in what may turn out to be a global trend.

51

Stakeholders Can Help Realize the Potential of Entrepreneurs in Hong Kong

Residents of the Ma On Shan squatter village have no legal rights to their homes.
Source: Wikimedia Commons

Hong Kong is an entrepreneurial city, so it is fitting that there are many references to micro-entrepreneurship in this book. Hernando de Soto's work on formalizing property rights for the poor is founded on the belief that they will in turn use the assets—more than one trillion's worth around the world—to start businesses. It should be no surprise that de Soto himself is a successful businessman in Peru.

Muhammad Yunus' work in microfinance, and the numerous institutions it inspired, appealed to people because their entrepreneurial drive cannot be met by traditional banks, who believed they are too risky or unprofitable. In separate chapters on microfinance and entrepreneurship in Africa, I pointed out the hurdles small business owners face, like civil wars and discrimination.

In British Columbia, I called for support for indigenous people who want to start business, as part of economic reconciliation with the government. Implicit in poor and elderly people obtaining access to the Internet, from New York City or Hong Kong, is that they would start businesses. I warned small business owners to be careful with credit risk.

As I mentioned in previous chapters, fighting poverty requires big, systemic ideas. Microfinance and legal property rights reform are two of them. They may be able to drive a new wave of entrepreneurs in Hong Kong.

Entrepreneurs in Hong Kong

Hong Kong is a young city built by entrepreneurs (people who start their own businesses). That entrepreneurial spirit is embodied in the great scions of business today. Li Ka-shing started a plastic flower business in 1950. Using the money that he made, he entered the telecommunications, ports, and properties businesses, among other ventures that permeate Hong Kongers' daily lives. Lee Shau-kee, meanwhile, made his fortune in the real estate market through Henderson Land, which he founded in 1976 and is one of the four largest developers in Hong Kong. Today, businesses started by university students and graduates that get the most attention seem to revolve around technology and are skill- and capital-intensive. This will leave Hong Kongers who are not in the middle class and university-educated behind. Does this mean the end of city's original entrepreneurial spirit?

As Hong Kong's wealth and education gaps increase, a generation of urban poor exists once again. It is time to empower them to become entrepreneurs, starting with access to credit. One can take as example microfinance NGOs, which support poor people who cannot borrow from traditional banks with small loans. Another model to replicate is property rights reform, which helps poor squatters gain legal recognition for their informally claimed piece of land, in essence entitling them access to the mortgage and credit market.

Microfinance

Microfinance is predicated on the poor's ability to start innovative and profitable businesses. The goal, said the founder of FINCA's John Hatch, is to 'give poor communities the opportunities, then get out of the way!' To do that, FINCA has allied with major NGOs and banks. For example, FINCA borrowed US$3.5 million from Grameen Credit Agricole (many multinational banks have entered the microfinance business as philanthropic ventures) in early 2019 to lend to Zambians. On the ground, FINCA in Zambia makes HK$3,300 to HK$104,000 loans to business owners.

Grameen Bank is the gold standard in microfinance. Not only does it help the extremely poor people in developing countries, it extends microloans to the urban poor in developed economies like the United States. In 2018, Grameen Nippon was established in Japan, funding small groups of people with as much as HK$14,600 per borrower. In Hong Kong, the Grameen Bank has inspired the Hong Kong Mortgage Corporation's Microfinance Scheme, which has benefitted 216 groups since 2012. Its average loan size is HK$250,000, which is much higher than Grameen Nippon or Grameen America, which lends HK$27,000 on average.

Other Ways to Access Capital Markets

Sometimes, the poor can become entrepreneurs if they can obtain money through a home mortgage on their home. In poor communities around Peru, the great Peruvian economist Hernando de Soto found that people often do not have formal land titles, that is, a legal claim to their homes. But they have squatted there for a long time, and their neighbours (and dogs) recognize their ownership. So once the government gives them formal titles to their land, they can take out mortgages and loans from banks for entrepreneurship. In Hong Kong, there are still squatter villages in Chai Wan, Pok Fu Lam, and the New Territories, among other places. If these homes' ownership are legally recognized, potentially thousands of people can use their properties to take out mortgage for starting businesses.

According to Yunus, we are all entrepreneurs by nature. He has told the story of giving money and wares to beggars and seeing them transform into vendors. He has served roughly 160 million people all over the world in microcredit, mostly women, who have since started their own businesses. De Soto is optimistic that they are entrepreneurs, too. Even famed economists Esther Duflo and Abhijit Banerjee, who are cynical of the entrepreneurship-economic growth link, observed that poor people liked to start their own businesses. So it is reasonable, then, to give the micro-entrepreneurs in Hong Kong a chance as well.

<h1>52[17]</h1>

<h1>How Insuring the Poor in Hong Kong Is Becoming Big Business?</h1>

Microinsurance can protect Hong Kongers from climate-related events like typhoon and high humidity in the spring.
Source: Wikimedia Commons

When I introduced Muhammad Yunus in Chapter 4, I pointed out the variety of financial services for the poor he inspired. This

[17] An edited version of this chapter appeared in the *South China Morning Post* on October 18, 2020.

includes microinsurance, which helps mitigate the risks that poor people face. Like microcredit, it is an industry traditionally neglected by banks because of the small transactions involved.

Microinsurance is the most useful in health and climate related events, where the poor cannot afford large premiums. They may be part of the everyday solution for energy poverty, where the extremely poor cannot stomach fluctuations in heating and electricity prices.

There are already weather-related financial instruments available for farmers in developed countries; the poor, too, can benefit from insurance that hedge their crops and properties. When the poor and the elderly use the Internet for business, microinsurance can prevent loss from fraud, equipment failure, and criminal activities. This becomes more relevant as cities like Hong Kong plan for a 'smart' future, in a pandemic, when more people stay at home and go online, or as education becomes more accessible to the poor.

It can, in principle, also lower the credit risks of micro-entrepreneurs the way derivatives do for big businesses. Although microinsurance is not widely available in Hong Kong, it is a promising development for poverty alleviation in the city.

One of the major challenges in poverty alleviation is minimizing the risks that the poor face, in health, capital accumulation, and jobs, among other areas. A person with a higher income would normally buy insurance, but the premium is largely out of the reach for the poor. Banks and NGOs, in particular microfinance institutions, have stepped in in many parts of the world to provide low-income people with low-premium policies, with decent payouts, for a range of events in health, life, and natural disasters.

Banks and NGOs Offer a Variety of Microinsurance Products

Every country seems to have a different experience with microfinance. Bangladesh, home of the Grameen Bank, has a large market for microinsurance, with over 25 million customers. A variety of groups offer microinsurance products in loan, life, health, livestock, and health insurance, although microfinance institutions have better premium rates than traditional insurance companies and professional societies (like the International Network of Alternative Financial Institutions) that offer microfinance solutions. An academic study, using data from the Grameen Bank, showed that the poor benefits from microinsurance, using measures such as household income, health and nutritional status, and the poverty rate.

In Indonesia, the most populous country in Southeast Asia, many multinationals sell microinsurance products, including the Indonesian subsidiary of Allianz Life, which offers Sekoci, whose premiums can be paid over the cell phone. The target customer for this particular product has an income of US$136 per month.

Indonesia is also innovating in terms of climate change-related products. 95 per cent of Jakarta could be submerged due to climate change by 2050. The poor cluster in vulnerable coastal cities. Microinsurance provides protection for their homes and crops, available through the cell phone, in this large Muslim country with a notoriously low insurance penetration rate, which is around 3 per cent.

In Singapore, NTUC Income (established by the National Trades Union Congress's) schemes are directed towards the poor. The core plan pays out $3,700 in case of death or total and permanent disability of a parent or guardian. Grab, a startup, signed with China's Zhong An in 2020 to provide insurance products to micro-entrepreneurs in Southeast Asia, 9 million of whom the company has served in the last 6 years. In addition it will offer medical insurance to drivers in its ride-hailing service.

Microinsurance in Hong Kong

Hong Kong's microinsurance market, by comparison, is less mature. DBS Bank has decided to break from the traditional areas of coverage and introduced a digital microinsurance that offers protection against online crimes such as identity theft, online privacy invasion, tech support, hacking, harassment, and cyberbullying. This development is good for the poor. The policies will encourage them to log on to the Internet, form communities for political engagement, and conduct business online by lowering their risks at an affordable price.

But the government, NGOs, and banks can do more. For example, they can develop a greater selection of microinsurance products covering life and property for low-income residents and those who are vulnerable to the city's high cost of living. Climate-related events like typhoon and high humidity in the spring, whose damages to Hong Kongers' homes, land, and businesses are a fact of life, should be insurable for all.

Microinsurance seems to fill in a niche that traditional banks and governments once did not find profitable and so did not operate in. As the market for the poor is gathering into a critical mass, banks and startups are now entering the business that was reserved for non-profits. This is good news for the poor in Hong Kong, who should expect to find more competitively-priced products tailored made for their needs.

53

The Economics of Hong Kong's Parkland

Lantau South is Hong Kong's largest country park by area.
Source: Wikimedia Commons

Most measures of poverty will consider the amount a person spends on housing. Buying a home is, at worst, prohibitive in Hong Kong and is a burden for the poor. There are few options available to remedy high home prices. Most involve reclaiming land for apartment buildings. As I write this book, the government has just announced a major, HK$624 billion project to develop land on the large Lantau Island.

Moving to nearby cities in the Greater Bay Area, where homes are cheaper, is a possibility. Many massive infrastructure projects are going on that can one day move thousands of workers and their families to and from Hong Kong each day. These so-called 'one to two hour living circles' and 'three hour living circles' can make commuting from Mainland China more convenient than living in Hong Kong's rural fringes.

Developing country park land is another option. There are many of them. The benefits of building homes on them far outweigh how much people are willing to pay to conserve them. The supply and demand of real estate in Hong Kong crushes any concerns for biodiversity and the environment.

Country Parks in Hong Kong

1. *Size*

Country parks are everywhere in Hong Kong. Comprising 24 parks and 22 conservation areas they cover 443 square kilometres in the city. The largest parks are those in Lantau South, Tai Lam, and Plover Cove. The smallest is in Lung Fu Shan, which has an area of only 47 hectares. Their designation, development, and management are prescribed by the Country Parks Ordinance, which also established the Country and Marine Parks Board to advise the Director of Agriculture, Fisheries and Conservation.

2. *Features of the Parks*

The Shing Mun Country Park encompasses the Shing Mun Reservoir, which has been a water supply for urban Kowloon since 1937. Kam Shan and Tai Tam Country Parks have four reservoirs each. As reported in 2002, there are over 487 km of footpaths in the country parks. There are four long hiking trails in the country parks: the MacLehose Trail (100 km), the Wilson Trail (78 km), the Lantau Trail (70 km), and the Hong Kong Trail (50 km).

There are picnic areas, barbecue sites, mountain biking loops and trails, and jogging trails. A government survey found that 39 per cent of the visitors to Hong Kong's country parks came to barbecue, 14 per cent to picnic, 12 per cent to stroll, and 8 per cent to hike. Visitor centres and education efforts exist to help people gain better appreciation of Hong Kong's countryside. Centres have been established at Ngong Ping, Aberdeen, Sai Kung, Clear Water Bay, Shing Mun, Tai Mo Shan, Quarry Bay, and Sai Kung.

The Shing Mun Arboretum has a collection of about 300 plant species. 579,400 people participated in conservation education programs in 2017, in activities such as hiking, planting, and enjoying nature in guided tours. This is close to a 2.9-time increase from 2008.

3. *Biodiversity*

Streams often crisscross hiking trails, and mineral deposits can be found in country parks like Shing Mun and Tai Lam. Various common and exotic species of macaques, bamboo, dragonflies, and the plant life they feed on populate the country parks. Protected species like the Hong Kong Newt, the Hanging Bells tree, and the Chinese White Dolphin are found within the vicinities. In sum, Hong Kong has 48 species of mammals, 240 species of birds, 206 species of butterflies, 2135 species of plants, 75 species of reptiles, and 23 species of amphibians, a large portion of which can be found in the city's country parks.

4. *Scenery and Visitors*

From some parks, visitors can see the Victoria Harbor and Hong Kong's cityscape. From other points, hikers can see, like at Kam Shan Country Park, the highest peak in Hong Kong. Many of the top views of Hong Kong can be seen in and from country parks, like the Ho Pui Reservoir in Tai Lam Country Park.

In 2018, 12.3 million people visited Hong Kong's country parks, roughly the same level as 2008 but a 5.4 per cent decrease from 2017. The amount of garbage collected reflects the traffic through the country parks—3,000 tons in 2010, although, like the number of visitors, the number has remained steady through the years.

Real Estate Development on Country Parkland

1. *Land Shortage in Hong Kong*

But there are calls for land development on country park land. According to Our Hong Kong Foundation, a think tank, Hong Kong will possibly need more than 9,000 hectares of land for new housing over the next 30 years, instead of 4,800 hectares as estimated by the government. The total area of developed land in the city increased by 7,800 hectares from 1995 to 2004, but decreased sharply to 1,100 hectares from 2005 to 2015.

The Country Parks Ordinance has locked up the land for real estate development, totaling 16 times Hong Kong's total developed land area. While having green space is important for the city, the boundaries of the parks, as prescribed by the Country Parks Ordinance, should be reassessed to see if land that is originally protected can be developed. Biodiversity can be redistributed to areas that are currently low in ecological value.

2. *Fringe Development*

In May 2017, the government had asked the Housing Society, a non-profit group, to oversee the study on developing public housing and senior residences on two country parks' fringes. Two 20-hectare sites were chosen outside Tai Lam and Ma On Shan Country Parks. The assessment would take 12 to 14 months and involve an environmental, ecological, and recreational valuation. The head of the Housing Society, Wong Kit Loong, said that the organization had been a housing laboratory for Hong Kong and had carried out different housing experiments in the past.

The Value of Country Parks

Economic valuations of the country parks vary. One, based on the most recent study by the non-profit Civic Exchange, gives a figure of HK$183.4 million (in 2002 dollars). Another estimates the bequest, existence, and altruistic values of park land by asking survey respondents how much they are willing to pay services from and access to it. Using this method, visitors—based on three country parks—will pay an average of HK$101.1 per year to visit, making the valuation of all parklands HK$1.497 billion.

These estimates are dwarfed by the valuations of the country parks, using any economic measure, if they are developed for public housing and other forms of private residences. This is good news for real estate developers and Hong Kongers, and bad news for the environment. This is expect, as the status quo— as represented by the resource curse in Africa and conservative business practices during the 'lost decades' of Japan—is always the juggernaut to reformers. Australia, which had dealt admirably with a sudden influx of income from gold and other minerals, seemed to be the exception to the rule.

Agencies like the Environment Bureau are urging stakeholders to engage, 'recognize, and consider biodiversity concerns together with other socio-economic issues' and to set up scientific standards to review whether park boundaries should be redrawn for new housing. If the builders have their way, Hong Kongers will enjoy a larger real estate supply and lower rental and housing prices. And, as in most cities in the world, most people in the city want cheap housing.

54[18]

What the Poor Should Be Thankful for?

The Hong Kong government has ensured that the poor has equal access to a
variety of preventive healthcare.
Source: Wikimedia Commons

When I discussed Africa in Part II, I mentioned diseases that
burden Hong Kongers, most of which are skewed against the

---

[18] An edited version of this chapter appeared as an op-ed in
the *South China Morning Post* on September 13, 2020.

poor: non-communicable ailments like obesity, diabetes, and cardiovascular diseases, HIV/AIDS, dengue fever, and Japanese encephalitis. That is the wish list of what needs to be prevented, made less expensive to treat, and even eradicated.

This chapter is what Hong Kong got right, and the level at which public health management should aspire to. There is universal and free immunization for children for a host of diseases. Drinking water is up to international standards of cleanliness. Maternal mortality is virtually non-existent.

There are ways to alleviate the health inequality that still exists in the city. Academics in Canada suggest that activism is an effective strategy to address poverty as the source of health inequity. When the government needs to step in, they can use conditional cash transfer programs as in Brazil, instead of cash handouts, to entice the poor to get vaccinations and booster shots, and poor, pregnant mothers to receive medical checkups.

Healthcare can be expensive, and governments have learned along the way that prevention is the best way to avoid medical procedures and treatment. Unfortunately, in many parts of the world even access to preventive medicine—including immunization, establishment of a clean water supply, and ante- and post-natal care for mothers—there still exists a discrepancy between the rich and the poor. Hong Kongers should be thankful that they are all entitled to these public health measures.

Immunization

The Hong Kong government has ensured that the poor has equal access to immunization. Under the Hong Kong Childhood Immunization Program, over 95 per cent of eligible young people are protected, free of charge, against 11 communicable diseases through a regime of shots and booster shots from birth through sixth grade. Children from families that receive social assistance are also eligible, along with other children, for free flu vaccinations, a scheme that benefitted 1,900 people in the 2017/2018 flu season.

The WHO has been working with a group of multilateral, bilateral, and government agencies to bring diseases like polio and measles under control in Bangladesh, where only three-quarters of children under the age of one have received all the required immunization.

In Laos, only 87 per cent of children received all three required doses of the diphtheria-tetanus-pertussis vaccine. The government is still working hard to control diseases like measles, rubella, and hepatitis B. Agencies seem to have trouble delivering vaccines in rural communities. Hong Kong's public health system, by comparison, is much more inclusive.

Clean Water

Hong Kong also has some of the cleanest drinking water in the world. The Water Supplies Department created the Hong Kong Drinking Water Standards so that the city's drinking water complies with the WHO's standards, which include limiting the amount of metals like arsenic, lead, and mercury; pesticides like DDT; disinfectants and their by-products like chlorine; inorganic chemicals like fluoride and nitrate; organic chemicals like benzenes; organisms like *E. coli*; and radioactive material. Concerns about the city's water supply in recent years comes from the last leg of the water's journey, in the uncleanliness of the water pipes in public housing estates. But those seemed to be isolated cases that have been dealt with.

The cleanliness of the water supply is much worse in other Asian countries. In Pakistan, for example, 22 per cent of the water supply in the capital city was found to be non-chlorinated. Without clean water, people often fall sick to diarrhea, a major killer in the developing world. Those who do not die become undernourished, since they have trouble absorbing the nutrients from the food they eat.

In neighbouring India, Water.org estimates that more than one-tenth of the population lacks access to clean water, and 21 per cent of communicable diseases there are linked to their unsafe water supply. Like in many developing countries, non-profit organizations and government agencies often resort to passing out bottles of chlorine bleach to cleanse drinking water at home, a reality that is unthinkable in Hong Kong.

Maternal Care

Another area in which the Hong Kong government has been taking care of everyone, regardless of wealth, is maternal health. Maternal mortality has always been low in the city, and in the 1980s has already dipped below 10 deaths per 100,000 births, or the level where Singapore is today. Thanks to good healthcare for pregnant women, there was only one registered maternal death in 2017, or a ratio of 1.8 deaths per 100,000 births.

In nearby Burma, maternal mortality is over 2,800 in the latest census year, translating to 282 deaths per 100,000 births. New mothers there still grapple with obtaining access to antenatal and postnatal care and receiving treatment to treatable conditions like pre-eclampsia, a form of high blood pressure.

The latest World Bank data states that Indonesia's maternal mortality ratio is 126 deaths per 100,000 births. A study conducted by the Ministry of Health and the United Nations Population Fund found that eclampsia and hemorrhage are the main causes, and half of these cases were preventable. Drugs and a ready supply of blood are essential but lacking in the country. In Hong Kong, there is free access to ante- and post-natal services for all residents, which help them identify life-threatening medical conditions and receive treatment.

It is agreed upon among experts that there are relatively inexpensive and easy programs to institute to improve population health, including immunizing children, cleaning the drinking water, and checking up on women before and after they give birth. But even among Hong Kong's neighbours in Asia, it is not a fact of life. In this city where the wealth gap is increasing, equality in access to public health programs is certainly one thing to commend on.

It's Not Just About Money: Effective Philanthropy in Hong Kong Needs More Effort from Everyone

Hong Kongers are generous, but they fall behind other countries in hands-on volunteerism.
Source: Wikimedia Commons

---

[19] This chapter appeared as an op-ed in *Hong Kong Free Press* on December 22, 2018.

This book, for the most part, has been about the big ideas in poverty alleviation. But what can the average person do to fight poverty and lessen inequalities in Hong Kong? There are the usual suspects: donations to a favourite charity, helping out a random stranger, volunteering, and organizing philanthropic communities. The choice is personal, although the observation I made in regard to the Aboriginal people in British Columbia—that a society is judged by how well it treats its weakest members—is still an apt guide to follow.

By many measures, Hong Kongers are generous. According to the Home Affairs Department, the number of tax-exempt charities has risen from 3,250 in 2000 to 8,831 in 2016.

The amount of individual and corporate donations, as a percentage of GDP, rose from 0.22 per cent in 2000-1 to 0.52 per cent (HK$11.7 billion) in 2014-5.

The government cited a ranking by Charities Aid Foundation (CAF), a British charity, in a recent report. CAF has ranked 147 countries in the level of their generosity, by three categories and a meta-score called the World Giving Index.

The data has been collected by Gallup, as part of its World Poll Initiative, since the index's inception 9 years ago.

Trends in Philanthropy in Hong Kong

Here are a few observations from the results from 2015 to 2018. In the past three available editions, Hong Kong's ranking has remained steady between 26th and 30th. This has kept the city above egalitarian Sweden and Finland, and below high trust societies like the United States, Australia, and Canada.

Hong Kong has consistently performed better in rankings of 'donated money to a charity?' in which Hong Kong ranked

11th among the surveyed countries and dropped to 21st before rising to 18th in 2018, than in 'Helped a stranger, or someone you didn't know who needed help?' or 'Volunteered your time to an organization?'

By absolute scores, Hong Kong is a long way from the top. In 2018, Hong Kong has a score of 44 per cent in the World Giving Index. Indonesia, which places first, scores 59 per cent. On willingness to help a stranger, Hong Kong scored 60 per cent, which is much lower than Libya's 83 per cent.

Hong Kong has a 'willingness to donate' score of 55 per cent, which is much lower than Myanmar's 88 per cent. This category, by the way, is where Hong Kong holds the highest rank. Finally, Hong Kong scores 19 per cent in time committed to volunteering, which is abysmal compared with Indonesia's 53 per cent.

How Should Success in Philanthropy Be Measured?

Hong Kong's goal should not be just to improve relative to other countries. It should also try to obtain higher index scores in each of the three categories as well as the conglomerate total.

This is most important because it leads to that measure of inequality in a society, the Gini coefficient. Hong Kong's Gini coefficient is relatively high—denoting a high level of inequality—at 0.539 in 2017, compared to 0.415 in 2016 in the US and 0.292 in 2015 in Sweden.

How well private individuals and companies conduct philanthropy demonstrates how well we combat inequality: a city-wide effort to reallocate time and resources from the mega-rich and rich to the less fortunate—and the average person to the poor.

The government can play a role in promoting philanthropy at all social levels. Encouraging the creation of civic organizations and the development of community sports and music can foster trust and goodwill between people in a community. People who are closely bonded are more likely to help each other in times of need and to volunteer.

It can sponsor classes and workshops to teach and support more people who want to set up charities—or strategic, effective, venture, and student philanthropy. Generous Hong Kongers would want to donate to charities with which they can identify and to which they are emotionally attached (in fact, many large donations in the city continue to be to a wealthy benefactor's alma mater). A match is more likely if a greater variety of causes are available to them.

A Final Word on Giving

Hong Kong's lopsided focus on giving monetary gifts rather than on-the-ground and hands-on volunteerism is also worrying. After all, what is the use of donating more money if there is a lack of volunteers? What if there are not enough volunteers willing to supervise the clothing collection site or stock the food pantry?

Would a Good Samaritan who feeds a homeless man be more useful than the cache of money that floods in when he falls sick from the cold? We must remember that the goal of philanthropy, apart from narrowing the income gap, is to make us more human.

Conclusion

This book began with a meditation on the most horrific war in the twentieth century and the crucial role that the economy played in drumming up support for it. Fast forward to today, and another transnational, and domestic, threat looms in Europe. If poverty does not cause it, does terrorism have an economic effect on the poor?

Catalonia was an interesting study, because its administrative status in relations to the federal government in Madrid is analogous to Hong Kong and Beijing. The issue there is whether raising the minimum wage there, which depending on whom one asks may or may not help the poor, would affect Catalonia's crime rate.

Africa is a large continent with over one billion people. It is a large battleground in the fight against extreme poverty that requires a concerted, large-scaled effort. Health is a good indicator of how developed countries are. A huge underlying cause of poverty is corruption, but some argue that countries there suffer from the resource curse, a chronic lack of economic growth despite having an enormous cache of natural resources. Political accountability may be one solution; multilateralists would call for cooperation between different stakeholders on various levels to bring resources to Africans. While Fair Trade advocates call for product certifications to help the poor, others suggest microfinance and business-friendly policies as more effective tools. Technocrats may say more collaborations are needed between technology and telecommunications companies and governments. I end the discussion on Africa with climate change, which impacts the poor through farming and armed conflicts.

There are several popular issues in Canada, across the Atlantic, in regards to poverty. The country is known for its universal healthcare, but poverty inequality seems to affect health outcomes for the poor population. British Columbia is a western province with a unique set of problems, chronic Aboriginal unemployment. Western alienation is a persistent regional problem, and I considered the effect of macroeconomic policies on Alberta, the energy and agricultural heartland of Canada.

In the US, three groups of people are economically vulnerable: illegal immigrants, military veterans, and those who do not have access to computers and the Internet. I also explored American corporate risk and energy policies to see how they affect company bankruptcies and the poor.

Around the Pacific Rim, I surveyed the popular conditional cash transfer program, made famous by Brazil's Bolsa Família (Family Grant). Australia suffers from a general form of the resource curse, the Dutch disease, which, if poorly managed, may affect economic growth. India, which has lifted over 271 million people out of poverty, is likely to help more in the US-China trade war. Japan's economic policies and business culture have a definite lesson for anti-poverty reformers. China is a large economy, with a variety of variables to consider. An important one is the global energy market's constraint on energy security, which Hong Kong can learn from.

I have selected a few topics, not meant to be exhaustive, for discussion about Hong Kong: gender equality, intergenerational income mobility, elderly poverty, the digital divide, the development of the Guangdong-Hong Kong-Macau Greater Bay Area, education reform, entrepreneurship, microcredit, real estate, health, and philanthropy. They involve a wide variety of problems and solutions.

The key takeaway from this survey is that there is a whole arsenal of large scale poverty-fighting ideas, some of which can be applied to Hong Kong. The Millennium Village model is one. Legal property rights reform, championed by Hernando de Soto, is another. Microfinance has been popularized by commercial banks and non-profit organizations. A corruption-free government is a requisite in resource-filled countries. A multilateral approach is necessary to attack energy poverty, a symptom of extreme poverty, although the shale revolution promises cheap energy to millions around the world. Activism is sometimes effective, as in the Fair Trade movement or healthcare reform in Canada.

Access to technology is important in advanced as well as developing economies, and so are the public-private partnerships that can make it happen. Education is, as generally accepted by development economists, critical in escaping the poverty trap and income inequality. When cash handouts become ineffective, conditional cash transfer programs have proven itself in many countries.

So this is my anti-poverty toolkit. Take your pick. Stay realistic about the pace of reform, and appreciate the myriad priorities on a government's agenda. Poverty and inequality in Hong Kong can be dramatically reduced in our lifetime.

Glossary

3D—3-dimensional

AI—artificial intelligence

AIDS—acquired immunodeficiency syndrome

Aski—Auslander Sonderkonten fuer Inlandszahlungen

BC—British Columbia

bcm—billion cubic metres

b/d—barrels per day

BOJ—Bank of Japan

BRI—Belt and Road Initiative

CAF—Charities Aid Foundation

CCT—conditional cash transfer

CDS—credit default swaps

CIA—Central Intelligence Agency

CIS—Commonwealth of Independent States

CNOOC—China National Offshore Oil Corporation

CNPC—China National Petroleum Corporation

COVID-19—Coronavirus Disease 19

CSR—corporate social responsibility

DDT—Dichloro-Diphenyl-Trichloroethane

EFCC—Economic and Financial Crimes Commission (Nigeria)

EGF—Globalization Adjustment Fund

EU—European Union

EUEI—European Union Energy Initiative for Poverty Eradication and Sustainable Development

FATF—Financial Action Task Force on Money Laundering

FDI—foreign direct investment

FINCA—Foundation for International Community Assistance

FINE—(F)airtrade Labelling Organizations International; (I)nternational Fair Trade Association; (N)etwork of European Worldshops; (E)uropean Fair Trade Association

FSU—Former Soviet Union

GDP—gross domestic product

GNP—gross national product

GSFI—government-sponsored financial institutions

HFI—household food insecurity

HIV—human immunodeficiency virus

HK GAAP—Hong Kong Generally Accepted Accounting Principle

HKFRS—Hong Kong International Financial Reporting Standards

IEE—intergenerational earnings elasticity

ILD—Institute for Liberty and Democracy

IMF—International Monetary Fund

INRA-ENPC—Institut national de la recherche agronomique/ École nationale des ponts et chaussées

INTERPOL—International Criminal Police Organization

ISP—Internet Service Provider

J-firm—Japanese firm

JIT—just-in-time

LA—Los Angeles

LegCo—Legislative Council

LTCB—Long-Term Credit Bank of Japan

MDG—Millennium Development Goal

Mefo—Metallurgische Forschung

MFI—microfinance institution

MTN—Mobile Telephone Network

NAFTA—North American Free Trade Agreement

NGO—non-governmental organization

NOC—National Oil Companies

NYU—New York University

OECD—Organization for Economic Co-operation and Development

OPEC—Oil Producing and Exporting Countries

P/E—price-per-earning ratio

RMB—renminbi

SAR—Special Administrative Region

SDOH—social determinants of health

SII—Structural Impediments Initiative

SME—small and medium-sized enterprises

TAA—Trade Adjustment Assistance

UC—University of California

UK—United Kingdom

UN—United Nations

UNICEF—United Nations International Children's Emergency Fund

US—United States

VTC—Vocational Training Council

WHO—World Health Organization

WTO—World Trade Organization

Bibliography

Adjei, Joseph, Thankom Arun, and Farhad Hossain. 2009. 'Asset Building and Poverty Reduction in Ghana: The Case of Microfinance.' *Savings and Development* 33(3): 265-91, http://www.jstor.org/stable/41406497.

Adusei, Michael. 2016. 'Does Entrepreneurship Promote Economic Growth in Africa?' *African Development Review* 28(2): 201-14.

Ahsan, Syed M., M.A.B. Khalily, Syed A. Hamid, Shubhasish Barua, and Suborna Barua. 'The Microinsurance Market in Bangladesh: An Analytical Overview.' *The Bangladesh Development Studies* 36(1): 1-54, https://www.jstor.org/stable/41968861.

Aideyan, Osaore. 2009. 'Microfinance and Poverty Reduction in Rural Nigeria.' *Savings and Development* 33(3): 293-317, http://www.jstor.org/stable/41406498.

Ainsworth, Martha, and Mead Over. 1994. 'AIDS and African Development.' *The World Bank Research Observer* 9(2): 203-40, http://www.jstor.org/stable/3986325.

Aker, Jenny C. 2010. 'Information from Markets Near and Far: Mobile Phones and Agricultural Markets in Niger.' *American Economic Journal: Applied Economics* 2(3): 46-59, http://www.jstor.org/stable/25760219.

Aker, Jenny C., and Isaac M. Mbiti. 2010. 'Mobile Phones and Economic Development in Africa.' *The Journal of Economic Perspectives* 24(3): 207-32, http://www.jstor.org/stable/20799163.

Alden, Edward, and Bryan Roberts. 2011. 'Are US Borders Secure? Why We Don't Know, and How to Find Out.' *Foreign Affairs* 90(4): 19-22, https://search-proquest-com.eproxy1.lib.hku.hk/docview / 873487195?accountid=14548.

Al-Tamimi, Naser. 2013. 'The Growing Roles of Asian Powers in the Gulf: A Saudi Perspective.' In *Asia-Gulf Economic Relations in the 21st Century*, edited by Tim Niblock and Monica Malik, 35-61. London: Gerlach Press, http://www.jstor.org/stable/j.ctt1df4hn2.5/. Dannreuther 2011.

Alvaredo, Facundo, Lucas Chancel, Thomas Piketty, Emmanuel Saez, and Gabriel Zucman. 2017. 'Global Inequality Dynamics: New Findings from WID.world.' Working Paper 23119. NBER, Cambridge: MA, http://www.nber.org/papers/w23119.

Anduanbessa, Tsegaye. 2009. 'Statistical Analysis of the Performance of Microfinance Institutions: The Ethiopian Case.' *Savings and Development* 33(2): 183-98, http://www.jstor.org/stable/41406492.

Annim, Samuel K. 2010. 'Sensitivity of Loan Size to Lending Rates: Evidence from Ghana's Microfinance Sector.' *African Review of Money, Finance, and Banking* 85-107, http://www.jstor.org/stable/41803207.

Anyanwu, John C., and Andrew E.O. Erhijakpor. 2009. 'Health Expenditures and Health Outcomes in Africa.' *African Development Review* 21(2): 400-33. doi:10.1111/j.1467-8268.2009.00215.x.

Aoki, Katsuki and Thomas T. Lennerfors. 2013. 'The New, Improved Keiretsu.' *Harvard Business Review* (September).

Aranta, Aris, and Reza Siregar. 1999. 'Social Safety Net Policies in Indonesia: Objectives and Shortcomings.' *ASEAN Economic Bulletin* 16(3): 344-59, https://www.jstor.org/stable/25773597.

Arif, G.M., Shujaat Farooq, Saman Nazir and Maryam Satti. 2014. 'Child Malnutrition and Poverty: The Case of Pakistan.' *The Pakistan Development Review* 53(2): 99-118, https://www.jstor.org/stable/24397882.

Asenso-Okyere, Kwadwo, Felix A. Asante, Jifar Tarek, and Kwaw S. Andam. 2011. 'A Review of the Economic Impact of Malaria in Agricultural Development.' *Agricultural Economics* 42: 293-304.

Ashton, Peter J. 2002. 'Avoiding Conflicts over Africa's Water Resources.' *Ambio* 31(3): 236-42, http://www.jstor.org/stable/4315243.

Associated Press. 2001. 'Finding Winners, Losers in Enron Debacle.' November 30, https://search.proquest.com/docview/259442239?accountid=37892.

Aterido, Reyes, and Mary Hallward-Driemeier. 2011. 'Whose Business is it Anyway?' *Small Business Economics* 37: 443-64. doi:10.1007/sll187-011-9375-y.

Autor, David, Frank Levy, and Richard Murnane.2003. 'The Skill Content of Recent Technological Change: An Empirical Exploration.' *Quarterly Journal of Economics* 118: 1279-1333.

Auxenfants, Marc. 2019. 'The Cost of Luxembourg's Free Public Transport Plan.' *BBC Worklife*, January 30, https://www.bbc.com/worklife/article/20190128-the-cost-of-luxembourgs-free-public-transport-plan.

Balaban, D. 2008. 'Going Mobile with Remittances, Technology, Mobile Banking.' *Cards and Payments*, http://www.cardsandpayments.net.

Banerjee, Abhijit, and Esther Duflo. 2011. *Poor Economics*. PublicAffairs: New York.

Barnett, J. 2000. 'Destabilizing the Environment-Conflict Thesis.' *Review of International Studies* 26(2): 271–88.

Barreca, Alan I. 2010. 'The Long-Term Economic Impact of In Utero and Postnatal Exposure to Malaria.' *The Journal of Human Resources* 45(4): 865-92, http://www.jstor.org/stable/25764792.

Bazilian, Morgan D. 2015. 'Power to the Poor: Provide Energy to Fight Poverty.' *Foreign Affairs* 94(2).

Berhane, Guush, and Cornelis Gardebroek. 2011. 'Does Microfinance Reduce Rural Poverty? Evidence Based on Household Panel Data from Northern Ethiopia.' *American Journal of Agricultural Economics* 93(1): 43-55, http://www.jstor.org/stable/41240259.

Beuving, J. Joost. 2004. 'Cotonou's Klondike: African Traders and Second-Hand Car Markets in Benin.' *The Journal of Modern African Studies* 42(4): 511-37, http://www.jstor.org/stable/3876137.

Bhagwati, Jagdish, and Francisco Rivera-Batiz. 2013. 'A Kinder, Gentler Immigration Policy: Forget Comprehensive Reform-Let the States Compete.' *Foreign Affairs* 92(6): 9-15, https://search-proquest-com.eproxy1.lib.hku.hk/docview/1450254093?accountid=14548.

Bhalla, A. 1990. 'Rural-Urban Disparities in India and China.' *World Development* 18: 1097-1110.

Billette, André. 1979. 'Poor Health and Poor Policies.' *Canadian Journal of Social Work Education (Revue canadienne d'Éducation en service social)* 5(1): 43-61.

Birol, Fatih. 2007. 'Energy Economics: A Place for Energy Poverty in the Agenda?' *The Energy Journal* 28(3): 1-6, http://www.jstor.org/stable/41323106.

Bleakley, Hoyt. 2009. 'Economic Effects of Childhood Exposure to Tropical Disease.' *The American Economic Review* 99(2): 218-23, http://www.jstor.org/stable/25592402.

Blinder, Alan S. 2007a. 'How Many US Jobs Might Be Offshorable?' Working Paper No. 142. CEPS, Center for Economic Policy Studies, Princeton University.

Blundy, Rachel. 2017. 'How Safe is Hong Kong's Water?' *South China Morning Post.* https://www.scmp.com/news/hong-kong/health-environment/article/2083874/how-safe-hong-kongs-water.

Botman, Dennis, and Zoltan Jakab. 2014. 'Abenomics—Time for a Push from Higher Wages.' *IMFBlog*, March 20, https://blogs.imf.org/2014/03/20/abenomics-time-for-a-push-from-higher-wages/.

Brahmbhatt, Milan, Otaviano Canuto, and Ekaterina Vostroknutova. 2010. 'Dealing with Dutch Disease.' *Economic Premise (The World Bank)* 16: 1-7.

Bretschger, Lucas, and Simone Valente. 2011. 'Climate Change and Uneven Development.' *The Scandinavian Journal of Economics* 113(4): 825-45, http://www.jstor.org/stable/41407747.

Broadman, Harry G. 2008. 'China and India Go to Africa: New Deals in the Developing World.' *Foreign Affairs* 87(2).

Brown, I., Z. Cajee, D. Davies, and S. Stroebel. 'Cell Phone Banking: Predictors of Adoption in South Africa—An Exploratory Study.' *International Journal of Information Management* 23: 381-94.

Brown, Jeffrey R., and Austan Goolsbee. 2002. 'Does the Internet Make Markets More Competitive? Evidence from the Life Insurance Industry.' *Journal of Political Economy* 110(3): 481-507.

Burgess, Robin, and Rohini Pande. 2005. 'Do Rural Banks Matter? Evidence from the Indian Social Banking Experiment.' *The American Economic Review* 95(3): 780-95.

Campus France. 2019. 'Tuition Rates in Public Institutions.' *Campus France*, https://www.campusfrance.org/en/tuition-fees-France.

Capponi, Agostino, and Jaksa Cvitanic. 2009. *International Journal of Theoretical and Applied Finance* 12: 1-29. https://ssrn.com/abstract=1318133.

Caves, R. E. 1982. *Multinational Enterprise and Economic Analysis.* Cambridge: Cambridge University Press.

CEIC. 2019. 'China Air: Passenger Traffic.' https://www.ceicdata.com/en/china/air-passenger-traffic (accessed January 22, 2020).

Chan, Lih-Shing, and Kee-Lee Chou. 2018. 'Poverty in Old Age: Evidence from Hong Kong.' *Aging & Society* 38: 37-55, doi:10.1017/S0144686X16000817.

Chávez, Karen, and Trevor Hughes. 2019. 'Trump: Park Rangers Will Patrol Mexican Border, Arrest Migrants.' *USA Today*, November 23, https://www.usatoday.com/story/news/2019/11/23/president-trump-sends-park-rangers-patrol-u-s-mexico-border/4166432002/.

Chen, Shaofeng. 2011. 'Has China's Foreign Energy Quest Enhanced Its Energy Security?' *The China Quarterly* 207: 600-25, http://www.jstor.org/stable/41305259/.

Chen, Yongwei, and Duhai Fu. 2015. Journal of Economic Inequality 13: 299-307.

Cheung, Alvin. 2019. 'A Brief Discussion on Global Intergenerational Earnings Elasticity Research.' Our Hong Kong Foundation, February 12.

China Daily. 2017. 'Second Belt and Road Summit Opens in HK.' *China Daily*. September 11, http://www.chinadaily.com.cn/hkedition/2017-09/11/content_31836854.htm.

2019. 'China's Mobile Payments Penetration Rate Highest in the World at 86%: PwC Report.' *China Banking News*, April 15, http://www.chinabankingnews.com/2019/04/15/chinas-mobile-payments-penetration-rate-highest-in-the-world-at-86-pwc-report/.

Chirwa, Ephraim W., Peter M. Mvula, Lucy Namata, and Evious K. Zgovu. 1999. 'Capacity Constraints, Management and Effectiveness of Poverty-Oriented Microfinance Institutions in Malawi.' *African Review of Money, Finance, and Banking* 21-48, http://www.jstor.org/stable/23026370.

Chiu, Peace. 2018. 'Record 1.37 Million People Living below Poverty Line in Hong Kong as Government Blames Rise on Ageing Population and Cityís Improving Economy.' *South China Morning Post*, November 19, https://www.scmp.com/news/hong-kong/society/article/2174006/record-13-million-people-living-below-poverty-line-hong-kong.

Cho, Sharon. 2017. 'Russia Reemerges as China's Top Oil Supplier Before OPEC Meet.' *Bloomberg*, April 25, https://www.bloomberg.

com/news/articles/2017-04-25/russia-reemerges-as-china-s-top-oil-supplier-before-opec-meet.

CIA The World Factbook. 2017. 'Crude Oil—Production.' Https://www.cia.gov/library/publications/the-world-factbook/rankorder/2241rank.html (accessed July 13)

------. 2017. 'Crude Oil—Proved Reserves.' Https://www.cia.gov/library/publications/the-world-factbook/rankorder/2244rank.html (assessed July 13).

Ćirković, Stevan. 2019. 'Bolsa Família in Brazil.' Great Policy Successes Case Study Series, Centre for Public Impact, https://www.centreforpublicimpact.org/case-study/bolsa-familia-in-brazil/.

CNBC. 2019. 'CCTV Script 15/10/19.' Https://www.cnbc.com/2019/12/24/cctv-script-151019.html (accessed January 20).

Collier, Paul, Gordon Conway, and Tony Venables. 2008. 'Climate Change and Africa.' *Oxford Review of Economic Policy* 24(2): 337-53, http://www.jstor.org/stable/23606648.

Collins, Patricia A., Elaine M. Power and Margaret H. Little. 2014. 'Municipal-Level Responses to Household Food Insecurity in Canada: A call for Critical, Evaluative Research.' *Canadian Journal of Public Health / Revue Canadienne de Santé Publique* 105(2): 138-41.

Comic, Miriam. 2017. '"We are All Entrepreneurs": Muhammad Yunus on Changing the World, One Microloan at a Time.' *The Guardian*, March 29, https://www.theguardian.com/sustainable-business/2017/mar/29/we-are-all-entrepreneurs-muhammad-yunus-on-changing-the-world-one-microloan-at-a-time.

Conly, Gladys N. 1975. *The Impact of Malaria on Economic Development: A Case Study.* Scientific Publication 297. Washington, D.C.: Pan American Health Organization, Pan American Sanitary Bureau, Regional Office of the World Health Organization.

Connell, Dan and Frank Smyth. 2013. 'Africa's New Bloc.' *Foreign Affairs* 77(2): 80-94.

Corden, W.M. 2012. 'Dutch Disease in Australia: Policy Options for a Three-Speed Economy.' *The Australian Economic Review* 45(3): 290-304, https://doi.org/10.1111/j.1467-8462.2012.00685.x.

Corden, W.M., and P.J. Neary. 1982. 'Booming Sector and Deindustrialization in a Small Open Economy.' *Economic Journal* 92: 825–48.

Cull, Robert, Asli Demirgüç-Kunt, and Jonathan Morduch. 2009. 'Microfinance Meets the Market.' *The Journal of Economic Perspectives* 23(1): 167-92, http://www.jstor.org/stable/27648299.

Daly, Tanvir R., and Panuel R. Prince. 2017. 'Making Microinsurance Work in Bangladesh: Three Takeaways.' *Action Center for Financial Inclusion Blog*, April 13, https://www.centerforfinancialinclusion. org/making-microinsurance-work-in-bangladesh-three-takeaways.

Dannreuther, Roland. 2011. 'China and Global Oil: Vulnerability and Opportunity.' *International Affairs* 87(6): 1345-364, http://www. jstor.org/stable/41306994/.

Dasgupta, Susmita, Somik Lall, and David Wheeler. 2001. 'Policy Reform, Economic Growth, and the Digital Divide: An Econometric Analysis.' World Bank Policy Research Paper no. 2567. World Bank, Washington, D.C.

DBS. 2019. 'DBS Hong Kong Offers Customers Cyber Insurance.' *Fin Extra*, https://www.finextra.com/pressarticle/77378/dbs-hong-kong-offers-customers-cyber-insurance.

De Brauw, Alan, Daniel Gilligan, John Hoddinott, Shalini Roy. 2011. 'The Impact of Bolsa Família on Education and Health Outcomes in Brazil.' Second Generation of CCTs Evaluations Conference, The World Bank, October 24.

Deeks, Steven G., Sharon R. Lewin, and Diane V. Havlir. 2013. 'The End of AIDS: HIV Infection as a Chronic Disease.' *Lancet* 382: 1525-533, http://dx.doi.org/10.1016/S0140-6736(13)61809-7.

Deuel, Wallace. 1942. *People under Hitler.* New York: Harcourt, Brace and Company.

Devarajan, Shantayanan, and Wolfgang Fengler. 2013. "Africa's Economic Boom: Why the Pessimists and the Optimists are Both Right." *Foreign Affairs* 92(3): 68-81.

Devitt, Conor, and Richard S.J. Tol. 2012. 'Civil War, Climate Change, and Development: A Scenario Study for Sub-Saharan Africa.' *Journal of Peace Research* 49(1): 129-45, http://www.jstor.org/stable/23141284.

DeWolf, Christopher. 2017. 'When Hong Kong Was a City of Villages: Squatter Settlements and Their Legacy.' *Zolima Citymag*, March 3.

Diamond, Larry, and Jack Mosbacher. 2013. 'Petroleum to the People: Africa's Coming Resource Curse—and How to Avoid It.' *Foreign Affairs* 92(5): 86-98.

DiChristopher, Tom. 2015. 'Sizing up the Trade Adjustment Assistance Program.' *CNBC*, June 26, https://www.cnbc.com/2015/06/26/is-aid-to-trade-displaced-workers-worth-the-cost.html.

Dixon, Simon, Simon McDonald, and Jennifer Roberts. 2001. 'AIDS and Economic Growth in Africa: A Panel Data Analysis.' *Journal of International Development* 13: 411-26. doi:10.1002/jid.795.

Dolan, Catherine S. 2010. 'Fractured Ties: The Business of Development in Kenyan Fair Trade Tea.' In *Fair Trade and Social Justice: Global Ethnographies*, edited by S. Lyon and M. Moberg, 147-75. New York: New York University Press.

Dolatyar, Mostafa, and T.S. Gray. 2000. 'The Politics of Water Scarcity in the Middle East.' *Environmental Politics* 9(3): 65–87.

Dow, Sandra, and Jean McGuire. 2011. 'Industrial Networks in Japan: Blessing or Curse?' *The European Financial Review* (February/March): 17-21.

Downs, Erica S. 2004. 'The Chinese Energy Security Debate.' *The China Quarterly* 177: 21-41, http://www.jstor.org/stable/20192303/.

Dragnet, Christian. 2016. 'China's Shifting Geo-economic Strategy.' *Survival* 58(3).

Drugge, S.E., and T.S. Veeman. 1980. 'Industrial Diversification in Alberta: Some Problems and Policies.' *Canadian Public Policy* 6: 221-28.

Duhig, Mary. 2004. 'Mitigating Credit Risk in Changing Times.' *Electric Perspectives* 29(2): 54-58, https://search.proquest.com/docview/217570954?accountid=37892.

Duncombe, Richard, and Boateng, Richard. 2009. 'Mobile Phones and Financial Services in Developing Countries: A Review of Concepts, Methods, Issues, Evidence and Future Research Directions.' *Third World Quarterly* 30(7): 1237-258, http://www.jstor.org/stable/40388181.

Du Preez, A. 2004. 'Misbehaving Tools: The Politics of Human-Technology Interactions.' In *South African Visual Culture*, edited by Van Eeden and A. Du Preez. Pretoria: Van Schaiks.

Elver, H. 2006. 'International Environmental Law, Water and the Future.' *Third World Quarterly* 27(5): 885–901.

Enright, M., E. Scott, and Enright, Scott & Associates. 2005. *The Greater Pearl River Delta*. Hong Kong: Invest Hong Kong.

Eshelby, Kate. 2007. 'Dying for a Drink.' *British Medical Journal* 334(7594):610-612, http://www.jstor.org/stable/20506718.

Etzo, Sebastiana, and Guy Collender. 2010. 'Briefing: The Mobile Phone 'Revolution' in Africa: Rhetoric or Reality?' *African Affairs* 109(437): 659-668, http://www.jstor.org/stable/40928368.

European Commission. 2019. 'European Globalisation Adjustment Fund (EGF).' Https://ec.europa.eu/social/main.jsp?catId=326 (accessed January 4).

Everaert, Luc, and Giovanni Ganelli. 2016. 'Japan: Time to Load a Fourth Arrow—Wage Increases,' *IMFBlog* (blog), March 13, https://blogs.imf.org/2016/03/13/japan-time-to-load-a-fourth-arrow-wage-increases/.

Falkenmark, M., and A. Jägerskog. 2010. 'Sustainability of Transnational Water Agreements in the Face of Socio-Economic and Environmental Change.' In *Transboundary Water Management: Principles and Practice*, edited by A. Earle, A. Jägerskog, and J. Öjendal, 157–71. London: Earthscan.

Fan, C.C. 1999. 'The Vertical and Horizontal Expansions of China's City System.' *Urban Geography* 20: 493-515.

Fang, H., K.N. Eggleston, and J.A. Rizzo. 2012. 'The Returns to Education in China: Evidence from the 1986 Compulsory Education Law.' Working paper No. 18189. National Bureau of Economic Research, Cambridge, MA.

Fannin, Rebecca A. 2019. 'US and China Superpower Race to Lead the Future of Technology Comes Down to $6 Billion.' *CNBC*, May 15, https://www.cnbc.com/2019/05/15/us-and-china-race-to-lead-future-of-tech-now-comes-down-to-6-billion.html.

FinMark Trust. 2008. 'FinScope in Africa: Supporting Financial Access.' Http://www.finscope.co.za/documents/2008/FSAfricaBrochure08.pdf.

Florida, Richard. 2018. 'The Rise of the Rest (of the World).' *CityLab*, April 19, https://www.citylab.com/life/2018/04/the-rise-of-the-rest-of-the-world/558401/.

Fontein, Joost. 2008. 'The Power of Water: Landscape, Water and the State in Southern and Eastern Africa: An Introduction.' *Journal of Southern African Studies* 34(4): 737-56, http://www.jstor.org/stable/40283191.

Fosfuri, A., M. Motta, and T. Rønde. 2001. "Foreign Direct Investment and Spillovers Through Workers Mobility." *Journal of International Economics* 53: 205–22.

Fredland, Richard A. 1998. 'AIDS and Development: An Inverse Correlation?' *The Journal of Modern African Studies* 36(4): 547-68, http://www.jstor.org/stable/161924.

Friedman, Thomas. 2012. *From Beirut to Jeruselum*. Picador: New York.

------. 2000. *The Lexus and the Olive Tree*. Picador: New York.

Fukao, Mitsuhiro. 2003. 'Japan's Lost Decade and Weaknesses in Its Corporate Governance Structure.' In *Japan's Economic Recovery*, edited by Robert M. Stern, 289-325. Edward Elgar Publishing: MA.

Fung, K.C. 1992. 'Some International Properties of Japanese Firms.' *Journal of the Japanese and International Economies* 6: 163-75.

------. 1991. 'Characteristics of Japanese Industrial Groups and Their Potential Impact on US-Japanese Trade.' In *Empirical Studies of Commercial Policy*, edited by Robert Baldwin, 137-68. Cambridge, MA: NBER Books.

------. 1989. 'Unemployment, Profit-sharing and Japan's Economic Success.' *European Economic Review* 33: 783-96.

Gaibulloev, Khusrav, and Todd Sandler. 2019. 'What We Have Learned about Terrorism since 9/11.' *Journal of Economic Literature* 57(2): 275-328, https://doi.org/10.1257/jel.20181444.

Gallardo, Joselito, Korotouomou Ouattara, Bikki Randhawa and William F. Steel. 2005. 'Microfinance Regulation: Lessons from Benin, Ghana, and Tanzania.' *Savings and Development* 29(1): 85-96, http://www.jstor.org/stable/25830885.

Garnaut, Ross, and Ligang Song. 2006. 'China's Resources Demand at the Turning Point.' In *The Turning Point in China's Economic Development*, edited by Ross Garnaut and Ligang Song, 276-93. Canberra: ANU Press, http://www.jstor.org/stable/j.ctt2jbj5d.22/.

Gerein, Nancy, Andrew Gree, and Stephen Pearson. 2006. 'The Implications of Shortages of Health Professionals for Maternal Health in Sub-Saharan Africa.' *Reproductive Health Matters* 14(27): 40-50, http://www.jstor.org/stable/3775848.

Giordano, M., A. Drieschova, J.A. Duncan, Y. Sayama, L. de Stefano, and A.T. Wolf. 2013. 'A Review of the Evolution and State of

Transboundary Freshwater Treaties.' *International Environmental Agreements: Politics, Law and Economics* 13: 1–22.

Glass, A., and K. Saggi. 2002. 'Multinational Firms and Technology Transfer.' *Scandinavian Journal of Economics* 104: 495–514.

Goldman Sachs Equity Research. 2017. 'Guangdong-Hong Kong-Macau: Creating Tomorrow's Greater Bay.' July. The Goldman Sachs Group.

Goldston, Robert. 1967. *The Life and Death of Nazi Germany.* London: Phoenix House.

Gompert, David C., and Bruce H. Stover. 2016. 'Creating a Sino-US Energy Relationship.' *Survival* 58(4).

Goodman, J., and V. Walia. 2007. 'Airtime Transfer Services in Egypt.' In *Vodafone, The Transformational Potential of m-Transactions.* Vodafone Policy Paper Series 6, Section 4, http://www.vodafone.com/m-transactions.

Gow, Jeff, Gavin George, Given Mutinta, Sylvia Mwamba, and Lutungu Ingombe. 2011. 'Health worker shortages in Zambia: An Assessment of Government Responses.' *Journal of Public Health Policy* 32(4): 476-88, http://www.jstor.org/stable/41342699.

Haaker, M. 1999. 'Spillovers from Foreign Direct Investment Through Labour Turnover: The Supply of Management Skills.' Discussion Paper. London School of Economics, London.

Hadfield, Amelia. 'Out of Africa: The Energy-Development Nexus.' In *The European Union in Africa,* edited by Maurizio Carbone, 209-37. Manchester, UK: Manchester University Press.

Hagopian, A., A. Ofosu, A. Fatusi, R. Biritwum, A. Essel, L.G. Hart, and C. Watts. 2005. ' "The Flight of Physicians from West Africa: Views of African Physicians and Implications for Policy.' *Social Science and Medicine* 61(8): 1750-60.

Hale, G., and C. Long. 2011. 'Are There Productivity Spillovers from Foreign Direct Investment in China?' *Pacific Economic Review* 16: 135–53.

Hambira, Wame L., and Jarkko Saarinen. 2015. 'Policy-Makers' Perceptions of the Tourism–Climate Change Nexus: Policy Needs and Constraints in Botswana.' *Development Southern Africa* 32(3): 350-62, http://dx.doi.org/10.1080/0376835X.2015.1010716.

Hamid, Syed A., Jennifer Roberts, and Paul Mosley. 2011. 'Can Micro Health Insurance Reduce Poverty? Evidence from Bangladesh.' *The*

Journal of Risk and Insurance 78(1): 57-82, https://www.jstor.org/stable/23019538.

Harman, Sophie. 2009. 'Fighting HIV and AIDS: Reconfiguring the State?' *Review of Africa Political Economy* 121: 353-67, doi: 10.1080/03056240903210846.

Hegener, M. 1995. 'Telecommunications in Africa via Internet in Particular.'. http://thing.at/texte/hegenerl.html (accessed May 25, 1998).

Helleiner, G.K. 1989. 'Transnational Corporations and Direct Foreign Investment.' In *Handbook of Development Economics*, edited by H. Chenery and T.N. Srinivasan. Amsterdam: North Holland.

Hermes, Niels, and Robert Lensink. 2007. 'Impact of Microfinance: A Critical Survey.' *Economic and Political Weekly* 42(6): 462-5, http://www.jstor.org/stable/4419226.

Herskovits, Jean. 2007. 'Nigeria's Rigged Democracy.' *Foreign Affairs* 86(4): 115-30.

Hertel, Thomas W., and Stephanie D. Rosch. 2010. 'Climate Change, Agriculture, and Poverty.' *Applied Economic Perspectives and Policy* 32(3): 355-85, http://www.jstor.org/stable/40864569.

Hill, Matthew, and Taonga C. Mitimingi. 2019. 'Zambia Faces an Electricity Crisis From Global Warming.' *Bloomberg Businessweek*, October 29, https://www.bloomberg.com/graphics/2019-new-economy-drivers-and-disrupters/zambia.html.

Hilson, Gavin. 2014. '"Constructing" Ethical Mineral Supply Chains in Sub-Saharan Africa: The Case of Malawian Fair Trade Rubies.' *Development and Change* 45(1): 53-78, doi:10.1111/dech.12069.

HKSAR. 2019. 'The Chief Executive's 2019 Policy Address: Embracing Public Health.' Https://www.policyaddress.gov.hk/2019/eng/p36.html.

------. 2018. 'Immunization for Children.' HKSAR Press Release, June 6, https://www.info.gov.hk/gia/general/201806/06/P2018060600702.htm.

HKSAR Census and Statistics Department (HKSAR CSD). 2019. 'Companies in Hong Kong with Parent Companies Located outside HK.' HKSAR CSD, https://www.censtatd.gov.hk/hkstat/sub/sp360.jsp?tableID=133&ID=0&productType=8.

------. 2018a. 'Employed Persons by Monthly Employment Earnings, Age Group and Sex.' Https://www.censtatd.gov.hk/FileManager/EN/Content_1149/T05_02.xls (accessed January 3, 2019).

------. 2018b. Hong Kong Poverty Situation Report 2017. HKSAR CSD: Hong Kong, https://www.censtatd.gov.hk/fd.jsp?file=B9XX0005E2017AN17E0100.pdf&product_id=B9XX0005&lang=1.

------. 2018c. 'Persons from the Mainland of China Having Resided in Hong Kong for Less than 7 Years by Sex and Duration of Residence in Hong Kong.' Https://www.censtatd.gov.hk/FileManager/EN/Content_1149/T01_14.xls (accessed January 3, 2019).

------. 2018d. 'Proportion of Working Population Aged 15 and Over From the Mainland of China Having Resided in Hong Kong for Less than 7 Years by Monthly Income from Main Employment and Sex.' Https://www.censtatd.gov.hk/FileManager/EN/Content_1149/T05_09.xls (accessed January 3, 2019).

------. 2018e. Thematic Household Survey. Report No. 64. Hong Kong: HKSAR CSD, https://www.statistics.gov.hk/pub/B11302642018XXXXB0100.pdf.

------. 2018f. Thematic Report: Persons from the Mainland Having Resided in Hong Kong for Less Than 7 Years. Hong Kong: HKSAR Census and Statistics Department.

------. 2018g. 'Women and Men in Hong Kong—Key Statistics.' HKSAR CSD: Hong Kong, https://www.statistics.gov.hk/pub/B11303032018AN18B0100.pdf.

------ 2017a. Hong Kong Poverty Situation Report 2017. Hong Kong: HKSAR CSD.

------. 2017b. 'Employed Persons by Monthly Employment Earnings, Age Group, and Sex.' Https://www.censtatd.gov.hk/hkstat/sub/gender/employment_earnings/.

HKSAR Department of Health. 2019a. 'Fees and Charges—For General Public." HKSAR DH Family Health Service.' Https://www.fhs.gov.hk/english/fee_cha/general_pub/general_pub.html.

------. 2019b. 'Maternal Mortality Ratio.' HealthyHK, Department of Health, https://www.healthyhk.gov.hk/phisweb/en/healthy_facts/health_indicators/maternal_mortality_ratio/.

HKSAR Education Bureau (HKSAR Ed). 2018a. 'Government Expenditure on Education.' Https://www.edb.gov.hk/en/about-edb/publications-stat/figures/gov-expenditure.html.

------. 2018b. 'Secondary Education.' Https://www.edb.gov.hk/en/about-edb/publications-stat/figures/sec.html.

HKSAR Environment Bureau. 2016. Hong Kong Biodiversity Strategy and Action Plan 2016-2021. Hong Kong: HKSAR Environment Bureau.

HKSAR Legislative Council (LegCo). 2019. 'Members' Biographies.' Https://www.legco.gov.hk/general/english/members/index.html.

HKSAR Office of the Communications Authority (HKSAR OCA). 2018. 'Key Communications Statistics.' Https://www.ofca.gov.hk/en/media_focus/data_statistics/key_stat (accessed July 5).

HKSAR Social Welfare Department (HKSAR SWD). 2018. 'Statistics on Child Abuse, Spouse/Cohabitant Battering and Sexual Violence Cases.' Https://www.swd.gov.hk/vs/english/stat.html.

HKSAR Trade and Industry Department. 2019. '2016/18 SME Mentorship Programme.' Https://www.success.tid.gov.hk/english/sme_men_pro/mentorship16.html (accessed January 4).

HKSAR Water Supplies Department. 2019. 'Hong Kong Drinking Water Standards.' HKSAR Water Supplies Department, https://www.wsd.gov.hk/en/core-businesses/water-quality/my-drinking-water-quality/hong-kong-drinking-water-standards/index.html#metals.

Hong Kong Mortgage Corporation. 2019. 'Microfinance Scheme Statistics.' Http://www.hkmc.com.hk/files/statistic_file/1/1231/mf_key_stat_eng.pdf.

Hong Kong Police Force. 2019. 'Crime Statistics Comparison.' https://www.police.gov.hk/ppp_en/09_statistics/csc.html (accessed January 20, 2020).

Hopkinson, Lisa. 2012. 'Developing a Biodiversity Strategy and Action Plan for Hong Kong.' Discussion Paper, Civic Exchange, Hong Kong.

Hopkinson, Lisa, and Rachel Stern. 2002. 'Wild but Not Free: An Economc Valuation of the Benefits of Nature Conservation in Hong Kong.' Discussion Paper. Civic Exchange, Hong Kong.

Hussain, A., P. Lanjouw, and N. Stern. 1994. 'Income Inequalities in China: Evidence from Household Survey Data.' World Development 22: 1947–57.

Hyde-Clarke, N. 2006. 'The Urban Digital Divide: A Comparative Analysis of Internet Cafés in Johannesburg, South Africa.' *Review*

of African Political Economy 33(107): 150-56, http://www.jstor.org/
stable/4007119.

Ilahiane, Hsain, and John Sherry. 2009. 'Economic and Social Effects
of Mobile Phone Use in Morocco.' *Ethnology* 48(2): 85-98, http://
www.jstor.org/stable/20754014.

Indonesian Ministry of Health and United Nations Population Fund.
2012. 'Disparity of Access and Quality: Review of Maternal Mortality
in Five Regions in Indonesia.' Indonesian Ministry of Health and
United Nations Population Fund, https://indonesia.unfpa.org/sites/
default/files/pub-pdf/Disparity_of_Access_Quality_Review_of_
Maternal_Mortality_in_5_Regions_in_Indonesia.pdf.

International Telecommunication Union. 2009. Information Society Statistical
Profiles 2009: Africa. Geneva: International Telecommunications
Union.

------. 2008. World Telecommunication Indicators Database. Geneva:
International Telecommunications Union.

Jack, William, and Tavneet Suri. 2009 'Mobile Money: The Economics of
M-Pesa.' http://www.mit.edu/~tavneet/M-PESA.pdf.

Jack, William, Tavneet Suri, and Robert Townsend. 2010. 'Monetary
Theory and Electronic Money: Reflections on the Kenyan
Experience.' *Economic Quarterly* 96(1): 83-122.

Jain, Purnendra, and Mito Takamichi. 2016. 'The Institutionalization of
Energy Cooperation in Asia.' In *Asia Designs*, edited by Saadia M.
Pekkanen, 135-157. Ithaca: Cornell University Press, http://www.
jstor.org/stable/10.7591/j.ctt1d2dnn1.12/.

Jensen, Robert. 2007. 'The Digital Provide: Information (Technology),
Market Performance, and Welfare in the South Indian Fisheries
Sector.' *Quarterly Journal of Economics* 122(3): 879-924.

Jiang, Xu, A.G.O. Yeh, and Jiang Xu. 2008. 'Regional Cooperation
in the Pan-Pearl River Delta: A Formulaic Aspiration or A New
Imagination?' *Built Environment* (1978-) 34(4): 408-26.

Johnson, Susan, and Steven Arnold. 2012. 'Inclusive Financial Markets:
Is Transformation Under Way in Kenya?' *Development Policy Review*
30(6): 719-748.

Jorion, Philip, and Gaiyan Zhang. 2009. 'Credit Contagion from
Counterparty Risk.' *The Journal of Finance* 64(5): 2053-87, https://
www.jstor.org/stable/27735165.

Juma, Calestous. 2015. 'What is Africa's Agricultural Potential?' *World Economic Forum Agenda*, September 3, https://www.weforum.org/agenda/2015/09/what-is-africas-agriculture-potential/.

Kalicki, Jan H. 2001. 'Caspian Energy at the Crossroads.' *Foreign Affairs* 80(5): 120-34, http://www.heinonline.org. eproxy1.lib.hku.hk/HOL/Page?handle=hein.journals/fora80&size=2&collection=journals&id=888.Kennedy 2011.

Kaplan, R.D. 1994. 'The Coming Anarchy: Globalization and the Challenges of a New Century—A Reader.' Indiana University Press: Bloomington.

Kapstein, Ethan B. 2009. 'Africa's Capitalist Revolution.' *Foreign Affairs* 88(4): 119-130.

Katlama, Christine, Steven G. Deeks, Brigitte Autran, Javier Martinez-Picado, Jan van Lunzen, Christine Rouzioux, Michael Miller et al. 2013. 'Barriers to a Cure for HIV: New Ways to Target and Eradicate HIV-1 Reservoirs.' *Lancet* 381: 2109-17, http://dx.doi.org/10.1016/S0140-6736(13)60104-X.

Kats, Rimma. 2018. 'Smartphone Usage in Japan Is Growing, but Feature Phones Arenít Going Away.' *eMarketer*, May 9, https://www.emarketer.com/content/smartphone-usage-in-japan-is-growing-but-feature-phones-aren-t-going-away.

Kaufmann, L. 1997. 'A Model of Spillovers Through Labour Recruitment.' *International Economic Journal* 11: 13–34.

Kaufmann, Robert K., Stephane Dees, Pavlos Karadeloglou, and Marcelo Sánchez. 2004. 'Does OPEC Matter? An Econometric Analysis of Oil Prices.' *The Energy Journal* 25(4): 67-90, http://www.jstor.org/stable/41323358/.

Kawakami, Tamami. 2018. 'Japan Version of Grameen Bank Launched to Help People Out of Poverty.' *The Manichi*, September 14, https://mainichi.jp/english/articles/20180914/p2a/00m/0na/007000c.

Kennedy, Andrew B. 2011. 'China's Petroleum Predicament: Challenges and Opportunities in Beijing's Search for Energy Security.' In *Rising China: Global Challenges and Opportunities*, edited by Jane Golley and Ligang Song, 121-135. Canberra: ANU Press, http://www.jstor.org/stable/j.ctt24hbk1.15/.Kissane 2015.

Kenny, Charles. 2003. 'Development's False Divide.' *Foreign Policy* January-February, http://www.jstor.org/stable/3183524.

Kissane, Carolyn. 2015. 'The Quest for Energy Security in the Central Asian "Neighborhood".' In *China, The United States*, and *The Future of Central Asia*, edited by David B.H. Denoon, 366-94. New York: NYU Press, http://www.jstor.org/stable/j.ctt15vt94p.17/.

Knight, P.T. 1995. 'The Telematics Revolution in Africa and the World Bank Group.' Http://www.knight-moore.com/html/telematicsin_africa.html (accessed April 25, 1998).

Kung, J., and Y. Lee. 2001. 'So What if There is Income Inequality? The Distributive Consequence of Nonfarm Employment in Rural China.' *Economic Development and Cultural Change* 50: 19–46.

Langa, G. 2002. 'Information and Communication Technology.' In *Public Attitudes in Contemporary South Africa*. Cape Town: Human Sciences Research Council.

Lanzafame, Matteo. 2014. 'Temperature, Rainfall, and Economic Growth in Africa.' *Empirical Economics* 46: 1-18, doi:10.1007/s00181-012-0664-3.

Lardy, N.R. 1995. 'The Role of Foreign Trade and Investment in China's Economic Transformation.' *The China Quarterly* 144: 1065–1082.

Largue, Pamela. 2019. 'Sub-Saharan Africa Requires Urgent Investment to Meet Energy Goals.' *ESI Africa*, October 23, https://www.esi-africa.com/industry-sectors/finance-and-policy/sub-saharan-africa-requires-urgent-investment-to-meet-energy-goals/.

Lee, Siu-Yau, and Kee-Lee Chou. 2016. 'Trends in Elderly Poverty in Hong Kong: A Decomposition Analysis.' *Social Indicators Research* 129: 551-64, doi:10.1007/s11205-015-1120-5.

Lee, Y.F. 2002. 'Tackling Cross-Border Environmental Problems in Hong Kong: Initial Responses and Institutional Constraints.' *The China Quarterly* 172: 986-1009.

Levenstein, Margaret C., and Valerie Y. Suslow. 2006. 'What Determines Cartel Success?' *Journal of Economic Literature* 44(1): 43-95, http://www.jstor.org/stable/30032296/.

Levin, Benjamin. 1990. 'Tuition Fees and University Accessibility.' *Canadian Public Policy* 16(1): 51-59, https://www.jstor.org/stable/3551258.

Levin, Richard C. 2010. 'Top of the Class.' *Foreign Affairs* 89(3): 63-75 http://web.a.ebscohost.com.eproxy1.lib.hku.hk/ehost/detail/detail?sid=0d0fef7f-2189-45db-aeba 200b9f0bdf3%40sessionmgr

4006&vid=2&hid=4112&bdata=JnNpdGU9ZWhvc3QtbGl2ZSZz
Y29wZT1zaXRl#AN=49154216&db=mth.

Levine, Ross. 2005 'Finance and Growth: Theory and Evidence.' In *Handbook of Economic Growth*, ed. Philippe Aghion and Steven Durlauf. The Netherlands: Elsevier Science.

Lewis, Leo, Tom Mitchell, and Yuan Yang. 2017. 'Is China's Economy Turning Japanese?' *Financial Times*, May 29, https://www.ft.com/content/a3564812-363c-11e7-99bd-13beb0903fa3? mhq5j=e3.

Lin, J., F. Cai, and Z. Li. 2003. *The China Miracle: Development Strategy and Economic Reform*. Hong Kong: Chinese University Press.

Liu, J.D. 2001. 'On Administrative Organization and Innovation of Management Model in Metropolitan Region in Mainland China—Reform on Administrative Setting in the Pearl River Delta.' *Economic Geography* 21(2): 201-212.

Loconto, Allison M., and Emmanuel F. Simbua. 2012. 'Making Room for Smallholder Cooperatives in Tanzanian Tea Production: Can Fairtrade Do That?' *Journal of Business Ethics* 108(4): 451-665, http://www.jstor.org/stable/23259284.

Los Angeles Times. 2018. *Mapping L.A.* http://maps.latimes.com/neighborhoods.

Lucas, Adrienne M. 2013. 'The Impact of Malaria Eradication on Fertility.' *Economic Development and Cultural Change* 61(3): 607-31, http://www.jstor.org/stable/10.1086/669261.

Luft, Gal. 2016. 'China's Infrastructure Play: Why Washington Should Accept the New Silk Road.' *Foreign Affairs*.

Lusaka Times. 2019. 'FINCA Zambia Borrows $3.5m from Grameen Credit Agricole Foundation for Microfinance Lending.'January 8, https://www.lusakatimes.com/2019/01/08/finca-zambia-borrows-3-5m-from-grameen-credit-agricole-foundation-for-microfinancelending/.

Mahadea, Darma. 2012. 'Prospects of Entrepreneurship to the Challenge of Job Creation in South Africa.' *Journal of Developmental Entrepreneurship* 17(4): 1-17, doi: 10.1142/S1084946712500203.

Manahan, Mary Ann. 2016. 'In Deep Water: Confronting the Climate and Water Crises.' In *The Secure and the Dispossessed*, edited by Nick Buxton and Ben Hayes. London: Pluto Press, http://www.jstor.org/stable/j.ctt18gzdk7.15.

Mann, Joseph. 2009. 'Russia's Policy Towards OPEC.' *Middle Eastern Studies* 45(6): 985-1005, http://www.jstor.org/stable/40647181/. Morse and Richard 2002.

Maseland, Robbert, and Albert de Vaal. 2002. 'How Fair is Fair Trade?' *De Economist* 150(3): 251-72.

Mastel, Greg. 2006. 'Why We Should Expand Trade Adjustment Assistance.' *Challenge* 49(4): 42-57.

McCarthy, Niall. 2019. 'Report: India Lifted 271 Million People Out of Poverty in a Decade.' *Forbes*, July 12, https://www.forbes.com/sites/niallmccarthy/2019/07/12/report-india-lifted-271-million-people-out-of-poverty-in-a-decade-infographic/#a6ddad92284b.

McDade, B.E., and A. Spring. 2005. 'The "New Generation of African Entrepreneurs": Networking to Change the Climate for Business and Private Sector-Led Development.' *Entrepreneurship and Regional Development* 17(1): 17-42.

McGeer, Bonnie. 2018. 'Grameen America Eyes Banks in Ambitious Push to Expand Microlending Effort.' *American Banker*, March 1, https://www.americanbanker.com/news/grameen-america-eyes-banks-in-ambitious-push-to-expand-microlending-effort.

McMahon, Patrice C. 2017. 'Cooperation Rules: Insights on Water and Conflict from International Relations.' In *Water Security in the Middle East*, edited by Jean Axelrad Cahan. London: Anthem Press, http://www.jstor.org/stable/j.ctt1jktqmk.7.

McVay, Ken. 2019. *The Nizkor Project: Nazi Conspiracy and Aggression*, Volume II, Chapter XVL, http://www.nizkor.org/hweb/imt/nca/nca-02/nca-02-16-12-index.html.

Meng, X. 2004. 'Economic Restructuring and Income Inequality in Urban China.' *Review of Income and Wealth* 50: 357–79, doi:10.1111/j.0034–6586.2004.00130.x.

Merrington, Louise. 2014. 'India and China: Strategic Engagements in Central Asia.' In *The Engagement of India*, edited by Ian Hall, 89-110. Washington, D.C.: Georgetown University Press, http://www.jstor.org/stable/j.ctt7zswn9.9/.

Miller, Cynthia, Rhiannon Miller, Nandita Verma, Nadine Dechausay, Edith Yang, Timothy Rudd, Jonathan Rodriguez, and Sylvie Honig. 2016. *Effects of a Modified Conditional Cash Transfer Program in Two American Cities*. New York: MDRC, https://www.mdrc.org/sites/

default/files/CEOSIF_Family_Rewards%20Report-Web-Final_
FR.pdf.

'Models of Mobile Banking.' 2010. *Economic and Political Weekly* January
30-February 5, http://www.jstor.org/stable/25664056.

Molony, Thomas. 2008. 'Running out of Credit: The Limitations of
Mobile Telephony in a Tanzanian Agricultural Marketing System.'
The Journal of Modern African Studies 46(4): 637-58, http://www.
jstor.org/stable/30224909.

Morawczynski, Olga, and Mark Pickens. 2009. 'Poor People Using
Mobile Financial Services: Observations on Customer Usage and
Impact from M-PESA.' CGAP Brief, http://www.cgap.org/gm/
document-1.9.36723/BR_Poor_People _Using_Mobile_Financial_
Services.pdf.

Morse, Edward L. 2014. 'Welcome to the Revolution: Why Shale is the
Next Shale.' *Foreign Affairs* 93(3).

Mukhopadhaya, Pundarik. 2013. 'Trends in Income Inequality in China:
The Effects of Various Sources of Income.' *Journal of the Asia Pacific
Economy* 18(2):304-17, http://dx.doi.org/10.1080/13547860.2013.
778158.

Munemo, Jonathan. 2012. 'Entrepreneurship in Developing Countries:
Is Africa Different?' *Journal of Developmental Entrepreneurship* 17(1):
1-12, doi:10.1142/S1084946712500045.

Naughton, Barry. 2017. 'Is China Socialist?' *Journal of Economic
Perspectives* 31(1): 3-24.

Neumann, Jeannette. 2019. 'Bank of Spain Cuts Economic Growth
Forecasts through 2021.' *Bloomberg*, September 24, https://www.
bloomberg.com/news/articles/2019-09-24/bank-of-spain-cuts-
economic-growth-forecasts-through-2021.

Noël, Pierre. 2016. 'The New Oil Regime.' *Survival* 58(5): 71-82, doi:
10.1080/00396338.2016.1231532.

Norwegian Petroleum. 2020. 'The Government's Revenues.'Https://
www.norskpetroleum.no/en/economy/governments-revenues/
(accessed January 20, 2020).

Nyaga, Joseph K. 2014. 'Mobile Banking Services in the East African
Community (EAC): Challenges to the Existing Legislative and
Regulatory Frameworks.' *Journal of Information Policy* 4: 270-95,
http://www.jstor.org/stable/10.5325/jinfopoli.4.2014.0270.

Odhiambo, Rhoda, 2017. 'Zambia Hospitals Overwhelmed with Too Many Patients, Fewer Doctors.' *Deutsche Welle*, August 28, https://www.dw.com/en/zambia-hospitals-overwhelmed-with-too-many-patients-fewer-doctors/a-40146334.

Ohmae, Kenichi. 1993. 'The Rise of the Region State.' *Foreign Affairs* 72(2): 78-87, https://search-proquest-com.eproxy2.lib.hku.hk/docview/214279549?accountid=14548.

Okey, Mawusse K.N. 2016. Corruption and Emigration of Physicians from Africa.' *Journal of Economic Development* 41(2): 27-52.

Olano, Gabriel. 2019a. 'Grab Enters Micro-Insurance, Other Financial Services in Singapore.' *Insurance Business*, March 21, https://www.insurancebusinessmag.com/asia/news/breaking-news/grab-enters-microinsurance-other-financial-services-in-singapore-162734.aspx.

------. 2019b. 'Indonesia Has Low Insurance Penetration but High Profitability—Report.' *Insurance Business*, July 28,https://www.insurancebusinessmag.com/asia/news/breaking-news/indonesia-has-low-insurance-penetration-but-high-profitability--report-107316.aspx.

------. 2016. 'Allianz Life Indonesia Launches Microinsurance Product.' *Insurance Business*, November 3, https://www.insurancebusinessmag.com/asia/news/breaking-news/allianz-life-indonesia-launches-microinsurance-product-50082.aspx.

Onazi, Oche. 2013. *Human Rights from Community*. Edinburgh, UK: Edinburgh University Press, http://www.jstor.org/stable/10.3366/j.ctt5hh359.10.

OPEC. 2020. 'Equatorial Guinea Facts and Figures.' Https://www.opec.org/opec_web/en/about_us/4319.htm (accessed January 20

------. 2019. 'OPEC Monthly Oil Market Report—September 2019.' Vienna: OPEC.

------. 2018. 'Saudi Arabia Facts and Figures.' Organization of the Petroleum Exporting Countries. https://www.opec.org/opec_web/en/about_us/169.htm (accessed December 25).

------. 2017. 'OPEC Share of World Crude Oil Reserves, 2016.' Http://www.opec.org/opec_web/en/data_graphs/330.htm (assessed July 13).

Oxfam Hong Kong. 2018. 'Hong Kong Inequality Report.' Oxfam Hong Kong: Hong Kong, https://www.oxfam.org.hk/en/f/news_and_publication/16372/Oxfam_inequality%20report_Eng_FINAL_3Oct.pdf.

Pachauri, Shonali, and Daniel Spreng. 2004. 'Energy Use and Energy Access in Relation to Poverty.' *Economic and Political Weekly* 39(3): 271-8, http://www.jstor.org/stable/4414526.

Packard, Randall M. 2009. '"Roll Back Malaria, Roll in Development?" Reassessing the Economic Burden of Malaria.' *Population and Development Review* 35(1): 53-87, http://www.jstor.org/stable/25487642.

Panagariya, Arvind. 2008. *India: The Emerging Giant.* Oxford: Oxford University Press.

Peberdy, Sally. 2000. 'Mobile Entrepreneurship: Informal Sector Cross-Border Trade and Street Trade in South Africa.' *Development Southern Africa* 17(2): 201-19.

Peng, C.H., Paul Yip, and Y.W. Law. 2018. 'Intergenerational Earnings Mobility and Returns to Education in Hong Kong: A Developed Society with High Economic Inequality.' *Social Indicators Research*: 1-24, doi: http://dx.doi.org/10.1007/s11205-018-1968-2.

Pickens, Sue, Paul Boumbulian, Ron J. Anderson, Samuel Ross, and Sharon Phillips. 2002. 'Community-Oriented Primary Care in Action: A Dallas Story.' *American Journal of Public Health* 92(11): 1728-32.

Piper, Karen. 2014. *The Price of Thirst.* Minneapolis: University of Minnesota Press, http://www.jstor.org/stable/10.5749/j.ctt7zw6d6.9.

Pohl, Benjamin, and Ashok Swain. 2017. 'Leveraging Diplomacy for Resolving Transboundary Water Problems.' In *Water Diplomacy in Action*, edited by Shafiqul Islam and Kaveh Madani. London: Anthem Press, http://www.jstor.org/stable/j.ctt1jktqgh.8.

Pohly, Michael, and James Vore. 2002. 'Insurers Eye Derivatives for Credit Risk.' *National Underwriter*, April 15, https://search.proquest.com/docview/228575544?accountid=37892.

Pomfred, R. 1997. 'Growth and Transition: Why Has China's Performance Been So Different?' *Journal of Comparative Economics* 25: 422–40.

Porteous, David. 2006. 'The Enabling Environment for Mobile Banking in Africa.' Paper Commissioned by United Kingdom Department for International Development (DFIP), http://www.bankablefrontier.com/assets/ee.mobil.banking.report.v3.1.pdf.

Preisendörfer, Peter, Ansgar Bitz, and Frans J. Bezuidenhout. 2012. 'In Search of Black Entrepreneurship: Why is There a Lack of

Entrepreneurial Activity among the Black Population in South Africa.' *Journal of Developmental Entrepreneurship* 17(1): 1-18, doi:10.1142/S1084946712500069.

Raphael, Dennis. 2015. 'The Political Economy of Health: A Research Agenda for Addressing Health Inequalities in Canada.' *Canadian Public Policy / Analyse de Politiques* 41(2): S17-S25.

------. 1998. 'Public Health Responses to Health Inequalities.' *Canadian Journal of Public Health / Revue Canadienne de Santé Publique* 89(6): 380-81

Rasella, Davide, Rosana Aquino, and Mauricio Lima Barreto. 2013. 'Impact of Income Inequality on Life Expectancy in a Highly Unequal Developing Country: The Case of Brazil.' *Journal of Epidemiology and Community Health* 67(8): 661-66.

Raval, Anjli. 2015. 'Russia Takes Over as Top Oil Supplier to China.' *Financial Times*, June 24, https://www.ft.com/content/9eda3756-19bc-11e5-8201-cbdb03d71480?mhq5j=e3.

Ravallion, M., and S. Chen. 2007. 'China's (Uneven) Progress against Poverty.' *Journal of Development Economics* 82: 1–42.

Rawlings, Samantha B. 2016. 'Gender, Race, and Heterogeneous Effects of Epidemic Malaria on Human Capital and Income.' *Economic Development and Cultural Change* 64(3): 509-43, doi:10.1086/684965.

Renaud, P. 1996. 'Un Exemple Burkinabe.' *Le Monde Diplomatique*, February 1, http://www.monde-diplomatique.fr/md/1996/02/RENAUD/2326.html.

------. n.d. 'Vers une Desertification Technologique du Sud?' http://antares.rio.net/forum/midrand/iridium.htm (accessed May 23, 1998).

Renaud, P., and Torres, A. 1995. 'Internet en Afrique: Partir de l'Existant et Developper les Capacites Locales.' http://antares.rio.net/interafrique/perso/publications/Cotonou95.html (accessed May 25, 1998).

Reuters. 2019. 'Gas Demand Growth in China Slows as Economy Hits Consumption.' Https://www.scmp.com/news/china/politics/article/3032974/gas-demand-growth-china-slows-economy-hits-consumption (accessed January 22, 2020).

Riccio, James, and Cynthia Miller. 2016. *New York's First Conditional Cash Transfer Program*. New York: MDRC, https://www.mdrc.org/sites/default/files/NYC_First_Conditional_Cash_Transfer_Full_Report_0.pdf.

Robst, John. 2001. 'A Note on the Relationship between Medical Care Resources and Mortality.' *Applied Economic Letters* 8: 737-9.

Rodriguez-Clare, A. 1996. 'Multinationals, Linkages, and Economic Development.' *American Economic Review* 86: 852–73.

Roemer, John E., and Pedro Rosa Dias. 2016. 'Barefoot and Footloose Doctors: Optimal Resource Allocation in Developing Countries with Medical Migration.' *Social Choice Welfare* 46: 335-58, doi:10.1007/s00355-015-0916-1.

Rogers, Jim. 1998. 'The Internet: Emerging Technologies in Two West African Countries.' *Educational Technology Research and Development* 46(3): 102-09, http://www.jstor.org/stable/30221068.

Roller, Lars-Hendrik, and Leonard Waverman. 2001. 'Telecommunications Infra structure and Economic Development: A Simultaneous Approach.' *American Economic Review* 91(4): 909-23.

Reuters. 2017. 'Russia Beats Saudi as Top China Oil Supplier for Second Month.' May 23.

Sachs, J., and P. Malaney. 2002. 'The Economic and Social Burden of Malaria.' *Nature* 415: 680-85.

Samuel, J., N. Shah, and W. Hadingham. 2005. 'Mobile Communications in South Africa, Tanzania, and Egypt: Results from Community and Business Surveys.' Http://www.vodafone.com/etc/medialib/attachments/cr_downloads.Par.78351.File.dat/GPP_SIM_paper_3.pdf.

Scheiber, Noam. 2002. 'Where the Oil Is.' *New York Times,* November 10, https://mobile.nytimes.com/2002/11/10/magazine/the-way-we-live-now-11-10-02-economics-of-oil-where-the-oil-is.html.

Schmeier, Susanne. 2013. *Governing International Watercourses: River Basin Organizations and the Sustainable Governance of Internationally Shared Rivers and Lakes.* New York: Routledge.

Shei, Amie, Federico Costa, Mitermayer G. Reis, and Albert I. Ko. 2014. 'The Impact of Brazil's Bolsa Família Conditional Cash Transfer Program on Children's Health Care Utilization and Health Outcomes.' *BMC International Health and Human Rights* 14(10).

Sheives, Kevin. 2006. 'China Turns West: Beijing's Contemporary Strategy Towards Central Asia.' *Pacific Affairs* 79(2): 205-24, http://www.jstor.org/stable/40022689/.

Sheng, Andrew, and Geng Xiao. 2017. 'The Promise of China's Pearl River Delta.' *Project Syndicate*, May 26, https://www.project-syndicate.org/

commentary/hong-kong-china-development-by-andrew-sheng-and-xiao-geng-2017-05.

------. 2014. 'Piketty with Chinese Characteristics.' July 2, https://www.project-syndicate.org/commentary/andrew-sheng-and-geng-xiao-apply-to-china-thomas-piketty-s-framework-for-understanding-the-country-s-rising-income-inequality.

Simon, Matt. 2019. 'The Sea Is Consuming Jakarta, and Its People Aren't Insured.' *Wired.com*, July 19, https://www.wired.com/story/jakarta-insurance/.

Sito, Peggy. 2018. 'From Plastic Flowers to Property and Ports: How Li Ka-shing Became a Symbol of Hong Kong.' *South China Morning Post*, March 16, https://www.scmp.com/business/companies/article/2137587/plastic-flowers-property-and-ports-how-li-ka-shing-became-symbol.

Soares, Fabio Veras, Rafael Perez Ribas and Rafael Guerreiro Osurio. 2010. ‚Evaluating the Impact of Brazil's Bosa Familia: Cash Transfer Programs in Comparative Perspective.' *Latin American Research Review* 45(2): 173-90.

Soldatkin, Vladimir. 2017. 'Russian Oil Output Declines, Almost at Global Pact Target.' Reuters, May 2, http://www.reuters.com/article/us-russia-energy-production-idUSKBN17Y0EQ.

Sorbonne University. 2018. *Guide des Associations et des Ateliers Artistiques UPMC*. Sorbonne University.

South China Morning Post. 2017. 'Medical Errors Must be Taken Seriously.' August 25, https://www.scmp.com/comment/insight-opinion/article/2108197/medical-errors-must-be-taken-seriously.

Stacey, Nevzer. 1998. 'Social Benefits of Education.' *The Annals of the American Academy of Political and Social Science* 559: 54-63. https://www.jstor.org/stable/1049606.

Starr, Joyce R. 1991. 'Water Wars.' *Foreign Policy* 82: 17-36, http://www.jstor.org/stable/1148639.

Statista. 2019a. 'Digital Payments.' *Statista*, https://www.statista.com/outlook/296/109/digital-payments/united-states.

------. 2019b. 'Number of Mobile Cell Phone Subscriptions in China from Janurary 2018 to February 2019 (in Millions).' *Statista*, https://www.statista.com/statistics/278204/china-mobile-users-by-month/.

Statista. 2019c. 'Number of students in Germany in the winter semester of 2018/2019, by type of university.' Https://www.statista.com/statistics/584067/student-numbers-by-type-of-university-germany/.

Statistics Canada. 2019. 'Labour Force Characteristics by Aboriginal Group and Educational Attainment.' *Statistics Canada*, https://www150.statcan.gc.ca/t1/tbl1/en/tv.action?pid=1410035901.

------. 2018a. 'Methods Used to Look for Work by Aboriginal Identity, Unemployed.' *Statistics Canada*, https://www150.statcan.gc.ca/t1/tbl1/en/tv.action?pid=4110001201&pickMembers%5B0%5D=1.1&pickMembers%5B1%5D=3.3&pickMembers%5B2%5D=5.2&pickMembers%5B3%5D=6.2.

------. 2018b. 'Reasons for Difficulty in Finding Work by Aboriginal Identity, Unemployed.' https://www150.statcan.gc.ca/t1/tbl1/en/tv.action?pid=4110001401&pickMembers%5B0%5D=1.1&pickMembers%5B1%5D=3.3&pickMembers%5B2%5D=5.1&pickMembers%5B3%5D=6.1.

------. 2016. 'Distribution of Population Aged 25 to 64 (Total and with Aboriginal Identity), by Sex and Educational Attainment.' Https://www150.statcan.gc.ca/t1/tbl1/en/tv.action?pid=3710010001.

Statistics SA. 2005. 'Table 1: 2001 Income Category by Geography per Person Weighted.' Accessed August 4, 2005 from Statistical Information Services, Pretoria.

Stern, Michelle. 2019. 'Market-Based Pricing Disappearing on Blue-Chip US Loans.' *Loan Pricing Corporation*, July 19, https://www.reuters.com/article/cds-bristolmyers/market-based-pricing-disappearing-on-blue-chip-us-loans-idUSL2N24J0QM.

Stetter, S. et al. 2011. 'Conflicts about Water: Securitizations in a Global Context.' *Cooperation and Conflict* 46(4): 441–59.

Stewart, Matthew. 2018. 'The 9.9 Percent is the New American Aristocracy.' *The Atlantic*, https://www.theatlantic.com/magazine/archive/2018/06/the-birth-of-a-new-american-aristocracy/559130/.

Stigler, George J. 1961. 'The Economics of Information.' *Journal of Political Economy* 69(3): 213-25.

Stiglitz, Joseph E. 2013. 'Japan is a Model, Not a Cautionary Tale,' *The Great Divide*, June 9, https://opinionator.blogs.nytimes.com/2013/06/09/japan-is-a-model-not-a-cautionary-tale/.

Stoddart, Paul. 2011. 'Development through Fair Trade: Candour or Deception?' *Journal of Economic Affairs* March 8, 2011.

Stremlau, John. 2000. 'Ending Africa's Wars.' *Foreign Affairs* 79(4): 117-132.

Sun, Nikki. 2019. 'Hong Kong Property Patriarch Leaves Sons with $64bn Question.' *Nikkei Asian Review*, May 17, https://asia.nikkei.com/Spotlight/Asian-Family-Conglomerates/Hong-Kong-property-patriarch-leaves-sons-with-64bn-question.

Superville, Darlene. 2018. 'Trump to Sign Bill Extending HIV/AIDS Program, Pence Says.' *Associated Press*, November 30, https://apnews.com/211f31bcfa8d495192edb82243d662e2.

Swain, Ashok. 2004. *Managing Water Conflict: Asia, Africa and the Middle East*. London: Routledge.

Swain, A., R.B. Swain, A. Themnér, and F. Krampe. 2011. *Climate Change and the Risk of Violent Conflicts in Southern Africa*. Pretoria: Global Crisis Solutions.

Sylla, Ndongo S. 2014. *The Fair Trade Scandal*. London: Pluto Press, http://www.jstor.org/stable/j.ctt183p3b4.9.

Tan, Lorna. 2017. 'Better Insurance Cover for the Low-Income.' *The Straits Times*, June 4, https://www.straitstimes.com/singapore/better-insurance-cover-for-the-low-income.

Taub, Ben. 2017. 'Lake Chad: The World's Most Complex Humanitarian Disaster.' *The New Yorker*, November 27, https://www.newyorker.com/magazine/2017/12/04/lake-chad-the-worlds-most-complex-humanitarian-disaster.

Telhami, Shibley, and Fiona Hill. 2002. 'America's Vital Stakes in Saudi Arabia.' *Foreign Affairs* 81(6): 167-78, http://www.heinonline.org.eproxy1.lib.hku.hk/HOL/Page?handle=hein.journals/fora81&size=2&collection=journals&id=1060.

Teljeur, Ethèl, Mayuree Chetty, and Morné Hendriksz. 2017. 'Africa's Prospects for Infrastructure Development and Regional Integration: Energy Sector.' In *Infrastructure in Africa*, edited by Mthuli Ncube and Charles L. Lufumpa, 185-256. Bristol, UK: Policy Press, http://www.jstor.org/stable/j.ctt1t88xmm.15.

Tepperman, Jonathan. 2016. 'Brazil's Antipoverty Breakthrough.' *Foreign Affairs* 95(1).

Tessman, Brock, and Wojtek Wolfe. 2011. 'Great Powers and Strategic Hedging: The Case of Chinese Energy Security Strategy.'

International Studies Review 13(2): 214-40, http://www.jstor.org/stable/23017154/.

The Economist. 2019a. 'Free Public Transport in Estonia.' May 9, https://www.economist.com/europe/2019/05/09/free-public-transport-inestonia.

------. 2019b. 'Get Used to It.' July 20.

------. 2019c. 'How to Defeat AIDS, Malaria, and Tuberculosis.' October 10, https://www.economist.com/science-and-technology/2019/10/10/how-to-defeat-aids-malaria-and-tuberculosis.

------. 2019d. 'New Research Traces the Intricate Links between Policy and Politics.' May 9, https://www.economist.com/finance-andeconomics/2019/05/09/new-research-traces-the-intricate-linksbetween-policy-and-politics.

------. 2019e. 'Terminal Degrees.' July 20.

------. 2018a. 'How Developing Countries Weave Social Safety Nets.' April 14, https://www.economist.com/finance-andeconomics/2018/04/14/how-developing-countries-weave-socialsafety-nets.

------. 2018b. 'How a Small African Nation is Beating AIDS.' March 1, https://www.economist.com/middle-east-and-africa/2018/03/01/how-a-small-african-nation-is-beating-aids.

------. 2018c. 'Income-Share Agreements Are a Novel Way to Pay Tuition Fees.' July 19, https://www.economist.com/finance-andeconomics/2018/07/19/income-share-agreements-are-a-novel-wayto-pay-tuition-fees.

------. 2018d. 'Justin Trudeau's Climate Plans are Stuck in Alberta's Tar Sands.' December 13.

------. 2017a. 'A China that Works.' April 8, https://search.proquest.com/docview/1894701040?accountid=14548.

------. 2017b. 'Come Closer.' April 8, https://search.proquest.com/docview/1894701437?accountid=14548.

------. 2017c. 'Jewel in the Crown.' April 8, https://search.proquest.com/docview/1894701117?accountid=14548.

------. 2017d. 'Robots in the Rustbelt.' April 8, https://search.proquest.com/docview/1894701385?accountid=14548.

------. 2016a. 'The Class Ceiling.' June 4, https://www.economist.com/.../china/21699923-chinas-education-system-deeply-unfairclass-ceiling.

------. 2016b. 'Continental Disconnect; Telecommunications in Africa.' December 10, https://search-proquest-com.eproxy1.lib.hku.hk/docview/1847523512?accountid=14548.

------. 2016c. 'Of Profits and Prophesies.' February 6.

------. 2016d. 'Our Bulldozers, Our Rules.' July 2.

------. 2016e. 'Overhyped, Underappreciated.' July 30.

------. 2016f. 'A Report Shows HIV in Retreat in Many African Countries.' December 1. https://www.economist.com/middle-eastand-africa/2016/12/01/a-report-shows-hiv-in-retreat-in-manyafrican-countries.

------. 2016g. 'Three-Piece Dream Suit.' July 30.

------. 2016h. 'What are Sanctuary Cities?' November 22, https://www.economist.com/blogs/economist-explains/2016/11/economistexplains-13.

------. 2015. 'Go Forth and Multiply.' October 8, http://www.economist.com/news/business/21672290-crowded-home-market-encouragingsome-institutions-expand-abroad-go-forth-and-multiply.

------. 2014a. 'Difficult Transitions.' November 12.

------. 2014b. 'What Next?' December 4.

------. 2013a. 'A House Divided.' February 9, https://www.economist.com/. . ./china/21571460-chinas-government-unveils-sprawlingplan-fight-inequality-house-divided.

------. 2013b. 'Pennies from Heaven.' December 12, https://www.economist.com/international/2013/12/12/pennies-from-heaven.

------. 2013c. 'Secure Enough.' June 22, https://www.economist.com/news/united-states/21579828-spending-billions-more-fences-anddrones-will-do-more-harm-good-secure-enough.

------. 2012a. 'Crony Tigers, Divided Dragons.' October 13, www.economist.com/node/21564408.

------. 2012b. 'Upwardly Mobile; Innovation in Africa.' August 25, https://search-proquest-com.eproxy1.lib.hku.hk/docview/1034888306?accountid=14548.

------. 2011a. 'A Hard Homecoming.' December 17.

------. 2011b. 'Leaders: Africa Rising; The Hopeful Continent.' December 3, https://search-proquest-com.eproxy1.lib.hku.hk/docview/908037302?accountid=14548.

------. 2011c. 'Leave No Veteran Behind.' June 2.

------. 2011d. 'A Work in Progress.' March 17, http://www.economist. com/node/18359954.

------. 2010a. 'Give the Poor Money.' July 29, https://www.economist. com/leaders/2010/07/29/give-the-poor-money.

------. 2010b. 'How to Get Children Out of Jobs and into School.' July 29, https://www.economist.com/briefing/2010/07/29/how-to-getchildren-out-of-jobs-and-into-school.

------. 2010c. 'Not Just Another Fake.' January 16.

------. 2009. 'International: It May Make Life Easier and Cheaper; East Africa Gets Broadband.' June 20, https://search-proquest-com. eproxy1.lib.hku.hk/docview/223980908?accountid=14548.

------. 2007. '"International: The Digital Gap; Africa and the Internet.' October 20, https://search-proquest-com.eproxy1.lib.hku.hk/ docview/223994630?accountid=14548.

------. 2004. 'The Oil Wars: In the Pipeline.' May 1.

The Global Economy.com. 2019. 'Trade Openness—Country Rankings.' Https://www.theglobaleconomy.com/rankings/trade_openness/.

The Nazi Years: A Documentary History, ed. Joachimm Remak. 1969. Englewood Cliffs: Prentice-Hall.

Timiraos, Nick. 2015. '5 Questions on Trade Adjustment Assistance.' *WSJ.com*, June 15, https://blogs.wsj.com/briefly/2015/06/15/5-questions-on-trade-adjustment-assistance/.

Tolischus, Otto. 1969. 'Hitler Tightens His Control.' *Nazis and Fascists in Europe, 1918-1945*, ed. John Weiss. Chicago: Quadrangle Books.

Toobin, Jeffrey. 2015.'Why are So Many Veterans on Death Row?' *The New Yorker*, November 10.

Tunsjø, Øystein. 2013. *Hedging Against Risk*. New York: Columbia University Press, http://www.jstor.org/stable/10.7312/tuns16508.9/.

UNDP. 2002. Human Development Report 2002. New York: UNDP.

UNESCO. 2017. 'Education: Net Enrolment Rated by Level of Education.' Http://data.uis.unesco.org/Index.aspx?queryid=144.

United Nations. 2019. 'World Economic Situation and Prospects: October 2019 Briefing, No. 131.' Https://www.un.org/development/desa/dpad/publication/world-economic-situation-and-prospects-october-2019-briefing-no-131/ (accessed January 20, 2020).

United Nations Department of Economic and Social Affairs. 2018. '68% of the World Population Projected to Live in Urban Areas by 2050, Says UN.' United Nations, May 16, https://www.un.org/ development/desa/en/news/population/2018-revision-of-world-urbanization-prospects.html.

United Nations Population Fund. 2019. 'Safe Pregnancies for Displaced Mothers as Mobile Clinics Reach Deep into Kachin Camps.' UNPF, https://www.unfpa.org/news/safe-pregnancies-displaced-mothers-mobile-clinics-reach-deep-kachin-camps.

University of Bielefeld. 2019. 'The Courses Offered at Bielefeld University.' University of Bielefeld, https://ekvv.uni-bielefeld.de/ sinfo/publ/Home.jsp?lang=en.

Uppsala University. 2019. 'Major and Minor Fields of Study.' Uppsala University, https://www.uu.se/en/students/degrees-and-careers/degrees/ major-and-minor-fields-of-study/.

US Energy Information Administration. 2019. 'US Natural Gas Production Hit a New Record High in 2018.' https://www.eia.gov/ todayinenergy/detail.php?id=38692 (accessed January 22, 2020).

Vaughan, Pauline. 2007. 'Early Lessons from the Deployment of M-PESA, Vodafone's Own Mobile Transactions Service,' A section in The Transformational Potential of M-transactions. Vodaphone Policy Paper 6, 6-9.

Volberding, Paul A., and Steven G. Deeks. 2010. 'Antiretroviral Therapy and Management of HIV Infection.' *Lancet* 376: 49-62.

Vozoris, Nicholas T., and Valerie S. Tarasuk. 2004. 'The Health of Canadians on Welfare.' *Canadian Journal of Public Health / Revue Canadienne de Santé Publique* 95(2): 115-20.

VTC. 2019a. 'Employment Rate—Analysis by Level (2015/2016—2016/2017).' Http://statistics.vtc.edu.hk/summary2/IVE/IVEEmp/IVEEmpMain. jsp?ins=ive&pages=emp&type=emp&by4=level&lang=.

------. 2019b. 'Employment Rate of Graduates of Full-time Pre-employment Programmes—Analysis by Centre and Institute (2015/2016—2016/2017).' Http://statistics.vtc.edu.hk/summary2/TrC/TrCEmp/ TrCEmpMain.jsp?ins=trc&pages=emp&type=emp&by4=trc&lang=.

------. 2019c. 'No. of Students Enrolled (2016/2017—2017/2018).' Http://statistics.vtc.edu.hk/summary2/SHAPE/SHAPEEnrol/ SHAPEEnrolMain.jsp?ins=shape&pages=enrol&type=enrol&by4=sum.

------. 2019d. 'No. of Students Enrolled—Analysis by Mode (2017/2018—2018/2019).' Http://statistics.vtc.edu.hk/summary2/IVE/IVEEnrol/IVEEnrolMain.jsp?pages=enrol&type=enrol&by4=sum.

------. 2019e. 'No. of Trainees Enrolled in the Shine Skills Centres As at 30 September (2016/2017—2017/2018).' Http://statistics.vtc.edu.hk/summary2/SkCtr/SkCtrEnrol/SkCtrEnrolMain.jsp?pages=enrol&type=enrol&by4=sum.

------. 2019f. 'Statistics Section.' Http://statistics.vtc.edu.hk/summary2/index.jsp.

Wakefield, Jonny. 2017. 'Poverty Rate Down, Incomes Up, Albertans Saving More than Average, Census Statistics Show.' *Edmonton Sun*, September 13, https://edmontonsun.com/2017/09/13/poverty-rate-down-incomes-up-albertans-saving-more-than-average-census-statistics-show/wcm/c17ee5ef-81b1-44ed-9983-0698c4b67622.

Wallsten, Scott. 2005. 'Regulation and Internet Use in Developing Countries.' *Economic Development and Cultural Change* 53(2): 501-23, http://www.jstor.org/stable/10.1086/425376.

Wamukonya, Njeri. 2005. 'Power Sector Reforms in Sub-Saharan Africa: Some Lessons.' *Economic and Political Weekly* 40(50): 5302-08.

Wang, Lirong. 2015. 'Sea Lanes and Chinese National Energy Security.' *Journal of Coastal Research* 73: 572-76, http://www.jstor.org/stable/43843329/.

Wang, Y., and M. Blomström. 1992. 'Foreign Investment and Technology Transfer: A Simple Model.' *European Economic Review* 36: 137–55.

Ward, Patrick. 2014. 'Measuring the Level and Inequality of Wealth: An Application to China.' *Review of Income and Wealth* 60(4): 613-35, doi:10.1111/roiw.12063.

Water.org. 2019. 'Our Impact—India.' Https://water.org/our-impact/india/.

Waverman, Leonard, Meloria Meschi, and Melvyn Fuss. 2005. 'The Impact of Telecoms on Economic Growth in Developing Countries.' In *Africa: The Impact of Mobile Phones*, Vodafone Policy Paper 3, 10-23.

Weitz, John. 1997. *Hitler's Banker*. Toronto: Little, Brown and Company.

Weitzman, M.L. 1985. 'Increasing Returns and the Foundations of Unemployment Theory: Reply.' *Journal of Post Keynesian Economics* 7.

------. 1983. 'Some Macroeconomic Implications of Alternative Compensation Systems.' *Economic Journal* 93: 763-783.

Wen, Yuyuan. 2014. 'The Spillover Effect of FDI and its Impact on Productivity in High Economic Output Regions: A Comparative Analysis of the Yangtze River Delta and the Pearl River Delta, China.' Papers in Regional Science 93(2): 341-65.

Wensley, Simon. 2013. 'China's Energy Demand Growth and the Energy Policy Trilemma.' In *A New Model for Growth and Development*, edited by Ross Garnaut, Cai Fang, and Ligang Song, 301-19. Canberra: ANU Press, http://www.jstor.org/stable/j.ctt46n2zv.21/.

Williamson, Deanna L. 2001. 'The Role of the Health Sector in Addressing Poverty.' *Canadian Journal of Public Health / Revue Canadienne de Santé Publique* 92(3): 178-83.

Wolf, Aaron T., Shira B. Yoffe and Mark Giordano. 2003. 'International Waters: Indicators for Identifying Basins at Risk.' *Water Policy* 5: 29–60.

Wong, K., and M. Yeung. 2019. 'Population Aging Trend in Hong Kong.' Economic Letter 2019/02, Office of the Government Economist, HKSAR.

World Bank. 2019. *Doing Business 2019*. Washington, D.C.: World Bank.

------. 2018. *The State of Social Safety Nets 2018*. Washington, D.C.: World Bank, https://openknowledge.worldbank.org/bitstream/handle/10986/29115/9781464812545.pdf.

------. 2001. *World Development Report 2000/2001*. Washington, D.C.: World Bank.

World Bank WDI. 2017a. 'Government Expenditure on Education, Total (% of GDP).' Https://data.worldbank.org/indicator/SE.XPD.TOTL.GD.ZS.

------. 2017b. 'Government Expenditure on Education, Total (% of Government Expenditure).' Https://data.worldbank.org/indicator/SE.XPD.TOTL.GB.ZS.

------. 2017c. 'School Enrollment, Secondary (% Net).' Https://data.worldbank.org/indicator/SE.PRM.NENR?view=map.

World Bank. 1999. *World Development Report 1999/2000*. New York: Oxford University Press.

World Health Organization. 2019. 'Density of Physicians (Total Number per 1000 Population, Latest Available Year.' WHO Global Health

Observatory Data, https://www.who.int/gho/health_workforce/physicians_density/en/.

World Health Organization Bangladesh. 2019. 'Immunization and Vaccine Development.' WHO Bangladesh, http://www.searo.who.int/bangladesh/areas/immunizationvaccine/en/.

World Health Organization Western Pacific Region. 2019. 'Immunization.' WHO Representative Office—Lao's People Democratic Republic, http://www.wpro.who.int/laos/topics/immunization/en/.

Wu, F. 2002. 'China's Changing Urban Governance in the Transition Towards a More Market-Oriented Economy.' *Urban Studies* 39(7): 1071-93.

Wu, F., Xu, J., and Yeh, A.G.O. 2007. Urban Development in Post-Reform China: State, Market and Space. Abingdon: Routledge.

Xie, Yu, and Xiang Zhou. 2014. *Proceedings of the National Academy of Sciences of the United States of America* 111(19): 6928-33.

Xinhua. 2017. 'China to Further Reform to Drive Innovation.' *People's Daily Online*, August 31, http://en.people.cn/n3/2017/0831/c90785-9262448.html.

Xu, J., and A.G.O. Yeh. 2005. 'City Repositioning and Competitiveness Building in Regional Development: New Development Strategies of Guangzhou, China.' *International Journal of Urban and Regional Research* 29(2): 283-308.

Yeung, Y.M. 2005. 'Emergence of the Pan-Pearl River Delta.' *Geografiska annaler Series* B(87): 75-9.

Yeung, Y.M., and Gordon Kee. 2011. 'Infrastructure Development in the Pan-Pearl River Delta: Opportunities and Challenges.' In *China's Pan-Pearl River Delta*, edited by Anthony G.O. Yeh and Jiang Xu, 159-179. Hong Kong: Hong Kong University Press.

Young, Alwyn. 2005. 'The Gift of the Dying: The Trigged of AIDS and the Welfare of Future African Generations.' *The Quarterly Journal of Economics* 120(2): 423-66.

Zhang, K.H. 2006. 'Foreign Direct Investment and Economic Growth in China: A Panel Data Study for 1992–2004.' Paper prepared for the conference of WTO, China and Asian Economies. UIBE, Beijing.

Zhang, Y., and G. Wan. 2006. 'The Impact of Growth and Inequality or Rural Poverty in China.' *Journal of Comparative Economics* 34: 694–712.

Zhang, Zhongxiang. 2012. 'Why Are the Stakes So High?: Misconceptions and Misunderstandings in China's Global Quest for Energy Security.' In *Rebalancing and Sustaining Growth in China*, edited by Huw McKay and Ligang Song, 329-56. Canberra: ANU Press, http://www.jstor.org/stable/j.ctt24hd16.22/.

Zhao, Wei. 2014. 'From Industrial Policy to Upgrading Strategy: Dilemma of Local Developmental State in China's Pearl River Delta.' *China Economic Policy Review* 3(1): 1450006-1-32.

Zheng, Xin. 2019. 'China's Energy Consumption Hits Five-Year Record.' *China Daily*, April 28, https://www.chinadaily.com.cn/a/201904/28/WS5cc59903a3104842260b8ed7.html.

Zheng, Xin. 2018. 'Nation's Reliance on Crude Oil Imports Set to Continue.' *China Daily*, June 5, https://www.chinadaily.com.cn/global/2019-06/05/content_37477320.htm.